Just The facts101

Textbook Key Facts

Samoa West Business and
Investment Opportunities
Yearbook

by Cram101
Textbook NOT Included

Table of Contents

Just The Facts101

Exam Prep for

Samoa West Business and Investment Opportunities Yearbook

Just The Facts101 Exam Prep is your link from
the texbook and lecture to your exams.

**Just The Facts101 Exam Preps are unauthorized and comprehensive reviews
of your textbooks.**

All material provided by CTI Publications (c) 2019

Textbook publishers and textbook authors do not particpate in or contribute to these reviews.

Just The Facts101 Exam Prep

eAIN 448997

Foundations of Business

A business, also known as an enterprise, agency or a firm, is an entity involved in the provision of goods and/or services to consumers. Businesses are prevalent in capitalist economies, where most of them are privately owned and provide goods and services to customers in exchange for other goods, services, or money.

:: Organizational behavior ::

_____ is the state or fact of exclusive rights and control over property, which may be an object, land/real estate or intellectual property. _____ involves multiple rights, collectively referred to as title, which may be separated and held by different parties.

Exam Probability: **High**

1. *Answer choices:*
(see index for correct answer)

- a. Conformity
- b. Administrative Behavior
- c. Managerial grid model
- d. Ownership

Guidance: level 1

:: Interest rates ::

An _____ is the amount of interest due per period, as a proportion of the amount lent, deposited or borrowed . The total interest on an amount lent or borrowed depends on the principal sum, the _____ , the compounding frequency, and the length of time over which it is lent, deposited or borrowed.

Exam Probability: **High**

2. *Answer choices:*
(see index for correct answer)

- a. Interest rate
- b. Amortising swap
- c. Effective interest rate
- d. Wall Street Journal prime rate

Guidance: level 1

:: Money ::

In economics, _____ is money in the physical form of currency, such as banknotes and coins. In bookkeeping and finance, _____ is current assets comprising currency or currency equivalents that can be accessed immediately or near-immediately . _____ is seen either as a reserve for payments, in case of a structural or incidental negative _____ flow or as a way to avoid a downturn on financial markets.

Exam Probability: **Low**

3. *Answer choices:*
(see index for correct answer)

- a. Leprosy colony money
- b. Lump sum
- c. World Money Fair
- d. Ideal money

Guidance: level 1

:: Marketing analytics ::

_____ is a long-term, forward-looking approach to planning with the fundamental goal of achieving a sustainable competitive advantage. Strategic planning involves an analysis of the company's strategic initial situation prior to the formulation, evaluation and selection of market-oriented competitive position that contributes to the company's goals and marketing objectives.

Exam Probability: **Medium**

4. *Answer choices:*
(see index for correct answer)

- a. Marketing strategy
- b. Return on marketing investment
- c. Perceptual map
- d. Marketing effectiveness

Guidance: level 1

:: Legal terms ::

_____ , a form of alternative dispute resolution , is a way to resolve disputes outside the courts. The dispute will be decided by one or more persons , which renders the " _____ award". An _____ award is legally binding on both sides and enforceable in the courts.

Exam Probability: **Low**

5. *Answer choices:*
(see index for correct answer)

- a. Impunity
- b. Arbitration
- c. Competent authority
- d. Date certain

Guidance: level 1

:: Rhetoric ::

_____ is the pattern of narrative development that aims to make vivid a place, object, character, or group. _____ is one of four rhetorical modes , along with exposition, argumentation, and narration. In practice it would be difficult to write literature that drew on just one of the four basic modes.

Exam Probability: **Medium**

6. *Answer choices:*
(see index for correct answer)

- a. Paromoiosis
- b. Rhetorical criticism
- c. Rhetoric of health and medicine
- d. Description

Guidance: level 1

:: Project management ::

Contemporary business and science treat as a _____ any undertaking, carried out individually or collaboratively and possibly involving research or design, that is carefully planned to achieve a particular aim.

Exam Probability: **High**

7. *Answer choices:*
(see index for correct answer)

- a. Global Alliance for Project Performance Standards
- b. Alexander Laufer
- c. Project
- d. Cost estimate

Guidance: level 1

:: Retailing ::

_____ is the process of selling consumer goods or services to customers through multiple channels of distribution to earn a profit. _____ ers satisfy demand identified through a supply chain. The term "_____ er" is typically applied where a service provider fills the small orders of a large number of individuals, who are end-users, rather than large orders of a small number of wholesale, corporate or government clientele. Shopping generally refers to the act of buying products. Sometimes this is done to obtain final goods, including necessities such as food and clothing; sometimes it takes place as a recreational activity. Recreational shopping often involves window shopping and browsing; it does not always result in a purchase.

Exam Probability: **High**

8. *Answer choices:*
(see index for correct answer)

- a. Specialist store
- b. Zeeman
- c. Dry goods
- d. Profitect

Guidance: level 1

:: Organizational theory ::

_____ is the process of groups of organisms working or acting together for common, mutual, or some underlying benefit, as opposed to working in competition for selfish benefit. Many animal and plant species cooperate both with other members of their own species and with members of other species .

Exam Probability: **Low**

9. *Answer choices:*
(see index for correct answer)

- a. Organizational theory
- b. Solid line reporting
- c. Cooperation
- d. Organization development

Guidance: level 1

:: Survey methodology ::

An _____ is a conversation where questions are asked and answers are given. In common parlance, the word " _____ " refers to a one-on-one conversation between an _____ er and an _____ ee. The _____ er asks questions to which the _____ ee responds, usually so information may be transferred from _____ ee to _____ er . Sometimes, information can be transferred in both directions. It is a communication, unlike a speech, which produces a one-way flow of information.

Exam Probability: **Medium**

10. *Answer choices:*
(see index for correct answer)

- a. Political forecasting
- b. Self-report study
- c. Census
- d. Interview

Guidance: level 1

:: ::

_____ is the production of products for use or sale using labour and machines, tools, chemical and biological processing, or formulation. The term may refer to a range of human activity, from handicraft to high tech, but is most commonly applied to industrial design, in which raw materials are transformed into finished goods on a large scale. Such finished goods may be sold to other manufacturers for the production of other, more complex products, such as aircraft, household appliances, furniture, sports equipment or automobiles, or sold to wholesalers, who in turn sell them to retailers, who then sell them to end users and consumers.

Exam Probability: **High**

11. *Answer choices:*
(see index for correct answer)

- a. surface-level diversity
- b. levels of analysis
- c. information systems assessment
- d. Manufacturing

Guidance: level 1

In accounting, _____ is the income that a business have from its normal business activities, usually from the sale of goods and services to customers. _____ is also referred to as sales or turnover. Some companies receive _____ from interest, royalties, or other fees. _____ may refer to business income in general, or it may refer to the amount, in a monetary unit, earned during a period of time, as in "Last year, Company X had _____ of $42 million". Profits or net income generally imply total _____ minus total expenses in a given period. In accounting, in the balance statement it is a subsection of the Equity section and _____ increases equity, it is often referred to as the "top line" due to its position on the income statement at the very top. This is to be contrasted with the "bottom line" which denotes net income .

Exam Probability: **Medium**

12. *Answer choices:*
(see index for correct answer)

- a. AICPA Statements of Position
- b. Fixed investment
- c. Revenue
- d. Indian Accounting Standards

Guidance: level 1

:: Office administration ::

An _____ is generally a room or other area where an organization's employees perform administrative work in order to support and realize objects and goals of the organization. The word " _____ " may also denote a position within an organization with specific duties attached to it ; the latter is in fact an earlier usage, _____ as place originally referring to the location of one's duty. When used as an adjective, the term " _____ " may refer to business-related tasks. In law, a company or organization has _____ s in any place where it has an official presence, even if that presence consists of a storage silo rather than an establishment with desk-and-chair. An _____ is also an architectural and design phenomenon: ranging from a small _____ such as a bench in the corner of a small business of extremely small size , through entire floors of buildings, up to and including massive buildings dedicated entirely to one company. In modern terms an _____ is usually the location where white-collar workers carry out their functions. As per James Stephenson, " _____ is that part of business enterprise which is devoted to the direction and co-ordination of its various activities."

Exam Probability: **High**

13. *Answer choices:*
(see index for correct answer)

- a. Fish! Philosophy
- b. Activity management
- c. Inter departmental communication
- d. Office

Guidance: level 1

:: Income ::

_____ is a ratio between the net profit and cost of investment resulting from an investment of some resources. A high ROI means the investment's gains favorably to its cost. As a performance measure, ROI is used to evaluate the efficiency of an investment or to compare the efficiencies of several different investments. In purely economic terms, it is one way of relating profits to capital invested. _____ is a performance measure used by businesses to identify the efficiency of an investment or number of different investments.

14. *Answer choices:*

(see index for correct answer)

- a. Return on investment
- b. Creative real estate investing
- c. Family income
- d. Income Per User

Guidance: level 1

:: Private equity ::

_____ is a type of private equity, a form of financing that is provided by firms or funds to small, early-stage, emerging firms that are deemed to have high growth potential, or which have demonstrated high growth . _____ firms or funds invest in these early-stage companies in exchange for equity, or an ownership stake, in the companies they invest in. _____ ists take on the risk of financing risky start-ups in the hopes that some of the firms they support will become successful. Because startups face high uncertainty, VC investments do have high rates of failure. The start-ups are usually based on an innovative technology or business model and they are usually from the high technology industries, such as information technology , clean technology or biotechnology.

15. *Answer choices:*

(see index for correct answer)

- a. Private equity in the 1980s
- b. Club deal
- c. Leveraged buyout
- d. Firstpex

Guidance: level 1

:: Insolvency ::

_____ is a legal process through which people or other entities who cannot repay debts to creditors may seek relief from some or all of their debts. In most jurisdictions, _____ is imposed by a court order, often initiated by the debtor.

Exam Probability: **High**

16. *Answer choices:*
(see index for correct answer)

- a. Bankruptcy
- b. Liquidation
- c. United Kingdom insolvency law
- d. Conservatorship

Guidance: level 1

:: Marketing techniques ::

_____ is the activity of dividing a broad consumer or business market, normally consisting of existing and potential customers, into sub-groups of consumers based on some type of shared characteristics. In dividing or segmenting markets, researchers typically look for common characteristics such as shared needs, common interests, similar lifestyles or even similar demographic profiles. The overall aim of segmentation is to identify high yield segments – that is, those segments that are likely to be the most profitable or that have growth potential – so that these can be selected for special attention .

Exam Probability: **Medium**

17. *Answer choices:*
(see index for correct answer)

- a. Continuity marketing
- b. Virtual event
- c. Market segmentation
- d. AIDA

Guidance: level 1

:: Business ::

_____ is a trade policy that does not restrict imports or exports; it can also be understood as the free market idea applied to international trade. In government, _____ is predominantly advocated by political parties that hold liberal economic positions while economically left-wing and nationalist political parties generally support protectionism, the opposite of _____.

Exam Probability: **Medium**

18. *Answer choices:*
(see index for correct answer)

- a. Casengo
- b. Business directory
- c. Free trade
- d. Operating subsidiary

Guidance: level 1

:: Export and import control ::

" _____ " means the Government Service which is responsible for the administration of _____ law and the collection of duties and taxes and which also has the responsibility for the application of other laws and regulations relating to the importation, exportation, movement or storage of goods.

Exam Probability: **Medium**

19. *Answer choices:*
(see index for correct answer)

- a. International Traffic in Arms Regulations
- b. Customs
- c. ATA Carnet
- d. Wassenaar Arrangement

Guidance: level 1

:: Management ::

_____ is the process of thinking about the activities required to achieve a desired goal. It is the first and foremost activity to achieve desired results. It involves the creation and maintenance of a plan, such as psychological aspects that require conceptual skills. There are even a couple of tests to measure someone's capability of _____ well. As such, _____ is a fundamental property of intelligent behavior. An important further meaning, often just called " _____ " is the legal context of permitted building developments.

Exam Probability: **Medium**

20. *Answer choices:*
(see index for correct answer)

- a. Planning
- b. Corporate foresight
- c. SimulTrain
- d. Balanced scorecard

Guidance: level 1

:: Bribery ::

_____ is the act of giving or receiving something of value in exchange for some kind of influence or action in return, that the recipient would otherwise not offer. _____ is defined by Black's Law Dictionary as the offering, giving, receiving, or soliciting of any item of value to influence the actions of an official or other person in charge of a public or legal duty. Essentially, _____ is offering to do something for someone for the expressed purpose of receiving something in exchange. Gifts of money or other items of value which are otherwise available to everyone on an equivalent basis, and not for dishonest purposes, is not _____ . Offering a discount or a refund to all purchasers is a legal rebate and is not _____ . For example, it is legal for an employee of a Public Utilities Commission involved in electric rate regulation to accept a rebate on electric service that reduces their cost for electricity, when the rebate is available to other residential electric customers. Giving the rebate to influence them to look favorably on the electric utility's rate increase applications, however, would be considered _____ .

Exam Probability: **High**

21. *Answer choices:*

- a. Bribery
- b. English football bribery scandal
- c. Holyland Case
- d. Kickback

Guidance: level 1

:: Payments ::

A _____ is the trade of value from one party to another for goods, or services, or to fulfill a legal obligation.

Exam Probability: **Medium**

22. *Answer choices:*

- a. Thirty pieces of silver
- b. Subsidy
- c. Direct Payments
- d. Payment

Guidance: level 1

:: Debt ::

_____ is the trust which allows one party to provide money or resources to another party wherein the second party does not reimburse the first party immediately , but promises either to repay or return those resources at a later date. In other words, _____ is a method of making reciprocity formal, legally enforceable, and extensible to a large group of unrelated people.

Exam Probability: **High**

23. *Answer choices:*

- a. Credit
- b. Asset protection
- c. Tax benefits of debt
- d. Legal liability

:: Project management ::

A _____ is a source or supply from which a benefit is produced and it has some utility. _____ s can broadly be classified upon their availability—they are classified into renewable and non-renewable _____ s.Examples of non renewable _____ s are coal ,crude oil natural gas nuclear energy etc. Examples of renewable _____ s are air,water,wind,solar energy etc. They can also be classified as actual and potential on the basis of level of development and use, on the basis of origin they can be classified as biotic and abiotic, and on the basis of their distribution, as ubiquitous and localized . An item becomes a _____ with time and developing technology. Typically, _____ s are materials, energy, services, staff, knowledge, or other assets that are transformed to produce benefit and in the process may be consumed or made unavailable. Benefits of _____ utilization may include increased wealth, proper functioning of a system, or enhanced well-being. From a human perspective a natural _____ is anything obtained from the environment to satisfy human needs and wants. From a broader biological or ecological perspective a _____ satisfies the needs of a living organism .

Exam Probability: **High**

24. *Answer choices:*

(see index for correct answer)

- a. Collaborative project management
- b. Resource
- c. Risk management plan
- d. Multidisciplinary approach

:: Financial crises ::

A _____ is any of a broad variety of situations in which some financial assets suddenly lose a large part of their nominal value. In the 19th and early 20th centuries, many financial crises were associated with banking panics, and many recessions coincided with these panics. Other situations that are often called financial crises include stock market crashes and the bursting of other financial bubbles, currency crises, and sovereign defaults. Financial crises directly result in a loss of paper wealth but do not necessarily result in significant changes in the real economy .

25. *Answer choices:*

(see index for correct answer)

- a. The Vienna Initiative
- b. Copper Panic of 1789
- c. Panic of 1826
- d. Financial crisis

Guidance: level 1

:: Materials ::

A _____ , also known as a feedstock, unprocessed material, or primary commodity, is a basic material that is used to produce goods, finished products, energy, or intermediate materials which are feedstock for future finished products. As feedstock, the term connotes these materials are bottleneck assets and are highly important with regard to producing other products. An example of this is crude oil, which is a _____ and a feedstock used in the production of industrial chemicals, fuels, plastics, and pharmaceutical goods; lumber is a _____ used to produce a variety of products including all types of furniture. The term " _____ " denotes materials in minimally processed or unprocessed in states; e.g., raw latex, crude oil, cotton, coal, raw biomass, iron ore, air, logs, or water i.e. "...any product of agriculture, forestry, fishing and any other mineral that is in its natural form or which has undergone the transformation required to prepare it for internationally marketing in substantial volumes."

26. *Answer choices:*

(see index for correct answer)

- a. Kovar
- b. Whitetopping
- c. Raw material
- d. Radar-absorbent material

Guidance: level 1

:: Market research ::

A _____ is a small, but demographically diverse group of people and whose reactions are studied especially in market research or political analysis in guided or open discussions about a new product or something else to determine the reactions that can be expected from a larger population. It is a form of qualitative research consisting of interviews in which a group of people are asked about their perceptions, opinions, beliefs, and attitudes towards a product, service, concept, advertisement, idea, or packaging. Questions are asked in an interactive group setting where participants are free to talk with other group members. During this process, the researcher either takes notes or records the vital points he or she is getting from the group. Researchers should select members of the _____ carefully for effective and authoritative responses.

Exam Probability: **Low**

27. *Answer choices:*
(see index for correct answer)

- a. Frugging
- b. IModerate
- c. Qualtrics
- d. DigitalMR

Guidance: level 1

:: Alchemical processes ::

In chemistry, a _____ is a special type of homogeneous mixture composed of two or more substances. In such a mixture, a solute is a substance dissolved in another substance, known as a solvent. The mixing process of a _____ happens at a scale where the effects of chemical polarity are involved, resulting in interactions that are specific to solvation. The _____ assumes the phase of the solvent when the solvent is the larger fraction of the mixture, as is commonly the case. The concentration of a solute in a _____ is the mass of that solute expressed as a percentage of the mass of the whole _____ . The term aqueous _____ is when one of the solvents is water.

Exam Probability: **Medium**

28. *Answer choices:*
(see index for correct answer)

- a. Sublimation apparatus
- b. Fermentation
- c. Putrefaction
- d. Corporification

Guidance: level 1

:: ::

An _____ is a contingent motivator. Traditional _____ s are extrinsic motivators which reward actions to yield a desired outcome. The effectiveness of traditional _____ s has changed as the needs of Western society have evolved. While the traditional _____ model is effective when there is a defined procedure and goal for a task, Western society started to require a higher volume of critical thinkers, so the traditional model became less effective. Institutions are now following a trend in implementing strategies that rely on intrinsic motivations rather than the extrinsic motivations that the traditional _____ s foster.

Exam Probability: **Low**

29. *Answer choices:*
(see index for correct answer)

- a. surface-level diversity
- b. similarity-attraction theory
- c. interpersonal communication
- d. Incentive

:: Globalization-related theories ::

_____ is the process in which a nation is being improved in the sector of the economic, political, and social well-being of its people. The term has been used frequently by economists, politicians, and others in the 20th and 21st centuries. The concept, however, has been in existence in the West for centuries. "Modernization, "westernization", and especially "industrialization" are other terms often used while discussing _____ . _____ has a direct relationship with the environment and environmental issues. _____ is very often confused with industrial development, even in some academic sources.

Exam Probability: **High**

30. *Answer choices:*
(see index for correct answer)

- a. postmodernism
- b. post-industrial
- c. Capitalism

:: Business ::

A _____ is a mathematical object used to count, measure, and label. The original examples are the natural _____ s 1, 2, 3, 4, and so forth. A written symbol like "5" that represents a _____ is called a numeral. A numeral system is an organized way to write and manipulate this type of symbol, for example the Hindu–Arabic numeral system allows combinations of numerical digits like "5" and "0" to represent larger _____ s like 50. A numeral in linguistics can refer to a symbol like 5, the words or phrase that names a _____ , like "five hundred", or other words that mean a specific _____ , like "dozen". In addition to their use in counting and measuring, numerals are often used for labels , for ordering , and for codes . In common usage, _____ may refer to a symbol, a word or phrase, or the mathematical object.

Exam Probability: **Medium**

31. *Answer choices:*

- a. Closure
- b. Price-based selling
- c. Citizenship for life
- d. Number

Guidance: level 1

:: Marketing ::

_____ is based on a marketing concept which can be adopted by an organization as a strategy for business expansion. Where implemented, a franchisor licenses its know-how, procedures, intellectual property, use of its business model, brand, and rights to sell its branded products and services to a franchisee. In return the franchisee pays certain fees and agrees to comply with certain obligations, typically set out in a Franchise Agreement.

Exam Probability: **Medium**

32. *Answer choices:*

- a. Adobe Social
- b. Instant rebate
- c. Franchising
- d. Paddock girl

Guidance: level 1

:: Business ::

The seller, or the provider of the goods or services, completes a sale in response to an acquisition, appropriation, requisition or a direct interaction with the buyer at the point of sale. There is a passing of title of the item, and the settlement of a price, in which agreement is reached on a price for which transfer of ownership of the item will occur. The seller, not the purchaser typically executes the sale and it may be completed prior to the obligation of payment. In the case of indirect interaction, a person who sells goods or service on behalf of the owner is known as a salesman or saleswoman or salesperson, but this often refers to someone _____ goods in a store/shop, in which case other terms are also common, including salesclerk, shop assistant, and retail clerk.

33. *Answer choices:*

(see index for correct answer)

- a. Student@Home
- b. Ian McLeod
- c. Professional services
- d. Values scales

Guidance: level 1

:: Financial regulatory authorities of the United States ::

The _____ is the revenue service of the United States federal government. The government agency is a bureau of the Department of the Treasury, and is under the immediate direction of the Commissioner of Internal Revenue, who is appointed to a five-year term by the President of the United States. The IRS is responsible for collecting taxes and administering the Internal Revenue Code, the main body of federal statutory tax law of the United States. The duties of the IRS include providing tax assistance to taxpayers and pursuing and resolving instances of erroneous or fraudulent tax filings. The IRS has also overseen various benefits programs, and enforces portions of the Affordable Care Act.

34. *Answer choices:*

(see index for correct answer)

- a. Operation Choke Point
- b. National Futures Association
- c. Commodity Futures Trading Commission
- d. Internal Revenue Service

Guidance: level 1

:: Globalization-related theories ::

_____ is an economic system based on the private ownership of the means of production and their operation for profit. Characteristics central to _____ include private property, capital accumulation, wage labor, voluntary exchange, a price system, and competitive markets. In a capitalist market economy, decision-making and investment are determined by every owner of wealth, property or production ability in financial and capital markets, whereas prices and the distribution of goods and services are mainly determined by competition in goods and services markets.

Exam Probability: **Medium**

35. *Answer choices:*
(see index for correct answer)

- a. postmodernism
- b. Economic Development
- c. post-industrial

Guidance: level 1

:: Market research ::

_____ is an organized effort to gather information about target markets or customers. It is a very important component of business strategy. The term is commonly interchanged with marketing research; however, expert practitioners may wish to draw a distinction, in that marketing research is concerned specifically about marketing processes, while _____ is concerned specifically with markets.

Exam Probability: **Low**

36. *Answer choices:*
(see index for correct answer)

- a. Sociomapping
- b. Cambashi
- c. ISO 20252
- d. Market research and opinion polling in China

Guidance: level 1

:: ::

Some scenarios associate "this kind of planning" with learning "life skills".Schedules are necessary, or at least useful, in situations where individuals need to know what time they must be at a specific location to receive a specific service, and where people need to accomplish a set of goals within a set time period.

Exam Probability: **Low**

37. *Answer choices:*
(see index for correct answer)

- a. Scheduling
- b. surface-level diversity
- c. similarity-attraction theory
- d. process perspective

Guidance: level 1

:: Summary statistics ::

_____ is the number of occurrences of a repeating event per unit of time. It is also referred to as temporal _____ , which emphasizes the contrast to spatial _____ and angular _____ . The period is the duration of time of one cycle in a repeating event, so the period is the reciprocal of the _____ . For example: if a newborn baby's heart beats at a _____ of 120 times a minute, its period—the time interval between beats—is half a second . _____ is an important parameter used in science and engineering to specify the rate of oscillatory and vibratory phenomena, such as mechanical vibrations, audio signals , radio waves, and light.

Exam Probability: **High**

38. *Answer choices:*
(see index for correct answer)

- a. Location parameter
- b. Multiple of the median
- c. Quantile
- d. Robin Hood index

Guidance: level 1

:: Environmental economics ::

_____ is the process of people maintaining change in a balanced environment, in which the exploitation of resources, the direction of investments, the orientation of technological development and institutional change are all in harmony and enhance both current and future potential to meet human needs and aspirations. For many in the field, _____ is defined through the following interconnected domains or pillars: environment, economic and social, which according to Fritjof Capra is based on the principles of Systems Thinking. Sub-domains of sustainable development have been considered also: cultural, technological and political. While sustainable development may be the organizing principle for _____ for some, for others, the two terms are paradoxical . Sustainable development is the development that meets the needs of the present without compromising the ability of future generations to meet their own needs. Brundtland Report for the World Commission on Environment and Development introduced the term of sustainable development.

Exam Probability: **Low**

39. *Answer choices:*
(see index for correct answer)

- a. Gross national happiness
- b. Sustainability
- c. Futures techniques
- d. Emission intensity

Guidance: level 1

:: Management ::

In business, a _____ is the attribute that allows an organization to outperform its competitors. A _____ may include access to natural resources, such as high-grade ores or a low-cost power source, highly skilled labor, geographic location, high entry barriers, and access to new technology.

Exam Probability: **Low**

40. *Answer choices:*
(see index for correct answer)

- a. Quality control
- b. Discovery-driven planning
- c. Stakeholder
- d. Opera management

:: Commercial item transport and distribution ::

A _____ is a commitment or expectation to perform some action in general or if certain circumstances arise. A _____ may arise from a system of ethics or morality, especially in an honor culture. Many duties are created by law, sometimes including a codified punishment or liability for non-performance. Performing one's _____ may require some sacrifice of self-interest.

Exam Probability: **High**

41. *Answer choices:*
(see index for correct answer)

- a. Voice-directed warehousing
- b. Duty
- c. Port of entry
- d. Transshipment problem

:: Non-profit technology ::

Instituto del Tercer Mundo is a Non-Governmental Organization that performs information, communication and education activities. _____ , which was established in 1989, shares the same secretariat and coordinating personnel as Social Watch and is based in Montevideo, Uruguay.

Exam Probability: **Low**

42. *Answer choices:*
(see index for correct answer)

- a. INeedAPencil
- b. OpenDocument Foundation
- c. Katrina PeopleFinder Project
- d. TechSoup Global

:: Debt ::

_____ , in finance and economics, is payment from a borrower or deposit-taking financial institution to a lender or depositor of an amount above repayment of the principal sum , at a particular rate. It is distinct from a fee which the borrower may pay the lender or some third party. It is also distinct from dividend which is paid by a company to its shareholders from its profit or reserve, but not at a particular rate decided beforehand, rather on a pro rata basis as a share in the reward gained by risk taking entrepreneurs when the revenue earned exceeds the total costs.

Exam Probability: **High**

43. *Answer choices:*

(see index for correct answer)

- a. Crown debt
- b. Default trap
- c. Interest
- d. Perpetual subordinated debt

Guidance: level 1

:: Planning ::

_____ is a high level plan to achieve one or more goals under conditions of uncertainty. In the sense of the "art of the general," which included several subsets of skills including tactics, siegecraft, logistics etc., the term came into use in the 6th century C.E. in East Roman terminology, and was translated into Western vernacular languages only in the 18th century. From then until the 20th century, the word " _____ " came to denote "a comprehensive way to try to pursue political ends, including the threat or actual use of force, in a dialectic of wills" in a military conflict, in which both adversaries interact.

Exam Probability: **Medium**

44. *Answer choices:*

(see index for correct answer)

- a. Default effect
- b. Enterprise architecture planning
- c. Resource-Task Network
- d. Strategy

Guidance: level 1

_____ is asystematic determination of a subject's merit, worth and significance, using criteria governed by a set of standards. It can assist an organization, program, design, project or any other intervention or initiative to assess any aim, realisable concept/proposal, or any alternative, to help in decision-making; or to ascertain the degree of achievement or value in regard to the aim and objectives and results of any such action that has been completed. The primary purpose of _____ , in addition to gaining insight into prior or existing initiatives, is to enable reflection and assist in the identification of future change.

Exam Probability: **High**

45. *Answer choices:*
(see index for correct answer)

- a. Work etiquette
- b. Counterproductive work behavior
- c. Workplace health surveillance
- d. Evaluation

Guidance: level 1

_____ or globalisation is the process of interaction and integration among people, companies, and governments worldwide. As a complex and multifaceted phenomenon, _____ is considered by some as a form of capitalist expansion which entails the integration of local and national economies into a global, unregulated market economy. _____ has grown due to advances in transportation and communication technology. With the increased global interactions comes the growth of international trade, ideas, and culture. _____ is primarily an economic process of interaction and integration that's associated with social and cultural aspects. However, conflicts and diplomacy are also large parts of the history of _____ , and modern _____ .

Exam Probability: **High**

46. *Answer choices:*
(see index for correct answer)

- a. Indo-Roman relations
- b. Globalization
- c. International monetary systems
- d. Price band

Guidance: level 1

:: E-commerce ::

_____ is the activity of buying or selling of products on online services or over the Internet. Electronic commerce draws on technologies such as mobile commerce, electronic funds transfer, supply chain management, Internet marketing, online transaction processing, electronic data interchange , inventory management systems, and automated data collection systems.

Exam Probability: **Medium**

47. *Answer choices:*
(see index for correct answer)

- a. Playism
- b. E-commerce
- c. Tender notification
- d. DigiCash

Guidance: level 1

:: Business models ::

_____ es are privately owned corporations, partnerships, or sole proprietorships that have fewer employees and/or less annual revenue than a regular-sized business or corporation. Businesses are defined as "small" in terms of being able to apply for government support and qualify for preferential tax policy varies depending on the country and industry. _____ es range from fifteen employees under the Australian Fair Work Act 2009, fifty employees according to the definition used by the European Union, and fewer than five hundred employees to qualify for many U.S. _____ Administration programs. While _____ es can also be classified according to other methods, such as annual revenues, shipments, sales, assets, or by annual gross or net revenue or net profits, the number of employees is one of the most widely used measures.

48. *Answer choices:*
(see index for correct answer)

- a. Small business
- b. Lemonade stand
- c. Strategy map
- d. Microfranchising

Guidance: level 1

:: Unemployment ::

In economics, a _____ is a business cycle contraction when there is a general decline in economic activity. Macroeconomic indicators such as GDP , investment spending, capacity utilization, household income, business profits, and inflation fall, while bankruptcies and the unemployment rate rise. In the United Kingdom, it is defined as a negative economic growth for two consecutive quarters.

49. *Answer choices:*
(see index for correct answer)

- a. Recession
- b. Reserve army of labour
- c. Unemployment Convention, 1919
- d. Involuntary unemployment

Guidance: level 1

:: Energy and fuel journals ::

In physics, energy is the quantitative property that must be transferred to an object in order to perform work on, or to heat, the object. Energy is a conserved quantity; the law of conservation of energy states that energy can be converted in form, but not created or destroyed. The SI unit of energy is the joule, which is the energy transferred to an object by the work of moving it a distance of 1 metre against a force of 1 newton.

50. *Answer choices:*

(see index for correct answer)

- a. Journal of Power Sources
- b. Applied Thermal Engineering
- c. Energies
- d. Solar Energy Materials and Solar Cells

Guidance: level 1

:: Semiconductor companies ::

_____ Corporation is a Japanese multinational conglomerate corporation headquartered in Konan, Minato, Tokyo. Its diversified business includes consumer and professional electronics, gaming, entertainment and financial services. The company owns the largest music entertainment business in the world, the largest video game console business and one of the largest video game publishing businesses, and is one of the leading manufacturers of electronic products for the consumer and professional markets, and a leading player in the film and television entertainment industry. _____ was ranked 97th on the 2018 Fortune Global 500 list.

Exam Probability: **Low**

51. *Answer choices:*
(see index for correct answer)

- a. Semitool
- b. STMicroelectronics
- c. Sony
- d. Sharp Corporation

Guidance: level 1

:: Credit cards ::

A _____ is a payment card issued to users to enable the cardholder to pay a merchant for goods and services based on the cardholder's promise to the card issuer to pay them for the amounts plus the other agreed charges. The card issuer creates a revolving account and grants a line of credit to the cardholder, from which the cardholder can borrow money for payment to a merchant or as a cash advance.

Exam Probability: **Low**

52. *Answer choices:*

(see index for correct answer)

- a. Credit card
- b. Palladium Card
- c. EnRoute
- d. Smiley v. Citibank

Guidance: level 1

:: Consumer theory ::

_____ is the quantity of a good that consumers are willing and able to purchase at various prices during a given period of time.

Exam Probability: **Medium**

53. *Answer choices:*

(see index for correct answer)

- a. Rational addiction
- b. Cross elasticity of demand
- c. Demand
- d. Elasticity of substitution

Guidance: level 1

:: Macroeconomics ::

A foreign _____ is an investment in the form of a controlling ownership in a business in one country by an entity based in another country. It is thus distinguished from a foreign portfolio investment by a notion of direct control.

Exam Probability: **High**

54. *Answer choices:*

(see index for correct answer)

- a. Monetarism
- b. Direct investment
- c. Crisis theory
- d. Welfare cost of inflation

Guidance: level 1

:: Strategic alliances ::

A _____ is an agreement between two or more parties to pursue a set of agreed upon objectives needed while remaining independent organizations. A _____ will usually fall short of a legal partnership entity, agency, or corporate affiliate relationship. Typically, two companies form a _____ when each possesses one or more business assets or have expertise that will help the other by enhancing their businesses. _____ s can develop in outsourcing relationships where the parties desire to achieve long-term win-win benefits and innovation based on mutually desired outcomes.

Exam Probability: **Low**

55. *Answer choices:*
(see index for correct answer)

- a. Defensive termination
- b. Cross-licensing
- c. Management contract
- d. Bridge Alliance

Guidance: level 1

:: Stock market ::

_____ is a form of corporate equity ownership, a type of security. The terms voting share and ordinary share are also used frequently in other parts of the world; " _____ " being primarily used in the United States. They are known as Equity shares or Ordinary shares in the UK and other Commonwealth realms. This type of share gives the stockholder the right to share in the profits of the company, and to vote on matters of corporate policy and the composition of the members of the board of directors.

Exam Probability: **Medium**

56. *Answer choices:*
(see index for correct answer)

- a. Common stock
- b. Leading stock
- c. Depositary receipt
- d. Inet

Guidance: level 1

:: Real estate valuation ::

_____ or OMV is the price at which an asset would trade in a competitive auction setting. _____ is often used interchangeably with open _____ , fair value or fair _____ , although these terms have distinct definitions in different standards, and may or may not differ in some circumstances.

Exam Probability: **Medium**

57. *Answer choices:*
(see index for correct answer)

- a. Zillow
- b. Sales comparison approach
- c. Appraisal Standards Board
- d. Real estate appraisal

Guidance: level 1

:: Electronic feedback ::

_____ occurs when outputs of a system are routed back as inputs as part of a chain of cause-and-effect that forms a circuit or loop. The system can then be said to feed back into itself. The notion of cause-and-effect has to be handled carefully when applied to _____ systems.

Exam Probability: **Low**

58. *Answer choices:*
(see index for correct answer)

- a. Positive feedback
- b. feedback loop

Guidance: level 1

:: Project management ::

Some scenarios associate "this kind of planning" with learning "life skills". _____ s are necessary, or at least useful, in situations where individuals need to know what time they must be at a specific location to receive a specific service, and where people need to accomplish a set of goals within a set time period.

59. *Answer choices:*
(see index for correct answer)

- a. Arrow diagramming method
- b. Product description
- c. Defense Acquisition Workforce Improvement Act
- d. Theory X and Theory Y

Guidance: level 1

Management

Management is the administration of an organization, whether it is a business, a not-for-profit organization, or government body. Management includes the activities of setting the strategy of an organization and coordinating the efforts of its employees (or of volunteers) to accomplish its objectives through the application of available resources, such as financial, natural, technological, and human resources.

:: ::

_____ s and acquisitions are transactions in which the ownership of companies, other business organizations, or their operating units are transferred or consolidated with other entities. As an aspect of strategic management, M&A can allow enterprises to grow or downsize, and change the nature of their business or competitive position.

Exam Probability: **Medium**

1. *Answer choices:*
(see index for correct answer)

- a. empathy
- b. cultural
- c. corporate values
- d. Merger

Guidance: level 1

:: Marketing techniques ::

In industry, product lifecycle management is the process of managing the entire lifecycle of a product from inception, through engineering design and manufacture, to service and disposal of manufactured products. PLM integrates people, data, processes and business systems and provides a product information backbone for companies and their extended enterprise.

Exam Probability: **Low**

2. *Answer choices:*
(see index for correct answer)

- a. Product life cycle
- b. Micromarketing
- c. Flyposting
- d. Intent marketing

Guidance: level 1

:: ::

The _____ is a political and economic union of 28 member states that are located primarily in Europe. It has an area of 4,475,757 km2 and an estimated population of about 513 million. The EU has developed an internal single market through a standardised system of laws that apply in all member states in those matters, and only those matters, where members have agreed to act as one. EU policies aim to ensure the free movement of people, goods, services and capital within the internal market, enact legislation in justice and home affairs and maintain common policies on trade, agriculture, fisheries and regional development. For travel within the Schengen Area, passport controls have been abolished. A monetary union was established in 1999 and came into full force in 2002 and is composed of 19 EU member states which use the euro currency.

Exam Probability: **Medium**

3. *Answer choices:*
(see index for correct answer)

- a. deep-level diversity
- b. surface-level diversity
- c. open system
- d. European Union

Guidance: level 1

:: Employment discrimination ::

A _____ is a metaphor used to represent an invisible barrier that keeps a given demographic from rising beyond a certain level in a hierarchy.

Exam Probability: **Low**

4. *Answer choices:*
(see index for correct answer)

- a. MacBride Principles
- b. Employment Non-Discrimination Act
- c. Glass ceiling
- d. Employment discrimination law in the European Union

Guidance: level 1

:: Marketing ::

_____ or stock control can be broadly defined as "the activity of checking a shop's stock." However, a more focused definition takes into account the more science-based, methodical practice of not only verifying a business' inventory but also focusing on the many related facets of inventory management "within an organisation to meet the demand placed upon that business economically." Other facets of _____ include supply chain management, production control, financial flexibility, and customer satisfaction. At the root of _____ , however, is the _____ problem, which involves determining when to order, how much to order, and the logistics of those decisions.

Exam Probability: **High**

5. *Answer choices:*
(see index for correct answer)

- a. Customer value proposition
- b. Processing fluency theory of aesthetic pleasure
- c. Inventory control
- d. Business marketing

Guidance: level 1

:: Employment ::

The _____ is an individual's metaphorical "journey" through learning, work and other aspects of life. There are a number of ways to define _____ and the term is used in a variety of ways.

Exam Probability: **High**

6. *Answer choices:*
(see index for correct answer)

- a. Career
- b. My Secret Life on the McJob
- c. organizational socialization
- d. Multiple careers

Guidance: level 1

:: ::

In mathematics, a _____ is a relationship between two numbers indicating how many times the first number contains the second. For example, if a bowl of fruit contains eight oranges and six lemons, then the _____ of oranges to lemons is eight to six . Similarly, the _____ of lemons to oranges is 6:8 and the _____ of oranges to the total amount of fruit is 8:14 .

Exam Probability: **Medium**

7. *Answer choices:*
(see index for correct answer)

- a. Sarbanes-Oxley act of 2002
- b. Ratio
- c. functional perspective
- d. similarity-attraction theory

Guidance: level 1

:: Electronic feedback ::

_____ occurs when outputs of a system are routed back as inputs as part of a chain of cause-and-effect that forms a circuit or loop. The system can then be said to feed back into itself. The notion of cause-and-effect has to be handled carefully when applied to _____ systems.

Exam Probability: **Medium**

8. *Answer choices:*
(see index for correct answer)

- a. Feedback
- b. Positive feedback

Guidance: level 1

:: ::

_____ is the assignment of any responsibility or authority to another person to carry out specific activities. It is one of the core concepts of management leadership. However, the person who delegated the work remains accountable for the outcome of the delegated work. _____ empowers a subordinate to make decisions, i.e. it is a shifting of decision-making authority from one organizational level to a lower one. _____ , if properly done, is not fabrication. The opposite of effective _____ is micromanagement, where a manager provides too much input, direction, and review of delegated work. In general, _____ is good and can save money and time, help in building skills, and motivate people. On the other hand, poor _____ might cause frustration and confusion to all the involved parties. Some agents, however, do not favour a _____ and consider the power of making a decision rather burdensome.

Exam Probability: **Low**

9. *Answer choices:*
(see index for correct answer)

- a. Delegation
- b. deep-level diversity
- c. similarity-attraction theory
- d. levels of analysis

Guidance: level 1

The _____ , now also known as the First _____ , was the transition to new manufacturing processes in Europe and the US, in the period from about 1760 to sometime between 1820 and 1840. This transition included going from hand production methods to machines, new chemical manufacturing and iron production processes, the increasing use of steam power and water power, the development of machine tools and the rise of the mechanized factory system. The _____ also led to an unprecedented rise in the rate of population growth.

Exam Probability: **High**

10. *Answer choices:*
(see index for correct answer)

- a. The Condition of the Working Class in England
- b. Industrial Revolution
- c. Capital intensive industry
- d. Bernat Mill

Guidance: level 1

:: ::

_____ involves the development of an action plan designed to motivate and guide a person or group toward a goal. _____ can be guided by goal-setting criteria such as SMART criteria. _____ is a major component of personal-development and management literature.

Exam Probability: **Medium**

11. *Answer choices:*
(see index for correct answer)

- a. cultural
- b. hierarchical
- c. Goal setting
- d. imperative

Guidance: level 1

:: Human resource management ::

An organizational chart is a diagram that shows the structure of an organization and the relationships and relative ranks of its parts and positions/jobs. The term is also used for similar diagrams, for example ones showing the different elements of a field of knowledge or a group of languages.

Exam Probability: **Low**

12. *Answer choices:*
(see index for correct answer)

- a. Compensation and benefits
- b. Occupational Information Network
- c. Chief human resources officer
- d. Progress, plans, problems

Guidance: level 1

:: Statistical terminology ::

_____ is the ability to avoid wasting materials, energy, efforts, money, and time in doing something or in producing a desired result. In a more general sense, it is the ability to do things well, successfully, and without waste. In more mathematical or scientific terms, it is a measure of the extent to which input is well used for an intended task or function . It often specifically comprises the capability of a specific application of effort to produce a specific outcome with a minimum amount or quantity of waste, expense, or unnecessary effort. _____ refers to very different inputs and outputs in different fields and industries.

Exam Probability: **Low**

13. *Answer choices:*
(see index for correct answer)

- a. Completeness
- b. Efficiency
- c. Proportional reporting ratio
- d. Noncentrality parameter

Guidance: level 1

:: Management occupations ::

_____ is the process of designing, launching and running a new business, which is often initially a small business. The people who create these businesses are called entrepreneurs.

Exam Probability: **High**

14. *Answer choices:*

(see index for correct answer)

- a. City manager
- b. Entrepreneurship
- c. Hayward
- d. Store manager

Guidance: level 1

:: Evaluation ::

_____ solving consists of using generic or ad hoc methods in an orderly manner to find solutions to _____ s. Some of the _____ -solving techniques developed and used in philosophy, artificial intelligence, computer science, engineering, mathematics, or medicine are related to mental _____ -solving techniques studied in psychology.

Exam Probability: **Medium**

15. *Answer choices:*

(see index for correct answer)

- a. Health technology assessment
- b. Transferable skills analysis
- c. Shifting baseline
- d. American Evaluation Association

Guidance: level 1

:: ::

A _____ , or also known as foreman, overseer, facilitator, monitor, area coordinator, or sometimes gaffer, is the job title of a low level management position that is primarily based on authority over a worker or charge of a workplace. A _____ can also be one of the most senior in the staff at the place of work, such as a Professor who oversees a PhD dissertation. Supervision, on the other hand, can be performed by people without this formal title, for example by parents. The term _____ itself can be used to refer to any personnel who have this task as part of their job description.

Exam Probability: **Low**

16. *Answer choices:*

(see index for correct answer)

- a. hierarchical
- b. interpersonal communication
- c. surface-level diversity
- d. Supervisor

Guidance: level 1

:: Project management ::

_____ and Theory Y are theories of human work motivation and management. They were created by Douglas McGregor while he was working at the MIT Sloan School of Management in the 1950s, and developed further in the 1960s. McGregor's work was rooted in motivation theory alongside the works of Abraham Maslow, who created the hierarchy of needs. The two theories proposed by McGregor describe contrasting models of workforce motivation applied by managers in human resource management, organizational behavior, organizational communication and organizational development. _____ explains the importance of heightened supervision, external rewards, and penalties, while Theory Y highlights the motivating role of job satisfaction and encourages workers to approach tasks without direct supervision. Management use of _____ and Theory Y can affect employee motivation and productivity in different ways, and managers may choose to implement strategies from both theories into their practices.

Exam Probability: **Medium**

17. *Answer choices:*

(see index for correct answer)

- a. Theory Z
- b. Theory X
- c. Gregory T. Haugan
- d. Transfer of Burden

Guidance: level 1

:: Teams ::

A _____ usually refers to a group of individuals who work together from different geographic locations and rely on communication technology such as email, FAX, and video or voice conferencing services in order to collaborate. The term can also refer to groups or teams that work together asynchronously or across organizational levels. Powell, Piccoli and Ives define _____ s as "groups of geographically, organizationally and/or time dispersed workers brought together by information and telecommunication technologies to accomplish one or more organizational tasks." According to Ale Ebrahim et. al. , _____ s can also be defined as "small temporary groups of geographically, organizationally and/or time dispersed knowledge workers who coordinate their work predominantly with electronic information and communication technologies in order to accomplish one or more organization tasks."

Exam Probability: **Low**

18. *Answer choices:*
(see index for correct answer)

- a. Team-building
- b. team composition

Guidance: level 1

:: Rhetoric ::

_____ is the pattern of narrative development that aims to make vivid a place, object, character, or group. _____ is one of four rhetorical modes , along with exposition, argumentation, and narration. In practice it would be difficult to write literature that drew on just one of the four basic modes.

Exam Probability: **Low**

19. *Answer choices:*

- a. Periodic sentence
- b. Sophism
- c. Laconic phrase
- d. Description

Guidance: level 1

:: Employment ::

_____ is a relationship between two parties, usually based on a contract where work is paid for, where one party, which may be a corporation, for profit, not-for-profit organization, co-operative or other entity is the employer and the other is the employee. Employees work in return for payment, which may be in the form of an hourly wage, by piecework or an annual salary, depending on the type of work an employee does or which sector she or he is working in. Employees in some fields or sectors may receive gratuities, bonus payment or stock options. In some types of _____ , employees may receive benefits in addition to payment. Benefits can include health insurance, housing, disability insurance or use of a gym. _____ is typically governed by _____ laws, regulations or legal contracts.

Exam Probability: **High**

20. *Answer choices:*

- a. EuroMayDay
- b. Employment
- c. Ontario Disability Employment Network
- d. Attendance allowance

Guidance: level 1

:: Workplace ::

A _____ , also referred to as a performance review, performance evaluation, development discussion, or employee appraisal is a method by which the job performance of an employee is documented and evaluated. _____ s are a part of career development and consist of regular reviews of employee performance within organizations.

21. *Answer choices:*
(see index for correct answer)

- a. Evaluation
- b. Control freak
- c. 360-degree feedback
- d. Workplace romance

Guidance: level 1

:: ::

In business strategy, _____ is establishing a competitive advantage by having the lowest cost of operation in the industry. _____ is often driven by company efficiency, size, scale, scope and cumulative experience .A _____ strategy aims to exploit scale of production, well-defined scope and other economies , producing highly standardized products, using advanced technology.In recent years, more and more companies have chosen a strategic mix to achieve market leadership. These patterns consist of simultaneous _____ , superior customer service and product leadership. Walmart has succeeded across the world due to its _____ strategy. The company has cut down on exesses at every point of production and thus are able to provide the consumers with quality products at low prices.

22. *Answer choices:*
(see index for correct answer)

- a. interpersonal communication
- b. Character
- c. corporate values
- d. Cost leadership

Guidance: level 1

:: Human resource management ::

A _____ is a group of people with different functional expertise working toward a common goal. It may include people from finance, marketing, operations, and human resources departments. Typically, it includes employees from all levels of an organization. Members may also come from outside an organization .

Exam Probability: **Medium**

23. *Answer choices:*
(see index for correct answer)

- a. Cross-functional team
- b. Cultural capital
- c. Herrmann Brain Dominance Instrument
- d. Corporate Equality Index

Guidance: level 1

:: Marketing ::

_____ comes from the Latin neg and otsia referring to businessmen who, unlike the patricians, had no leisure time in their industriousness; it held the meaning of business until the 17th century when it took on the diplomatic connotation as a dialogue between two or more people or parties intended to reach a beneficial outcome over one or more issues where a conflict exists with respect to at least one of these issues. Thus, _____ is a process of combining divergent positions into a joint agreement under a decision rule of unanimity.

Exam Probability: **Medium**

24. *Answer choices:*
(see index for correct answer)

- a. Marketing myopia
- b. Negotiation
- c. Price
- d. Interactive collateral management

Guidance: level 1

:: ::

_____ is the amount of time someone works beyond normal working hours. The term is also used for the pay received for this time. Normal hours may be determined in several ways.

25. *Answer choices:*
(see index for correct answer)

- a. interpersonal communication
- b. Character
- c. Overtime
- d. hierarchical perspective

Guidance: level 1

:: Asset ::

In financial accounting, an _____ is any resource owned by the business. Anything tangible or intangible that can be owned or controlled to produce value and that is held by a company to produce positive economic value is an _____ . Simply stated, _____ s represent value of ownership that can be converted into cash . The balance sheet of a firm records the monetary value of the _____ s owned by that firm. It covers money and other valuables belonging to an individual or to a business.

26. *Answer choices:*
(see index for correct answer)

- a. Current asset
- b. Asset

Guidance: level 1

:: Industrial design ::

In physics and mathematics, the _____ of a mathematical space is informally defined as the minimum number of coordinates needed to specify any point within it. Thus a line has a _____ of one because only one coordinate is needed to specify a point on it for example, the point at 5 on a number line. A surface such as a plane or the surface of a cylinder or sphere has a _____ of two because two coordinates are needed to specify a point on it for example, both a latitude and longitude are required to locate a point on the surface of a sphere. The inside of a cube, a cylinder or a sphere is three- _____ al because three coordinates are needed to locate a point within these spaces.

Exam Probability: **Medium**

27. *Answer choices:*
(see index for correct answer)

- a. Dimension
- b. Industrial Arts Curriculum Project
- c. Injection molding
- d. Diffus Design

Guidance: level 1

:: E-commerce ::

_____ is the activity of buying or selling of products on online services or over the Internet. Electronic commerce draws on technologies such as mobile commerce, electronic funds transfer, supply chain management, Internet marketing, online transaction processing, electronic data interchange , inventory management systems, and automated data collection systems.

Exam Probability: **Medium**

28. *Answer choices:*
(see index for correct answer)

- a. Tor
- b. Intention economy
- c. DVD-by-mail
- d. Eagle Cash

Guidance: level 1

:: ::

A _____ or GM is an executive who has overall responsibility for managing both the revenue and cost elements of a company's income statement, known as profit & loss responsibility. A _____ usually oversees most or all of the firm's marketing and sales functions as well as the day-to-day operations of the business. Frequently, the _____ is responsible for effective planning, delegating, coordinating, staffing, organizing, and decision making to attain desirable profit making results for an organization .

Exam Probability: **Low**

29. *Answer choices:*
(see index for correct answer)

- a. interpersonal communication
- b. corporate values
- c. open system
- d. Character

Guidance: level 1

:: ::

A _____ is a problem offering two possibilities, neither of which is unambiguously acceptable or preferable. The possibilities are termed the horns of the _____ , a clichéd usage, but distinguishing the _____ from other kinds of predicament as a matter of usage.

Exam Probability: **Low**

30. *Answer choices:*
(see index for correct answer)

- a. Dilemma
- b. surface-level diversity
- c. corporate values
- d. interpersonal communication

Guidance: level 1

:: Project management ::

Some scenarios associate "this kind of planning" with learning "life skills".
_____ s are necessary, or at least useful, in situations where individuals
need to know what time they must be at a specific location to receive a
specific service, and where people need to accomplish a set of goals within a
set time period.

31. *Answer choices:*
(see index for correct answer)

- a. Operational bill
- b. TELOS
- c. Kickoff meeting
- d. Project blog

Guidance: level 1

:: Decision theory ::

Within economics the concept of _____ is used to model worth or value,
but its usage has evolved significantly over time. The term was introduced
initially as a measure of pleasure or satisfaction within the theory of
utilitarianism by moral philosophers such as Jeremy Bentham and John Stuart
Mill. But the term has been adapted and reapplied within neoclassical
economics, which dominates modern economic theory, as a _____ function
that represents a consumer's preference ordering over a choice set. As such, it
is devoid of its original interpretation as a measurement of the pleasure or
satisfaction obtained by the consumer from that choice.

32. *Answer choices:*
(see index for correct answer)

- a. Decision rule
- b. ELECTRE
- c. Weighted sum model
- d. Utility

Guidance: level 1

:: Outsourcing ::

_____ is the relocation of a business process from one country to another—typically an operational process, such as manufacturing, or supporting processes, such as accounting. Typically this refers to a company business, although state governments may also employ _____ . More recently, technical and administrative services have been offshored.

Exam Probability: **High**

33. *Answer choices:*
(see index for correct answer)

- a. PFSweb
- b. Government of Nova Scotia
- c. Service-level agreement
- d. Selfsourcing

Guidance: level 1

:: Human resource management ::

_____ is the strategic approach to the effective management of people in an organization so that they help the business to gain a competitive advantage. It is designed to maximize employee performance in service of an employer's strategic objectives. HR is primarily concerned with the management of people within organizations, focusing on policies and on systems. HR departments are responsible for overseeing employee-benefits design, employee recruitment, training and development, performance appraisal, and Reward management . HR also concerns itself with organizational change and industrial relations, that is, the balancing of organizational practices with requirements arising from collective bargaining and from governmental laws.

Exam Probability: **Low**

34. *Answer choices:*
(see index for correct answer)

- a. Corporate Equality Index
- b. Human resource management
- c. Talent management
- d. Joint Personnel Administration

Guidance: level 1

:: Autonomy ::

In developmental psychology and moral, political, and bioethical philosophy, _____ is the capacity to make an informed, uncoerced decision. Autonomous organizations or institutions are independent or self-governing. _____ can also be defined from a human resources perspective, where it denotes a level of discretion granted to an employee in his or her work. In such cases, _____ is known to generally increase job satisfaction. _____ is a term that is also widely used in the field of medicine — personal _____ is greatly recognized and valued in health care.

Exam Probability: **Low**

35. *Answer choices:*
(see index for correct answer)

- a. Stateless nation
- b. Anti-individualism
- c. Autonomy
- d. Equality of autonomy

Guidance: level 1

:: Cognitive biases ::

The _____ is a type of immediate judgement discrepancy, or cognitive bias, where a person making an initial assessment of another person, place, or thing will assume ambiguous information based upon concrete information. A simplified example of the _____ is when an individual noticing that the person in the photograph is attractive, well groomed, and properly attired, assumes, using a mental heuristic, that the person in the photograph is a good person based upon the rules of that individual's social concept. This constant error in judgment is reflective of the individual's preferences, prejudices, ideology, aspirations, and social perception. The _____ is an evaluation by an individual and can affect the perception of a decision, action, idea, business, person, group, entity, or other whenever concrete data is generalized or influences ambiguous information.

Exam Probability: **Low**

36. *Answer choices:*
(see index for correct answer)

- a. Depressive realism

- b. Fluency heuristic
- c. The Century of the Self
- d. Telescoping effect

Guidance: level 1

:: Business ::

The seller, or the provider of the goods or services, completes a sale in response to an acquisition, appropriation, requisition or a direct interaction with the buyer at the point of sale. There is a passing of title of the item, and the settlement of a price, in which agreement is reached on a price for which transfer of ownership of the item will occur. The seller, not the purchaser typically executes the sale and it may be completed prior to the obligation of payment. In the case of indirect interaction, a person who sells goods or service on behalf of the owner is known as a _____ man or _____ woman or _____ person, but this often refers to someone selling goods in a store/shop, in which case other terms are also common, including _____ clerk, shop assistant, and retail clerk.

Exam Probability: **Medium**

37. *Answer choices:*
(see index for correct answer)

- a. Disadvantaged business enterprise
- b. EPG Model
- c. Global Social Venture Competition
- d. Intangible asset finance

Guidance: level 1

:: ::

A _____ is an approximate imitation of the operation of a process or system; the act of simulating first requires a model is developed. This model is a well-defined description of the simulated subject, and represents its key characteristics, such as its behaviour, functions and abstract or physical properties. The model represents the system itself, whereas the _____ represents its operation over time.

Exam Probability: **Low**

38. *Answer choices:*
(see index for correct answer)

- a. co-culture
- b. similarity-attraction theory
- c. Simulation
- d. corporate values

Guidance: level 1

:: Business planning ::

_____ is an organization's process of defining its strategy, or direction, and making decisions on allocating its resources to pursue this strategy. It may also extend to control mechanisms for guiding the implementation of the strategy. _____ became prominent in corporations during the 1960s and remains an important aspect of strategic management. It is executed by strategic planners or strategists, who involve many parties and research sources in their analysis of the organization and its relationship to the environment in which it competes.

Exam Probability: **Low**

39. *Answer choices:*
(see index for correct answer)

- a. Customer Demand Planning
- b. Stakeholder management
- c. Strategic planning
- d. Gap analysis

Guidance: level 1

:: Management ::

In the field of management, _____ involves the formulation and implementation of the major goals and initiatives taken by an organization's top management on behalf of owners, based on consideration of resources and an assessment of the internal and external environments in which the organization operates.

Exam Probability: **High**

40. *Answer choices:*

(see index for correct answer)

- a. Functional management
- b. Strategic management
- c. Capability management
- d. Tata Management Training Centre

Guidance: level 1

:: Decision theory ::

A _____ is a deliberate system of principles to guide decisions and achieve rational outcomes. A _____ is a statement of intent, and is implemented as a procedure or protocol. Policies are generally adopted by a governance body within an organization. Policies can assist in both subjective and objective decision making. Policies to assist in subjective decision making usually assist senior management with decisions that must be based on the relative merits of a number of factors, and as a result are often hard to test objectively, e.g. work-life balance _____ . In contrast policies to assist in objective decision making are usually operational in nature and can be objectively tested, e.g. password _____ .

Exam Probability: **Low**

41. *Answer choices:*
(see index for correct answer)

- a. Ellsberg paradox
- b. Probability matching
- c. Simple prioritization
- d. Kelly criterion

Guidance: level 1

:: Human resource management ::

_____ involves improving the effectiveness of organizations and the individuals and teams within them. Training may be viewed as related to immediate changes in organizational effectiveness via organized instruction, while development is related to the progress of longer-term organizational and employee goals. While _____ technically have differing definitions, the two are oftentimes used interchangeably and/or together. _____ has historically been a topic within applied psychology but has within the last two decades become closely associated with human resources management, talent management, human resources development, instructional design, human factors, and knowledge management.

Exam Probability: **Low**

42. *Answer choices:*
(see index for correct answer)

- a. human resource
- b. Training and development
- c. war for talent
- d. Leadership development

Guidance: level 1

:: Regression analysis ::

A _____ often refers to a set of documented requirements to be satisfied by a material, design, product, or service. A _____ is often a type of technical standard.

Exam Probability: **High**

43. *Answer choices:*
(see index for correct answer)

- a. Multinomial logistic regression
- b. Specification
- c. Zero-inflated model
- d. Nonlinear regression

Guidance: level 1

:: Project management ::

A _____ is a source or supply from which a benefit is produced and it has some utility. _____ s can broadly be classified upon their availability—they are classified into renewable and non-renewable _____ s.Examples of non renewable _____ s are coal ,crude oil natural gas nuclear energy etc. Examples of renewable _____ s are air,water,wind,solar energy etc. They can also be classified as actual and potential on the basis of level of development and use, on the basis of origin they can be classified as biotic and abiotic, and on the basis of their distribution, as ubiquitous and localized . An item becomes a _____ with time and developing technology. Typically, _____ s are materials, energy, services, staff, knowledge, or other assets that are transformed to produce benefit and in the process may be consumed or made unavailable. Benefits of _____ utilization may include increased wealth, proper functioning of a system, or enhanced well-being. From a human perspective a natural _____ is anything obtained from the environment to satisfy human needs and wants. From a broader biological or ecological perspective a _____ satisfies the needs of a living organism .

Exam Probability: **Low**

44. *Answer choices:*
(see index for correct answer)

- a. Case competition
- b. Resource
- c. Hart Mason Index
- d. Sunk costs

Guidance: level 1

:: Organizational behavior ::

In organizational behavior and industrial and organizational psychology, _____ is an individual`s psychological attachment to the organization. The basis behind many of these studies was to find ways to improve how workers feel about their jobs so that these workers would become more committed to their organizations. _____ predicts work variables such as turnover, organizational citizenship behavior, and job performance. Some of the factors such as role stress, empowerment, job insecurity and employability, and distribution of leadership have been shown to be connected to a worker`s sense of _____ .

45. *Answer choices:*

(see index for correct answer)

- a. Organizational storytelling
- b. Organizational commitment
- c. Administrative Behavior
- d. Organizational behavior management

Guidance: level 1

:: Management accounting ::

_____ s are costs that change as the quantity of the good or service that a business produces changes. _____ s are the sum of marginal costs over all units produced. They can also be considered normal costs. Fixed costs and _____ s make up the two components of total cost. Direct costs are costs that can easily be associated with a particular cost object. However, not all _____ s are direct costs. For example, variable manufacturing overhead costs are _____ s that are indirect costs, not direct costs. _____ s are sometimes called unit-level costs as they vary with the number of units produced.

46. *Answer choices:*

(see index for correct answer)

- a. Variable cost
- b. Holding cost
- c. Institute of Cost and Management Accountants of Bangladesh
- d. Inventory valuation

Guidance: level 1

:: Business process ::

A _____ or business method is a collection of related, structured activities or tasks by people or equipment which in a specific sequence produce a service or product for a particular customer or customers. _____ es occur at all organizational levels and may or may not be visible to the customers. A _____ may often be visualized as a flowchart of a sequence of activities with interleaving decision points or as a process matrix of a sequence of activities with relevance rules based on data in the process. The benefits of using _____ es include improved customer satisfaction and improved agility for reacting to rapid market change. Process-oriented organizations break down the barriers of structural departments and try to avoid functional silos.

Exam Probability: **Medium**

47. *Answer choices:*
(see index for correct answer)

- a. Real-time enterprise
- b. Communication-enabled business process
- c. Business process
- d. Change order

Guidance: level 1

:: Meetings ::

A _____ is a body of one or more persons that is subordinate to a deliberative assembly. Usually, the assembly sends matters into a _____ as a way to explore them more fully than would be possible if the assembly itself were considering them. _____ s may have different functions and their type of work differ depending on the type of the organization and its needs.

Exam Probability: **Low**

48. *Answer choices:*
(see index for correct answer)

- a. Annual general meeting
- b. Awayday
- c. Committee
- d. 2006 Russian March

Guidance: level 1

:: Management ::

_____ is a method of quality control which employs statistical methods to monitor and control a process. This helps to ensure that the process operates efficiently, producing more specification-conforming products with less waste . SPC can be applied to any process where the "conforming product" output can be measured. Key tools used in SPC include run charts, control charts, a focus on continuous improvement, and the design of experiments. An example of a process where SPC is applied is manufacturing lines.

Exam Probability: **High**

49. *Answer choices:*
(see index for correct answer)

- a. I-VMS
- b. Central administration
- c. Certified Project Management Professional
- d. Statistical process control

Guidance: level 1

:: Unemployment ::

In economics, a _____ is a business cycle contraction when there is a general decline in economic activity. Macroeconomic indicators such as GDP , investment spending, capacity utilization, household income, business profits, and inflation fall, while bankruptcies and the unemployment rate rise. In the United Kingdom, it is defined as a negative economic growth for two consecutive quarters.

Exam Probability: **Medium**

50. *Answer choices:*
(see index for correct answer)

- a. JobBridge
- b. Employment-to-population ratio
- c. Recession
- d. NAIRU

Guidance: level 1

_____ is a family of procedures to identify the content of a job in terms of activities involved and attributes or job requirements needed to perform the activities. _____ provides information of organizations which helps to determine which employees are best fit for specific jobs. Through _____ , the analyst needs to understand what the important tasks of the job are, how they are carried out, and the necessary human qualities needed to complete the job successfully.

Exam Probability: **Low**

51. *Answer choices:*
(see index for correct answer)

- a. Job design
- b. Vendor management system
- c. Competency-based recruitment
- d. Bradford Factor

Guidance: level 1

:: ::

_____ or haggling is a type of negotiation in which the buyer and seller of a good or service debate the price and exact nature of a transaction. If the _____ produces agreement on terms, the transaction takes place. _____ is an alternative pricing strategy to fixed prices. Optimally, if it costs the retailer nothing to engage and allow _____ , s/he can divine the buyer's willingness to spend. It allows for capturing more consumer surplus as it allows price discrimination, a process whereby a seller can charge a higher price to one buyer who is more eager . Haggling has largely disappeared in parts of the world where the cost to haggle exceeds the gain to retailers for most common retail items. However, for expensive goods sold to uninformed buyers such as automobiles, _____ can remain commonplace.

Exam Probability: **High**

52. *Answer choices:*
(see index for correct answer)

- a. empathy
- b. corporate values

- c. Bargaining
- d. personal values

Guidance: level 1

:: Management ::

A _____ is when two or more people come together to discuss one or more topics, often in a formal or business setting, but _____ s also occur in a variety of other environments. Many various types of _____ s exist.

Exam Probability: **High**

53. *Answer choices:*
(see index for correct answer)

- a. Virtual customer environment
- b. Organizational conflict
- c. Meeting
- d. Certified management consultant

Guidance: level 1

:: ::

The _____ or just chief executive , is the most senior corporate, executive, or administrative officer in charge of managing an organization especially an independent legal entity such as a company or nonprofit institution. CEOs lead a range of organizations, including public and private corporations, non-profit organizations and even some government organizations . The CEO of a corporation or company typically reports to the board of directors and is charged with maximizing the value of the entity, which may include maximizing the share price, market share, revenues or another element. In the non-profit and government sector, CEOs typically aim at achieving outcomes related to the organization's mission, such as reducing poverty, increasing literacy, etc.

Exam Probability: **High**

54. *Answer choices:*
(see index for correct answer)

- a. deep-level diversity
- b. Chief executive officer

- c. process perspective
- d. Character

Guidance: level 1

:: Employee relations ::

_____ ownership, or employee share ownership, is an ownership interest in a company held by the company's workforce. The ownership interest may be facilitated by the company as part of employees' remuneration or incentive compensation for work performed, or the company itself may be employee owned.

Exam Probability: **Medium**

55. *Answer choices:*
(see index for correct answer)

- a. Employee surveys
- b. Employee morale
- c. Employee stock
- d. Employee motivation

Guidance: level 1

:: ::

In a supply chain, a _____ , or a seller, is an enterprise that contributes goods or services. Generally, a supply chain _____ manufactures inventory/stock items and sells them to the next link in the chain. Today, these terms refer to a supplier of any good or service.

Exam Probability: **High**

56. *Answer choices:*
(see index for correct answer)

- a. empathy
- b. Vendor
- c. similarity-attraction theory
- d. open system

Guidance: level 1

:: ::

Some scenarios associate "this kind of planning" with learning "life skills".Schedules are necessary, or at least useful, in situations where individuals need to know what time they must be at a specific location to receive a specific service, and where people need to accomplish a set of goals within a set time period.

Exam Probability: **High**

57. *Answer choices:*
(see index for correct answer)

- a. co-culture
- b. personal values
- c. Scheduling
- d. surface-level diversity

Guidance: level 1

:: Statistical terminology ::

_____ is the magnitude or dimensions of a thing. _____ can be measured as length, width, height, diameter, perimeter, area, volume, or mass.

Exam Probability: **High**

58. *Answer choices:*
(see index for correct answer)

- a. Raw score
- b. Size
- c. Probable error
- d. Data generating process

Guidance: level 1

:: Training ::

_____ is action or inaction that is regulated to be in accordance with a particular system of governance. _____ is commonly applied to regulating human and animal behavior, and furthermore, it is applied to each activity-branch in all branches of organized activity, knowledge, and other fields of study and observation. _____ can be a set of expectations that are required by any governing entity including the self, groups, classes, fields, industries, or societies.

Exam Probability: **Low**

59. *Answer choices:*

(see index for correct answer)

- a. Teletraining
- b. Training workshop
- c. Arts-based training
- d. Discipline

Guidance: level 1

Business law

Corporate law (also known as business law) is the body of law governing the rights, relations, and conduct of persons, companies, organizations and businesses. It refers to the legal practice relating to, or the theory of corporations. Corporate law often describes the law relating to matters which derive directly from the life-cycle of a corporation. It thus encompasses the formation, funding, governance, and death of a corporation.

:: Legal terms ::

_____ , or non-absolute contributory negligence outside the United States, is a partial legal defense that reduces the amount of damages that a plaintiff can recover in a negligence-based claim, based upon the degree to which the plaintiff's own negligence contributed to cause the injury. When the defense is asserted, the factfinder, usually a jury, must decide the degree to which the plaintiff's negligence and the combined negligence of all other relevant actors all contributed to cause the plaintiff's damages. It is a modification of the doctrine of contributory negligence that disallows any recovery by a plaintiff whose negligence contributed even minimally to causing the damages.

Exam Probability: **Low**

1. *Answer choices:*
(see index for correct answer)

- a. Crime against nature
- b. Comparative negligence
- c. Attendant circumstance
- d. Appropriation

Guidance: level 1

:: ::

In financial markets, a share is a unit used as mutual funds, limited partnerships, and real estate investment trusts. The owner of _____ in the corporation/company is a shareholder of the corporation. A share is an indivisible unit of capital, expressing the ownership relationship between the company and the shareholder. The denominated value of a share is its face value, and the total of the face value of issued _____ represent the capital of a company, which may not reflect the market value of those _____ .

Exam Probability: **Low**

2. *Answer choices:*

- a. personal values
- b. interpersonal communication
- c. Shares
- d. process perspective

Guidance: level 1

:: Euthenics ::

_____ is an ethical framework and suggests that an entity, be it an organization or individual, has an obligation to act for the benefit of society at large. _____ is a duty every individual has to perform so as to maintain a balance between the economy and the ecosystems. A trade-off may exist between economic development, in the material sense, and the welfare of the society and environment, though this has been challenged by many reports over the past decade. _____ means sustaining the equilibrium between the two. It pertains not only to business organizations but also to everyone whose any action impacts the environment. This responsibility can be passive, by avoiding engaging in socially harmful acts, or active, by performing activities that directly advance social goals. _____ must be intergenerational since the actions of one generation have consequences on those following.

Exam Probability: **High**

3. *Answer choices:*

- a. Social responsibility
- b. Euthenics

- c. Home economics
- d. Minnie Cumnock Blodgett

:: ::

A _____ is a person who trades in commodities produced by other people. Historically, a _____ is anyone who is involved in business or trade. _____ s have operated for as long as industry, commerce, and trade have existed. During the 16th-century, in Europe, two different terms for _____ s emerged: One term, meerseniers, described local traders such as bakers, grocers, etc.; while a new term, koopman (Dutch: koopman, described _____ s who operated on a global stage, importing and exporting goods over vast distances, and offering added-value services such as credit and finance.

Exam Probability: **Low**

4. *Answer choices:*
(see index for correct answer)

- a. Merchant
- b. interpersonal communication
- c. personal values
- d. hierarchical perspective

:: Legal doctrines and principles ::

_____ is a defense in the law of torts, which bars or reduces a plaintiff's right to recovery against a negligent tortfeasor if the defendant can demonstrate that the plaintiff voluntarily and knowingly assumed the risks at issue inherent to the dangerous activity in which he was participating at the time of his or her injury.

Exam Probability: **Low**

5. *Answer choices:*
(see index for correct answer)

- a. Act of state
- b. Parol evidence
- c. Attractive nuisance

- d. Assumption of risk

:: ::

A _____ , or trial by jury, is a lawful proceeding in which a jury makes
a decision or findings of fact. It is distinguished from a bench trial in which
a judge or panel of judges makes all decisions.

Exam Probability: **Low**

6. *Answer choices:*
(see index for correct answer)

- a. Jury Trial
- b. empathy
- c. deep-level diversity
- d. process perspective

:: Business law ::

A _____ is an arrangement where parties, known as partners, agree to
cooperate to advance their mutual interests. The partners in a _____ may
be individuals, businesses, interest-based organizations, schools, governments
or combinations. Organizations may partner to increase the likelihood of each
achieving their mission and to amplify their reach. A _____ may result in
issuing and holding equity or may be only governed by a contract.

Exam Probability: **Medium**

7. *Answer choices:*
(see index for correct answer)

- a. Tax patent
- b. Double ticketing
- c. Partnership
- d. Tacit relocation

:: Stock market ::

_____ is freedom from, or resilience against, potential harm caused by others. Beneficiaries of _____ may be of persons and social groups, objects and institutions, ecosystems or any other entity or phenomenon vulnerable to unwanted change by its environment.

Exam Probability: **Low**

8. *Answer choices:*
(see index for correct answer)

- a. American depositary receipt
- b. Security
- c. Red herring prospectus
- d. Profit warning

Guidance: level 1

:: Project management ::

_____ is the right to exercise power, which can be formalized by a state and exercised by way of judges, appointed executives of government, or the ecclesiastical or priestly appointed representatives of a God or other deities.

Exam Probability: **Medium**

9. *Answer choices:*
(see index for correct answer)

- a. Technology roadmap
- b. Authority
- c. Work package
- d. Pre-construction services

Guidance: level 1

:: ::

The Sherman Antitrust Act of 1890 was a United States antitrust law that regulates competition among enterprises, which was passed by Congress under the presidency of Benjamin Harrison.

10. *Answer choices:*

(see index for correct answer)

- a. Character
- b. hierarchical perspective
- c. empathy
- d. information systems assessment

Guidance: level 1

:: Writs ::

In common law, a _____ is a formal _____ ten order issued by a body with administrative or judicial jurisdiction; in modern usage, this body is generally a court. Warrants, prerogative _____ s, and subpoenas are common types of _____ , but many forms exist and have existed.

Exam Probability: **High**

11. *Answer choices:*

(see index for correct answer)

- a. Writ
- b. Qui tam
- c. Writ of execution

Guidance: level 1

:: ::

A _____ is a law passed by a legislative body in a common law system to set the maximum time after an event within which legal proceedings may be initiated.

Exam Probability: **High**

12. *Answer choices:*

(see index for correct answer)

- a. open system
- b. imperative
- c. Sarbanes-Oxley act of 2002
- d. similarity-attraction theory

Guidance: level 1

_____ is a process of negotiation between employers and a group of employees aimed at agreements to regulate working salaries, working conditions, benefits, and other aspects of workers' compensation and rights for workers. The interests of the employees are commonly presented by representatives of a trade union to which the employees belong. The collective agreements reached by these negotiations usually set out wage scales, working hours, training, health and safety, overtime, grievance mechanisms, and rights to participate in workplace or company affairs.

Exam Probability: **Medium**

13. *Answer choices:*
(see index for correct answer)

- a. Common rule awards
- b. Collaborative bargaining
- c. In Place of Strife
- d. Collective bargaining

Guidance: level 1

A _____ is an individual or institution that legally owns one or more shares of stock in a public or private corporation. _____ s may be referred to as members of a corporation. Legally, a person is not a _____ in a corporation until their name and other details are entered in the corporation's register of _____ s or members.

Exam Probability: **Medium**

14. *Answer choices:*
(see index for correct answer)

- a. hierarchical
- b. Shareholder
- c. interpersonal communication
- d. levels of analysis

Guidance: level 1

:: Legal terms ::

A _____ is any "lesser" criminal act in some common law legal systems. _____ s are generally punished less severely than felonies, but theoretically more so than administrative infractions and regulatory offences. Many _____ s are punished with monetary fines.

Exam Probability: **Medium**

15. *Answer choices:*
(see index for correct answer)

- a. McKenzie friend
- b. Natural person
- c. Misdemeanor
- d. Punitive damages

Guidance: level 1

:: Intention ::

_____ is the mental element of a person's intention to commit a crime; or knowledge that one's action or lack of action would cause a crime to be committed. It is a necessary element of many crimes.

Exam Probability: **Medium**

16. *Answer choices:*
(see index for correct answer)

- a. bona fide
- b. Letter of Intent

Guidance: level 1

:: ::

The _____ is one of the several United States Uniform Acts proposed by the National Conference of Commissioners on Uniform State Laws . Forty-seven states, the District of Columbia, and the U.S. Virgin Islands have adopted the UETA. Its purpose is to harmonize state laws concerning retention of paper records and the validity of electronic signatures.

17. *Answer choices:*

(see index for correct answer)

- a. surface-level diversity
- b. cultural
- c. personal values
- d. information systems assessment

Guidance: level 1

:: Competition regulators ::

The _____ is an independent agency of the United States government, established in 1914 by the _____ Act. Its principal mission is the promotion of consumer protection and the elimination and prevention of anticompetitive business practices, such as coercive monopoly. It is headquartered in the _____ Building in Washington, D.C.

Exam Probability: **Low**

18. *Answer choices:*

(see index for correct answer)

- a. Competition Commission of India
- b. Commerce Commission
- c. Federal Cartel Office
- d. Federal Trade Commission

Guidance: level 1

:: Business ::

_____ is a trade policy that does not restrict imports or exports; it can also be understood as the free market idea applied to international trade. In government, _____ is predominantly advocated by political parties that hold liberal economic positions while economically left-wing and nationalist political parties generally support protectionism, the opposite of _____ .

Exam Probability: **Low**

19. *Answer choices:*

(see index for correct answer)

- a. American Environmental Assessment and Solutions Inc.
- b. Free trade
- c. Resource slack
- d. Counter trade

Guidance: level 1

:: ::

A concept of English law, a _____ is an untrue or misleading statement of fact made during negotiations by one party to another, the statement then inducing that other party into the contract. The misled party may normally rescind the contract, and sometimes may be awarded damages as well

-

Exam Probability: **Medium**

20. *Answer choices:*
(see index for correct answer)

- a. Misrepresentation
- b. empathy
- c. co-culture
- d. deep-level diversity

Guidance: level 1

:: Business law ::

An _____ is a clause in a contract that requires the parties to resolve their disputes through an arbitration process. Although such a clause may or may not specify that arbitration occur within a specific jurisdiction, it always binds the parties to a type of resolution outside the courts, and is therefore considered a kind of forum selection clause.

Exam Probability: **High**

21. *Answer choices:*
(see index for correct answer)

- a. Teck Corp. Ltd. v. Millar
- b. Family and Medical Leave Act of 1993
- c. Free agent
- d. Operating lease

:: ::

The _____ is an intergovernmental organization that is concerned with the regulation of international trade between nations. The WTO officially commenced on 1 January 1995 under the Marrakesh Agreement, signed by 124 nations on 15 April 1994, replacing the General Agreement on Tariffs and Trade , which commenced in 1948. It is the largest international economic organization in the world.

Exam Probability: **High**

22. *Answer choices:*
(see index for correct answer)

- a. personal values
- b. levels of analysis
- c. World Trade Organization
- d. Character

:: ::

A _____ is a request to do something, most commonly addressed to a government official or public entity. _____ s to a deity are a form of prayer called supplication.

Exam Probability: **High**

23. *Answer choices:*
(see index for correct answer)

- a. similarity-attraction theory
- b. surface-level diversity
- c. Petition
- d. interpersonal communication

:: Contract law ::

In the United States, the _____ rule refers to the legal right for a buyer of goods to insist upon "_____" by the seller. In a contract for the sale of goods, if the goods fail to conform exactly to the description in the contract the buyer may nonetheless accept the goods, or reject the goods, or reject the nonconforming part of the tender and accept the conforming part. The buyer does not have an unfettered ability to reject tender.

Exam Probability: **Medium**

24. *Answer choices:*
(see index for correct answer)

- a. Extended warranty
- b. Perfect tender
- c. Baseball business rules
- d. Job order contracting

Guidance: level 1

:: Business law ::

A _____ is a group of people who jointly supervise the activities of an organization, which can be either a for-profit business, nonprofit organization, or a government agency. Such a board's powers, duties, and responsibilities are determined by government regulations and the organization's own constitution and bylaws. These authorities may specify the number of members of the board, how they are to be chosen, and how often they are to meet.

Exam Probability: **High**

25. *Answer choices:*
(see index for correct answer)

- a. Business.gov
- b. Statutory authority
- c. Board of directors
- d. Leave of absence

Guidance: level 1

:: Contract law ::

Offer and acceptance analysis is a traditional approach in contract law. The offer and acceptance formula, developed in the 19th century, identifies a moment of formation when the parties are of one mind. This classical approach to contract formation has been modified by developments in the law of estoppel, misleading conduct, misrepresentation and unjust enrichment.

Exam Probability: **Low**

26. *Answer choices:*

- a. Franchisor
- b. Offeror
- c. Piggy-back
- d. Pre-existing duty rule

Guidance: level 1

:: Labour relations ::

_____ is a field of study that can have different meanings depending on the context in which it is used. In an international context, it is a subfield of labor history that studies the human relations with regard to work – in its broadest sense – and how this connects to questions of social inequality. It explicitly encompasses unregulated, historical, and non-Western forms of labor. Here, _____ define "for or with whom one works and under what rules. These rules determine the type of work, type and amount of remuneration, working hours, degrees of physical and psychological strain, as well as the degree of freedom and autonomy associated with the work."

Exam Probability: **Medium**

27. *Answer choices:*

- a. Delta Board Council
- b. Two-tier system
- c. Labor relations
- d. Eurocadres

Guidance: level 1

:: Consumer theory ::

A _____ is a technical term in psychology, economics and philosophy usually used in relation to choosing between alternatives. For example, someone prefers A over B if they would rather choose A than B.

Exam Probability: **Medium**

28. *Answer choices:*
(see index for correct answer)

- a. Consumer sovereignty
- b. Permanent income hypothesis
- c. Consumption
- d. Lexicographic preferences

Guidance: level 1

:: ::

_____ Motor Company is an American multinational automaker that has its main headquarter in Dearborn, Michigan, a suburb of Detroit. It was founded by Henry _____ and incorporated on June 16, 1903. The company sells automobiles and commercial vehicles under the _____ brand and most luxury cars under the Lincoln brand. _____ also owns Brazilian SUV manufacturer Troller, an 8% stake in Aston Martin of the United Kingdom and a 32% stake in Jiangling Motors. It also has joint-ventures in China , Taiwan , Thailand , Turkey , and Russia . The company is listed on the New York Stock Exchange and is controlled by the _____ family; they have minority ownership but the majority of the voting power.

Exam Probability: **Medium**

29. *Answer choices:*
(see index for correct answer)

- a. cultural
- b. open system
- c. hierarchical perspective
- d. surface-level diversity

Guidance: level 1

:: Utilitarianism ::

_____ is a family of consequentialist ethical theories that promotes actions that maximize happiness and well-being for the majority of a population. Although different varieties of _____ admit different characterizations, the basic idea behind all of them is to in some sense maximize utility, which is often defined in terms of well-being or related concepts. For instance, Jeremy Bentham, the founder of _____ , described utility as

Exam Probability: **Medium**

30. *Answer choices:*
(see index for correct answer)

- a. Utilitarianism
- b. Mere addition paradox
- c. Hedonism
- d. Consequentialism

Guidance: level 1

:: Insurance law ::

_____ exists when an insured person derives a financial or other kind of benefit from the continuous existence, without repairment or damage, of the insured object . A person has an _____ in something when loss of or damage to that thing would cause the person to suffer a financial or other kind of loss.Normally, _____ is established by ownership, possession, or direct relationship. For example, people have _____ s in their own homes and vehicles, but not in their neighbors' homes and vehicles, and almost certainly not those of strangers.

Exam Probability: **High**

31. *Answer choices:*
(see index for correct answer)

- a. QC clause
- b. Insurable interest
- c. Marine Insurance Act 1906
- d. Hangarter v. Provident

Guidance: level 1

:: Legal terms ::

_____ , or exemplary damages, are damages assessed in order to punish the defendant for outrageous conduct and/or to reform or deter the defendant and others from engaging in conduct similar to that which formed the basis of the lawsuit. Although the purpose of _____ is not to compensate the plaintiff, the plaintiff will receive all or some of the _____ award.

Exam Probability: **Low**

32. *Answer choices:*
(see index for correct answer)

- a. Age of majority
- b. Party
- c. Punitive damages
- d. Judicial estoppel

Guidance: level 1

:: Generally Accepted Accounting Principles ::

Expenditure is an outflow of money to another person or group to pay for an item or service, or for a category of costs. For a tenant, rent is an _____ . For students or parents, tuition is an _____ . Buying food, clothing, furniture or an automobile is often referred to as an _____ . An _____ is a cost that is "paid" or "remitted", usually in exchange for something of value. Something that seems to cost a great deal is "expensive". Something that seems to cost little is "inexpensive". "_____ s of the table" are _____ s of dining, refreshments, a feast, etc.

Exam Probability: **Low**

33. *Answer choices:*
(see index for correct answer)

- a. Expense
- b. Completed-contract method
- c. Standard Business Reporting
- d. Cost pool

Guidance: level 1

:: Commercial item transport and distribution ::

_____ s may be negotiable or non-negotiable. Negotiable _____ s allow transfer of ownership of that commodity without having to deliver the physical commodity. See Delivery order.

Exam Probability: **Low**

34. *Answer choices:*
(see index for correct answer)

- a. Blue Water Trucking
- b. Warehouse receipt
- c. Trade facilitation
- d. Hold

Guidance: level 1

:: Marketing ::

A _____ is an overall experience of a customer that distinguishes an organization or product from its rivals in the eyes of the customer. _____ s are used in business, marketing, and advertising. Name _____ s are sometimes distinguished from generic or store _____ s.

Exam Probability: **Low**

35. *Answer choices:*
(see index for correct answer)

- a. Paddock girl
- b. Market orientation
- c. Mystery shopping
- d. Non-price competition

Guidance: level 1

:: Business law ::

_____ is where a person's financial liability is limited to a fixed sum, most commonly the value of a person's investment in a company or partnership. If a company with _____ is sued, then the claimants are suing the company, not its owners or investors. A shareholder in a limited company is not personally liable for any of the debts of the company, other than for the amount already invested in the company and for any unpaid amount on the shares in the company, if any. The same is true for the members of a _____ partnership and the limited partners in a limited partnership. By contrast, sole proprietors and partners in general partnerships are each liable for all the debts of the business .

Exam Probability: **Low**

36. *Answer choices:*

- a. Retained interest
- b. Limited liability
- c. Forged endorsement
- d. License

Guidance: level 1

:: ::

In law, an _____ is the process in which cases are reviewed, where parties request a formal change to an official decision. _____ s function both as a process for error correction as well as a process of clarifying and interpreting law. Although appellate courts have existed for thousands of years, common law countries did not incorporate an affirmative right to _____ into their jurisprudence until the 19th century.

Exam Probability: **Low**

37. *Answer choices:*

- a. interpersonal communication
- b. Appeal
- c. information systems assessment
- d. process perspective

Guidance: level 1

:: Stock market ::

The _____ of a corporation is all of the shares into which ownership of the corporation is divided. In American English, the shares are commonly known as "_____ s". A single share of the _____ represents fractional ownership of the corporation in proportion to the total number of shares. This typically entitles the _____ holder to that fraction of the company's earnings, proceeds from liquidation of assets , or voting power, often dividing these up in proportion to the amount of money each _____ holder has invested. Not all _____ is necessarily equal, as certain classes of _____ may be issued for example without voting rights, with enhanced voting rights, or with a certain priority to receive profits or liquidation proceeds before or after other classes of shareholders.

Exam Probability: **High**

38. *Answer choices:*
(see index for correct answer)

- a. Next: The Future Just Happened
- b. Buy side
- c. Stock
- d. The Congressional Effect

Guidance: level 1

:: Treaties ::

A _____ is an agreement under international law entered into by actors in international law, namely sovereign states and international organizations. A _____ may also be known as an agreement, protocol, covenant, convention, pact, or exchange of letters, among other terms. Regardless of terminology, all of these forms of agreements are, under international law, equally considered treaties and the rules are the same.

Exam Probability: **Low**

39. *Answer choices:*
(see index for correct answer)

- a. Guillotine clause
- b. Alliance
- c. Clausula rebus sic stantibus
- d. Secret treaty

:: ::

Employment is a relationship between two parties, usually based on a contract where work is paid for, where one party, which may be a corporation, for profit, not-for-profit organization, co-operative or other entity is the employer and the other is the employee. Employees work in return for payment, which may be in the form of an hourly wage, by piecework or an annual salary, depending on the type of work an employee does or which sector she or he is working in. Employees in some fields or sectors may receive gratuities, bonus payment or stock options. In some types of employment, employees may receive benefits in addition to payment. Benefits can include health insurance, housing, disability insurance or use of a gym. Employment is typically governed by employment laws, regulations or legal contracts.

Exam Probability: **High**

40. *Answer choices:*
(see index for correct answer)

- a. Personnel
- b. information systems assessment
- c. Sarbanes-Oxley act of 2002
- d. process perspective

:: ::

A contract is a legally-binding agreement which recognises and governs the rights and duties of the parties to the agreement. A contract is legally enforceable because it meets the requirements and approval of the law. An agreement typically involves the exchange of goods, services, money, or promises of any of those. In the event of breach of contract, the law awards the injured party access to legal remedies such as damages and cancellation.

Exam Probability: **High**

41. *Answer choices:*
(see index for correct answer)

- a. Sarbanes-Oxley act of 2002

- b. empathy
- c. deep-level diversity
- d. personal values

Guidance: level 1

:: Debt ::

A _____ is a party that has a claim on the services of a second party. It is a person or institution to whom money is owed. The first party, in general, has provided some property or service to the second party under the assumption that the second party will return an equivalent property and service. The second party is frequently called a debtor or borrower. The first party is called the _____ , which is the lender of property, service, or money.

Exam Probability: **Low**

42. *Answer choices:*
(see index for correct answer)

- a. Creditor
- b. Debtors Anonymous
- c. Perpetual subordinated debt
- d. Least developed country

Guidance: level 1

:: ::

A _____ is an organization, usually a group of people or a company, authorized to act as a single entity and recognized as such in law. Early incorporated entities were established by charter . Most jurisdictions now allow the creation of new _____ s through registration.

Exam Probability: **Medium**

43. *Answer choices:*
(see index for correct answer)

- a. interpersonal communication
- b. corporate values
- c. Corporation
- d. Sarbanes-Oxley act of 2002

:: Statutory law ::

_____ or statute law is written law set down by a body of legislature or by a singular legislator . This is as opposed to oral or customary law; or regulatory law promulgated by the executive or common law of the judiciary. Statutes may originate with national, state legislatures or local municipalities.

Exam Probability: **High**

44. *Answer choices:*
(see index for correct answer)

- a. ratification
- b. Statutory Law
- c. Statute of repose
- d. incorporation by reference

:: Information technology audit ::

_____ is the act of using a computer to take or alter electronic data, or to gain unlawful use of a computer or system. In the United States, _____ is specifically proscribed by the _____ and Abuse Act, which criminalizes computer-related acts under federal jurisdiction. Types of _____ include.

Exam Probability: **Low**

45. *Answer choices:*
(see index for correct answer)

- a. Mobile device forensics
- b. Host protected area
- c. Information technology audit
- d. Computer fraud

:: Business ::

An _____ is a key document used by limited liability companies to outline the business` financial and functional decisions including rules, regulations and provisions. The purpose of the document is to govern the internal operations of the business in a way that suits the specific needs of the business owners. Once the document is signed by the members of the limited liability company, it acts as an official contract binding them to its terms.

_____ is mandatory as per laws only in 5 states - California, Delaware, Maine, Missouri, and New York LLCs operating without an _____ are governed by the state's default rules contained in the relevant statute and developed through state court decisions. An _____ is similar in function to corporate by-laws, or analogous to a partnership agreement in multi-member LLCs. In single-member LLCs, an _____ is a declaration of the structure that the member has chosen for the company and sometimes used to prove in court that the LLC structure is separate from that of the individual owner and thus necessary so that the owner has documentation to prove that he or she is indeed separate from the entity itself.

Exam Probability: **Medium**

46. *Answer choices:*
(see index for correct answer)

- a. Business analysis
- b. Operating agreement
- c. Disadvantaged business enterprise
- d. Attribution

Guidance: level 1

:: ::

Industrial espionage, _____, corporate spying or corporate espionage is a form of espionage conducted for commercial purposes instead of purely national security. While _____ is conducted or orchestrated by governments and is international in scope, industrial or corporate espionage is more often national and occurs between companies or corporations.

Exam Probability: **High**

47. *Answer choices:*
(see index for correct answer)

- a. cultural
- b. imperative
- c. interpersonal communication
- d. Sarbanes-Oxley act of 2002

Guidance: level 1

:: Patent law ::

A _____ is generally any statement intended to specify or delimit the
scope of rights and obligations that may be exercised and enforced by parties
in a legally recognized relationship. In contrast to other terms for legally
operative language, the term _____ usually implies situations that
involve some level of uncertainty, waiver, or risk.

Exam Probability: **Medium**

48. *Answer choices:*

(see index for correct answer)

- a. Disclaimer
- b. Industrial applicability
- c. Internet as a source of prior art
- d. Patentability

Guidance: level 1

:: Criminal law ::

_____ is the body of law that relates to crime. It proscribes conduct
perceived as threatening, harmful, or otherwise endangering to the property,
health, safety, and moral welfare of people inclusive of one's self. Most
_____ is established by statute, which is to say that the laws are enacted
by a legislature. _____ includes the punishment and rehabilitation of
people who violate such laws. _____ varies according to jurisdiction, and
differs from civil law, where emphasis is more on dispute resolution and victim
compensation, rather than on punishment or rehabilitation. Criminal procedure
is a formalized official activity that authenticates the fact of commission of
a crime and authorizes punitive or rehabilitative treatment of the offender.

Exam Probability: **Low**

49. *Answer choices:*

(see index for correct answer)

- a. complicit
- b. Mala prohibita
- c. Criminal law
- d. mitigating factor

Guidance: level 1

:: Actuarial science ::

_____ is the possibility of losing something of value. Values can be gained or lost when taking _____ resulting from a given action or inaction, foreseen or unforeseen . _____ can also be defined as the intentional interaction with uncertainty. Uncertainty is a potential, unpredictable, and uncontrollable outcome; _____ is a consequence of action taken in spite of uncertainty.

Exam Probability: **Medium**

50. *Answer choices:*
(see index for correct answer)

- a. Risk
- b. Reliability theory
- c. Insurable risk
- d. Life expectancy

Guidance: level 1

:: Criminal procedure ::

In law, a verdict is the formal finding of fact made by a jury on matters or questions submitted to the jury by a judge. In a bench trial, the judge's decision near the end of the trial is simply referred to as a finding. In England and Wales, a coroner's findings are called verdicts .

Exam Probability: **High**

51. *Answer choices:*
(see index for correct answer)

- a. Exoneration
- b. Directed verdict

Guidance: level 1

The _____ for the Protection of Literary and Artistic Works, usually known as the _____ , is an international agreement governing copyright, which was first accepted in Berne, Switzerland, in 1886.

Exam Probability: **Medium**

52. *Answer choices:*
(see index for correct answer)

- a. Berne Convention
- b. Chemical leasing
- c. Regulation of chemicals
- d. Middle German Chemical Triangle

Guidance: level 1

:: ::

_____ is an abstract concept of management of complex systems according to a set of rules and trends. In systems theory, these types of rules exist in various fields of biology and society, but the term has slightly different meanings according to context. For example.

Exam Probability: **Medium**

53. *Answer choices:*
(see index for correct answer)

- a. levels of analysis
- b. hierarchical perspective
- c. functional perspective
- d. cultural

Guidance: level 1

:: Equity (law) ::

An assignment is a legal term used in the context of the law of contract and of property. In both instances, assignment is the process whereby a person, the assignor, transfers rights or benefits to another, the _____ . An assignment may not transfer a duty, burden or detriment without the express agreement of the _____ . The right or benefit being assigned may be a gift or it may be paid for with a contractual consideration such as money.

Exam Probability: **High**

54. *Answer choices:*
(see index for correct answer)

- a. assignor
- b. Assignee

Guidance: level 1

:: Ethically disputed business practices ::

_____ is the trading of a public company's stock or other securities by individuals with access to nonpublic information about the company. In various countries, some kinds of trading based on insider information is illegal. This is because it is seen as unfair to other investors who do not have access to the information, as the investor with insider information could potentially make larger profits than a typical investor could make. The rules governing _____ are complex and vary significantly from country to country. The extent of enforcement also varies from one country to another. The definition of insider in one jurisdiction can be broad, and may cover not only insiders themselves but also any persons related to them, such as brokers, associates and even family members. A person who becomes aware of non-public information and trades on that basis may be guilty of a crime.

Exam Probability: **High**

55. *Answer choices:*
(see index for correct answer)

- a. Tobashi scheme
- b. Insider trading
- c. Two sets of books
- d. Earnings management

Guidance: level 1

_____ is the assignment of any responsibility or authority to another person to carry out specific activities. It is one of the core concepts of management leadership. However, the person who delegated the work remains accountable for the outcome of the delegated work. _____ empowers a subordinate to make decisions, i.e. it is a shifting of decision-making authority from one organizational level to a lower one. _____ , if properly done, is not fabrication. The opposite of effective _____ is micromanagement, where a manager provides too much input, direction, and review of delegated work. In general, _____ is good and can save money and time, help in building skills, and motivate people. On the other hand, poor _____ might cause frustration and confusion to all the involved parties. Some agents, however, do not favour a _____ and consider the power of making a decision rather burdensome.

Exam Probability: **Low**

56. *Answer choices:*
(see index for correct answer)

- a. cultural
- b. levels of analysis
- c. hierarchical
- d. open system

Guidance: level 1

_____ is the trust which allows one party to provide money or resources to another party wherein the second party does not reimburse the first party immediately , but promises either to repay or return those resources at a later date. In other words, _____ is a method of making reciprocity formal, legally enforceable, and extensible to a large group of unrelated people.

Exam Probability: **High**

57. *Answer choices:*
(see index for correct answer)

- a. Charge-off
- b. Floating charge
- c. Zombie company
- d. Debt crisis

:: Judgment (law) ::

In law, a _____ is a judgment entered by a court for one party and against another party summarily, i.e., without a full trial. Such a judgment may be issued on the merits of an entire case, or on discrete issues in that case.

Exam Probability: **High**

58. *Answer choices:*
(see index for correct answer)

- a. Entry of judgment
- b. judgment as a matter of law

:: ::

_____ is the practice of protecting the natural environment by individuals, organizations and governments. Its objectives are to conserve natural resources and the existing natural environment and, where possible, to repair damage and reverse trends.

Exam Probability: **High**

59. *Answer choices:*
(see index for correct answer)

- a. Environmental Protection
- b. open system
- c. information systems assessment
- d. interpersonal communication

Finance

Finance is a field that is concerned with the allocation (investment) of assets and liabilities over space and time, often under conditions of risk or uncertainty. Finance can also be defined as the science of money management. Participants in the market aim to price assets based on their risk level, fundamental value, and their expected rate of return. Finance can be split into three sub-categories: public finance, corporate finance and personal finance.

:: ::

_____ is the process of making predictions of the future based on past and present data and most commonly by analysis of trends. A commonplace example might be estimation of some variable of interest at some specified future date. Prediction is a similar, but more general term. Both might refer to formal statistical methods employing time series, cross-sectional or longitudinal data, or alternatively to less formal judgmental methods. Usage can differ between areas of application: for example, in hydrology the terms "forecast" and "_____" are sometimes reserved for estimates of values at certain specific future times, while the term "prediction" is used for more general estimates, such as the number of times floods will occur over a long period.

Exam Probability: **Medium**

1. *Answer choices:*

(see index for correct answer)

- a. Sarbanes-Oxley act of 2002
- b. corporate values
- c. open system
- d. Forecasting

Guidance: level 1

:: Financial ratios ::

_____ is the difference between revenue and cost of goods sold divided by revenue. _____ is expressed as a percentage. Generally, it is calculated as the selling price of an item, less the cost of goods sold .

_____ is often used interchangeably with Gross Profit, but the terms are different. When speaking about a monetary amount, it is technically correct to use the term Gross Profit; when referring to a percentage or ratio, it is correct to use _____ . In other words, _____ is a percentage value, while Gross Profit is a monetary value.

Exam Probability: **Medium**

2. *Answer choices:*

(see index for correct answer)

- a. Gross margin
- b. Yield gap
- c. Omega ratio
- d. Financial ratio

Guidance: level 1

:: ::

A _____ is a fund into which a sum of money is added during an employee's employment years, and from which payments are drawn to support the person's retirement from work in the form of periodic payments. A _____ may be a "defined benefit plan" where a fixed sum is paid regularly to a person, or a "defined contribution plan" under which a fixed sum is invested and then becomes available at retirement age. _____ s should not be confused with severance pay; the former is usually paid in regular installments for life after retirement, while the latter is typically paid as a fixed amount after involuntary termination of employment prior to retirement.

Exam Probability: **High**

3. *Answer choices:*

(see index for correct answer)

- a. Pension
- b. deep-level diversity
- c. co-culture
- d. surface-level diversity

Guidance: level 1

_____ in capital budgeting refers to the period of time required to recoup the funds expended in an investment, or to reach the break-even point. For example, a $1000 investment made at the start of year 1 which returned $500 at the end of year 1 and year 2 respectively would have a two-year _____ . _____ is usually expressed in years. Starting from investment year by calculating Net Cash Flow for each year: Net Cash Flow Year 1 = Cash Inflow Year 1 - Cash Outflow Year 1. Then Cumulative Cash Flow = Accumulate by year until Cumulative Cash Flow is a positive number: that year is the payback year.

Exam Probability: **High**

4. *Answer choices:*
(see index for correct answer)

- a. Soft launch
- b. Price analysis
- c. Numeric distribution
- d. Payback period

Guidance: level 1

_____ of something is, in finance, the adding together of interest or different investments over a period of time. It holds specific meanings in accounting, where it can refer to accounts on a balance sheet that represent liabilities and non-cash-based assets used in _____ -based accounting. These types of accounts include, among others, accounts payable, accounts receivable, goodwill, deferred tax liability and future interest expense.

Exam Probability: **Low**

5. *Answer choices:*
(see index for correct answer)

- a. Fair value accounting
- b. Mark-to-market
- c. Accounts payable
- d. Accrual

Guidance: level 1

:: Accounting journals and ledgers ::

_____ is a daybook or journal which is used to record transactions relating to adjustment entries, opening stock, accounting errors etc. The source documents of this prime entry book are journal voucher, copy of management reports and invoices.

Exam Probability: **Medium**

6. *Answer choices:*
(see index for correct answer)

- a. Check register
- b. Subledger
- c. General journal
- d. Journal entry

Guidance: level 1

:: Financial economics ::

_____ , Inc. is an independent investment research and financial publishing firm based in New York City, New York, United States, founded in 1931 by Arnold Bernhard. _____ is best known for publishing The _____ Investment Survey, a stock analysis newsletter that is among the most highly regarded and widely used independent investment research resources in global investment and trading markets, tracking approximately 1,700 publicly traded stocks in over 99 industries.

Exam Probability: **High**

7. *Answer choices:*
(see index for correct answer)

- a. Consumer leverage ratio
- b. Investment protection
- c. MarHedge
- d. Value Line

Guidance: level 1

:: ::

In finance, return is a profit on an investment. It comprises any change in value of the investment, and/or cash flows which the investor receives from the investment, such as interest payments or dividends. It may be measured either in absolute terms or as a percentage of the amount invested. The latter is also called the holding period return.

Exam Probability: **High**

8. *Answer choices:*
(see index for correct answer)

- a. functional perspective
- b. interpersonal communication
- c. corporate values
- d. Rate of return

Guidance: level 1

:: Finance ::

_____ is a field that is concerned with the allocation of assets and liabilities over space and time, often under conditions of risk or uncertainty. _____ can also be defined as the art of money management. Participants in the market aim to price assets based on their risk level, fundamental value, and their expected rate of return. _____ can be split into three sub-categories: public _____ , corporate _____ and personal _____ .

Exam Probability: **Low**

9. *Answer choices:*
(see index for correct answer)

- a. Net insurance benefit
- b. Crowdfunding
- c. Life settlement
- d. Roll yield

Guidance: level 1

:: Marketing ::

A _____ is an overall experience of a customer that distinguishes an organization or product from its rivals in the eyes of the customer. _____ s are used in business, marketing, and advertising. Name _____ s are sometimes distinguished from generic or store _____ s.

10. *Answer choices:*
(see index for correct answer)

- a. Digital omnivore
- b. Gold party
- c. Marketing Week
- d. Brand

Guidance: level 1

:: Accounting ::

_____ is a process of providing relief to shared service organization's cost centers that provide a product or service. In turn, the associated expense is assigned to internal clients' cost centers that consume the products and services. For example, the CIO may provide all IT services within the company and assign the costs back to the business units that consume each offering.

11. *Answer choices:*
(see index for correct answer)

- a. Cost allocation
- b. Earnings surprise
- c. INPACT International
- d. ACSOI

Guidance: level 1

:: Cash flow ::

In corporate finance, _____ or _____ to firm is a way of looking at a business's cash flow to see what is available for distribution among all the securities holders of a corporate entity. This may be useful to parties such as equity holders, debt holders, preferred stock holders, and convertible security holders when they want to see how much cash can be extracted from a company without causing issues to its operations.

Exam Probability: **Low**

12. *Answer choices:*

(see index for correct answer)

- a. Valuation using discounted cash flows
- b. Cash flow forecasting
- c. Free cash flow
- d. Factoring

Guidance: level 1

:: Stock market ::

A _____ , securities exchange or bourse, is a facility where stock brokers and traders can buy and sell securities, such as shares of stock and bonds and other financial instruments. _____ s may also provide for facilities the issue and redemption of such securities and instruments and capital events including the payment of income and dividends. Securities traded on a _____ include stock issued by listed companies, unit trusts, derivatives, pooled investment products and bonds. _____ s often function as "continuous auction" markets with buyers and sellers consummating transactions via open outcry at a central location such as the floor of the exchange or by using an electronic trading platform.

Exam Probability: **High**

13. *Answer choices:*

(see index for correct answer)

- a. Non-voting stock
- b. MoneyBee
- c. Extended hours trading
- d. Stock exchange

Guidance: level 1

:: Debt ::

_____ is when something, usually money, is owed by one party, the borrower or _____ or, to a second party, the lender or creditor. _____ is a deferred payment, or series of payments, that is owed in the future, which is what differentiates it from an immediate purchase. The _____ may be owed by sovereign state or country, local government, company, or an individual. Commercial _____ is generally subject to contractual terms regarding the amount and timing of repayments of principal and interest. Loans, bonds, notes, and mortgages are all types of _____ . The term can also be used metaphorically to cover moral obligations and other interactions not based on economic value. For example, in Western cultures, a person who has been helped by a second person is sometimes said to owe a " _____ of gratitude" to the second person.

Exam Probability: **Medium**

14. *Answer choices:*
(see index for correct answer)

- a. Tax benefits of debt
- b. Borrowing base
- c. Debt
- d. Debt relief

Guidance: level 1

:: Banking ::

_____ refers to a broad area of finance involving the collection, handling, and usage of cash. It involves assessing market liquidity, cash flow, and investments.

Exam Probability: **High**

15. *Answer choices:*
(see index for correct answer)

- a. Cash management
- b. Short term deposit
- c. Bank account
- d. Currency packaging

Guidance: level 1

:: Generally Accepted Accounting Principles ::

_____ , or non-current liabilities, are liabilities that are due beyond
a year or the normal operation period of the company. The normal operation
period is the amount of time it takes for a company to turn inventory into
cash. On a classified balance sheet, liabilities are separated between current
and _____ to help users assess the company's financial standing in
short-term and long-term periods. _____ give users more information about
the long-term prosperity of the company, while current liabilities inform the
user of debt that the company owes in the current period. On a balance sheet,
accounts are listed in order of liquidity, so _____ come after current
liabilities. In addition, the specific long-term liability accounts are listed
on the balance sheet in order of liquidity. Therefore, an account due within
eighteen months would be listed before an account due within twenty-four
months. Examples of _____ are bonds payable, long-term loans, capital
leases, pension liabilities, post-retirement healthcare liabilities, deferred
compensation, deferred revenues, deferred income taxes, and derivative
liabilities.

Exam Probability: **Medium**

16. *Answer choices:*

- a. Long-term liabilities
- b. Insurance asset management
- c. Net profit
- d. Completed-contract method

Guidance: level 1

:: Banking ::

A _____ is a financial account maintained by a bank for a customer. A
_____ can be a deposit account, a credit card account, a current account,
or any other type of account offered by a financial institution, and represents
the funds that a customer has entrusted to the financial institution and from
which the customer can make withdrawals. Alternatively, accounts may be loan
accounts in which case the customer owes money to the financial institution.

Exam Probability: **Low**

17. *Answer choices:*

(see index for correct answer)

- a. Bank account
- b. Bank examiner
- c. Arranger
- d. Demand deposit

Guidance: level 1

:: Bonds (finance) ::

A _____ is a type of bond that allows the issuer of the bond to retain the privilege of redeeming the bond at some point before the bond reaches its date of maturity. In other words, on the call date, the issuer has the right, but not the obligation, to buy back the bonds from the bond holders at a defined call price. Technically speaking, the bonds are not really bought and held by the issuer but are instead cancelled immediately.

Exam Probability: **High**

18. *Answer choices:*

(see index for correct answer)

- a. Bond valuation
- b. Bond fund
- c. Floating rate note
- d. Zero-coupon bond

Guidance: level 1

:: Generally Accepted Accounting Principles ::

In accounting, an economic item's _____ is the original nominal monetary value of that item. _____ accounting involves reporting assets and liabilities at their _____ s, which are not updated for changes in the items' values. Consequently, the amounts reported for these balance sheet items often differ from their current economic or market values.

Exam Probability: **High**

19. *Answer choices:*

(see index for correct answer)

- a. Gross sales

- b. Operating profit
- c. Gross profit
- d. Fixed investment

:: Retirement ::

An _____ is a series of payments made at equal intervals. Examples of annuities are regular deposits to a savings account, monthly home mortgage payments, monthly insurance payments and pension payments. Annuities can be classified by the frequency of payment dates. The payments may be made weekly, monthly, quarterly, yearly, or at any other regular interval of time.

Exam Probability: **High**

20. *Answer choices:*
(see index for correct answer)

- a. Retirement Estimator
- b. Annuity
- c. Aging in place
- d. Retirement Funds Administrators

:: Cash flow ::

_____ s are narrowly interconnected with the concepts of value, interest rate and liquidity. A _____ that shall happen on a future day tN can be transformed into a _____ of the same value in t0.

Exam Probability: **Medium**

21. *Answer choices:*
(see index for correct answer)

- a. Cash flow loan
- b. Invoice discounting
- c. Free cash flow
- d. Valuation using discounted cash flows

:: ::

An _____ is a systematic and independent examination of books, accounts, statutory records, documents and vouchers of an organization to ascertain how far the financial statements as well as non-financial disclosures present a true and fair view of the concern. It also attempts to ensure that the books of accounts are properly maintained by the concern as required by law. _____ ing has become such a ubiquitous phenomenon in the corporate and the public sector that academics started identifying an " _____ Society". The _____ or perceives and recognises the propositions before them for examination, obtains evidence, evaluates the same and formulates an opinion on the basis of his judgement which is communicated through their _____ ing report.

Exam Probability: **High**

22. *Answer choices:*
(see index for correct answer)

- a. surface-level diversity
- b. process perspective
- c. cultural
- d. Audit

Guidance: level 1

:: ::

The U.S. _____ is an independent agency of the United States federal government. The SEC holds primary responsibility for enforcing the federal securities laws, proposing securities rules, and regulating the securities industry, the nation's stock and options exchanges, and other activities and organizations, including the electronic securities markets in the United States.

Exam Probability: **Low**

23. *Answer choices:*
(see index for correct answer)

- a. hierarchical perspective
- b. empathy
- c. information systems assessment
- d. Securities and Exchange Commission

Guidance: level 1

:: ::

A _____ is an individual or institution that legally owns one or more shares of stock in a public or private corporation. _____ s may be referred to as members of a corporation. Legally, a person is not a _____ in a corporation until their name and other details are entered in the corporation's register of _____ s or members.

Exam Probability: **High**

24. *Answer choices:*

(see index for correct answer)

- a. Character
- b. interpersonal communication
- c. Shareholder
- d. cultural

Guidance: level 1

:: ::

_____ or accountancy is the measurement, processing, and communication of financial information about economic entities such as businesses and corporations. The modern field was established by the Italian mathematician Luca Pacioli in 1494. _____ , which has been called the "language of business", measures the results of an organization's economic activities and conveys this information to a variety of users, including investors, creditors, management, and regulators. Practitioners of _____ are known as accountants. The terms " _____ " and "financial reporting" are often used as synonyms.

Exam Probability: **Low**

25. *Answer choices:*

(see index for correct answer)

- a. levels of analysis
- b. imperative
- c. process perspective
- d. Accounting

Guidance: level 1

A _____ loan or, simply, _____ is used either by purchasers of real property to raise funds to buy real estate, or alternatively by existing property owners to raise funds for any purpose, while putting a lien on the property being _____ d. The loan is "secured" on the borrower`s property through a process known as _____ origination. This means that a legal mechanism is put into place which allows the lender to take possession and sell the secured property to pay off the loan in the event the borrower defaults on the loan or otherwise fails to abide by its terms. The word _____ is derived from a Law French term used in Britain in the Middle Ages meaning "death pledge" and refers to the pledge ending when either the obligation is fulfilled or the property is taken through foreclosure. A _____ can also be described as "a borrower giving consideration in the form of a collateral for a benefit ".

Exam Probability: **High**

26. *Answer choices:*
(see index for correct answer)

- a. open system
- b. Mortgage
- c. interpersonal communication
- d. similarity-attraction theory

Guidance: level 1

:: International taxation ::

_____ is the levying of tax by two or more jurisdictions on the same declared income , asset , or financial transaction . Double liability is mitigated in a number of ways, for example.

Exam Probability: **High**

27. *Answer choices:*
(see index for correct answer)

- a. Departure tax
- b. World taxation system
- c. Double taxation
- d. International taxation

:: Generally Accepted Accounting Principles ::

In accrual accounting, the revenue recognition principle states that expenses should be recorded during the period in which they are incurred, regardless of when the transfer of cash occurs. Conversely, cash basis accounting calls for the recognition of an expense when the cash is paid, regardless of when the expense was actually incurred.

Exam Probability: **Medium**

28. *Answer choices:*

(see index for correct answer)

- a. Shares outstanding
- b. Indian Accounting Standards
- c. Generally Accepted Accounting Practice
- d. Matching principle

:: Stock market ::

The _____ of a corporation is all of the shares into which ownership of the corporation is divided. In American English, the shares are commonly known as "_____ s". A single share of the _____ represents fractional ownership of the corporation in proportion to the total number of shares. This typically entitles the _____ holder to that fraction of the company's earnings, proceeds from liquidation of assets , or voting power, often dividing these up in proportion to the amount of money each _____ holder has invested. Not all _____ is necessarily equal, as certain classes of _____ may be issued for example without voting rights, with enhanced voting rights, or with a certain priority to receive profits or liquidation proceeds before or after other classes of shareholders.

Exam Probability: **Medium**

29. *Answer choices:*

(see index for correct answer)

- a. Intellidex
- b. Stock

- c. Stock promoter
- d. Public offering without listing

Guidance: level 1

:: ::

_____ is the study and management of exchange relationships. _____ is the business process of creating relationships with and satisfying customers. With its focus on the customer, _____ is one of the premier components of business management.

Exam Probability: **High**

30. *Answer choices:*
(see index for correct answer)

- a. Marketing
- b. Sarbanes-Oxley act of 2002
- c. corporate values
- d. Character

Guidance: level 1

:: Government bonds ::

A _____ or sovereign bond is a bond issued by a national government, generally with a promise to pay periodic interest payments called coupon payments and to repay the face value on the maturity date. The aim of a _____ is to support government spending. _____ s are usually denominated in the country's own currency, in which case the government cannot be forced to default, although it may choose to do so. If a government is close to default on its debt the media often refer to this as a sovereign debt crisis.

Exam Probability: **Medium**

31. *Answer choices:*
(see index for correct answer)

- a. Gilt-edged
- b. Risk-free bond
- c. Brady Bonds
- d. South Carolina v. Baker

:: Financial accounting ::

_____ is the value of all the non-financial and financial assets owned by an institutional unit or sector minus the value of all its outstanding liabilities. Since financial assets minus outstanding liabilities equal net financial assets, _____ can also be conveniently expressed as non-financial assets plus net financial assets. _____ can apply to companies, individuals, governments or economic sectors such as the sector of financial corporations or to entire countries.

Exam Probability: **Medium**

32. *Answer choices:*
(see index for correct answer)

- a. Net worth
- b. Convenience translation
- c. Controlling interest
- d. Associate company

:: International trade ::

In finance, an _____ is the rate at which one currency will be exchanged for another. It is also regarded as the value of one country's currency in relation to another currency. For example, an interbank _____ of 114 Japanese yen to the United States dollar means that ¥114 will be exchanged for each US$1 or that US$1 will be exchanged for each ¥114. In this case it is said that the price of a dollar in relation to yen is ¥114, or equivalently that the price of a yen in relation to dollars is $1/114.

Exam Probability: **High**

33. *Answer choices:*
(see index for correct answer)

- a. Balanced trade
- b. Food power
- c. Import quota
- d. Modalities

:: Hazard analysis ::

Broadly speaking, a _____ is the combined effort of 1. identifying and analyzing potential events that may negatively impact individuals, assets, and/or the environment ; and 2. making judgments "on the tolerability of the risk on the basis of a risk analysis" while considering influencing factors . Put in simpler terms, a _____ analyzes what can go wrong, how likely it is to happen, what the potential consequences are, and how tolerable the identified risk is. As part of this process, the resulting determination of risk may be expressed in a quantitative or qualitative fashion. The _____ is an inherent part of an overall risk management strategy, which attempts to, after a _____ , "introduce control measures to eliminate or reduce" any potential risk-related consequences.

Exam Probability: **Low**

34. *Answer choices:*
(see index for correct answer)

- a. Swiss cheese model
- b. Hazard identification
- c. Risk assessment

:: Bonds (finance) ::

A _____ is a fund established by an economic entity by setting aside revenue over a period of time to fund a future capital expense, or repayment of a long-term debt.

Exam Probability: **High**

35. *Answer choices:*
(see index for correct answer)

- a. 360-day calendar
- b. Revolver bond
- c. Covered bond
- d. Sinking fund

:: Business economics ::

A _____ is a term used primarily in cost accounting to describe something to which costs are assigned. Common examples of _____ s are: product lines, geographic territories, customers, departments or anything else for which management would like to quantify cost.

Exam Probability: **Low**

36. *Answer choices:*
(see index for correct answer)

- a. Cost object
- b. Inclusive business finance
- c. Creditor Reference
- d. Cost of equity

Guidance: level 1

:: Actuarial science ::

_____ is the addition of interest to the principal sum of a loan or deposit, or in other words, interest on interest. It is the result of reinvesting interest, rather than paying it out, so that interest in the next period is then earned on the principal sum plus previously accumulated interest. _____ is standard in finance and economics.

Exam Probability: **High**

37. *Answer choices:*
(see index for correct answer)

- a. Risk aversion
- b. Extreme value theory
- c. Medical underwriting
- d. Compound interest

Guidance: level 1

:: Markets (customer bases) ::

In economics, _____ is the economic price for which a good or service is offered in the marketplace. It is of interest mainly in the study of microeconomics. Market value and _____ are equal only under conditions of market efficiency, equilibrium, and rational expectations.

Exam Probability: **High**

38. *Answer choices:*
(see index for correct answer)

- a. Vertical market
- b. Competitive equilibrium
- c. Market system
- d. Market price

Guidance: level 1

:: Accounting terminology ::

_____ are liabilities that reflect expenses that have not yet been paid or logged under accounts payable during an accounting period; in other words, a company's obligation to pay for goods and services that have been provided for which invoices have not yet been received. Examples would include accrued wages payable, accrued sales tax payable, and accrued rent payable.

Exam Probability: **Medium**

39. *Answer choices:*
(see index for correct answer)

- a. Accrued liabilities
- b. Accounts payable
- c. Adjusting entries
- d. revenue recognition principle

Guidance: level 1

:: Business law ::

The expression " _____ " is somewhat confusing as it has a different meaning based on the context that is under consideration.From a product characteristic stand point, this type of a lease, as distinguished from a finance lease, is one where the lessor takes residual risk. As such, the lease is non full payout. From an accounting stand point, this type of lease results in off balance sheet financing.

Exam Probability: **High**

40. *Answer choices:*
(see index for correct answer)

- a. Valuation using the Market Penetration Model
- b. Retroactive overtime
- c. Examinership
- d. Company mortgage

Guidance: level 1

:: Investment ::

_____ , and investment appraisal, is the planning process used to determine whether an organization's long term investments such as new machinery, replacement of machinery, new plants, new products, and research development projects are worth the funding of cash through the firm's capitalization structure . It is the process of allocating resources for major capital, or investment, expenditures. One of the primary goals of _____ investments is to increase the value of the firm to the shareholders.

Exam Probability: **High**

41. *Answer choices:*
(see index for correct answer)

- a. Market exposure
- b. Personal pension scheme
- c. Index fund
- d. Capital budgeting

Guidance: level 1

:: ::

Pharmaceutical _____ is the creation of a particular pharmaceutical product to fit the unique need of a patient. To do this, _____ pharmacists combine or process appropriate ingredients using various tools.

Exam Probability: **Medium**

42. *Answer choices:*
(see index for correct answer)

- a. cultural
- b. Compounding
- c. surface-level diversity
- d. levels of analysis

Guidance: level 1

:: Expense ::

An _____ , operating expenditure, operational expense, operational expenditure or opex is an ongoing cost for running a product, business, or system. Its counterpart, a capital expenditure , is the cost of developing or providing non-consumable parts for the product or system. For example, the purchase of a photocopier involves capex, and the annual paper, toner, power and maintenance costs represents opex. For larger systems like businesses, opex may also include the cost of workers and facility expenses such as rent and utilities.

Exam Probability: **High**

43. *Answer choices:*
(see index for correct answer)

- a. Operating expense
- b. Corporate travel
- c. Accretion expense
- d. Interest expense

Guidance: level 1

:: Social security ::

_____ is "any government system that provides monetary assistance to people with an inadequate or no income." In the United States, this is usually called welfare or a social safety net, especially when talking about Canada and European countries.

Exam Probability: **Low**

44. *Answer choices:*
(see index for correct answer)

- a. Social security
- b. Social Security Act 1938
- c. Baby bonus
- d. Shidu

Guidance: level 1

:: Financial statements ::

In financial accounting, a _____ or statement of financial position or statement of financial condition is a summary of the financial balances of an individual or organization, whether it be a sole proprietorship, a business partnership, a corporation, private limited company or other organization such as Government or not-for-profit entity. Assets, liabilities and ownership equity are listed as of a specific date, such as the end of its financial year. A _____ is often described as a "snapshot of a company's financial condition". Of the four basic financial statements, the _____ is the only statement which applies to a single point in time of a business' calendar year.

Exam Probability: **Medium**

45. *Answer choices:*
(see index for correct answer)

- a. Statement on Auditing Standards No. 55
- b. quarterly report
- c. Statement on Auditing Standards No. 70: Service Organizations
- d. Balance sheet

Guidance: level 1

:: Capital gains taxes ::

A _____ refers to profit that results from a sale of a capital asset, such as stock, bond or real estate, where the sale price exceeds the purchase price. The gain is the difference between a higher selling price and a lower purchase price. Conversely, a capital loss arises if the proceeds from the sale of a capital asset are less than the purchase price.

Exam Probability: **High**

46. *Answer choices:*
(see index for correct answer)

- a. Capital gains tax
- b. Capital gain
- c. Capital Cost Allowance

Guidance: level 1

:: Fraud ::

In law, _____ is intentional deception to secure unfair or unlawful gain, or to deprive a victim of a legal right. _____ can violate civil law , a criminal law , or it may cause no loss of money, property or legal right but still be an element of another civil or criminal wrong. The purpose of _____ may be monetary gain or other benefits, for example by obtaining a passport, travel document, or driver's license, or mortgage _____ , where the perpetrator may attempt to qualify for a mortgage by way of false statements.

Exam Probability: **Medium**

47. *Answer choices:*
(see index for correct answer)

- a. Health care fraud
- b. Lebanese loop
- c. Hijacked journal
- d. Fraud

Guidance: level 1

:: Financial markets ::

For an individual, a _____ is the minimum amount of money by which the expected return on a risky asset must exceed the known return on a risk-free asset in order to induce an individual to hold the risky asset rather than the risk-free asset. It is positive if the person is risk averse. Thus it is the minimum willingness to accept compensation for the risk.

Exam Probability: **Low**

48. *Answer choices:*
(see index for correct answer)

- a. Fundamentally based indexes
- b. Risk premium
- c. Financial instrument
- d. Flight-to-quality

Guidance: level 1

:: Decision theory ::

A _____ is a deliberate system of principles to guide decisions and achieve rational outcomes. A _____ is a statement of intent, and is implemented as a procedure or protocol. Policies are generally adopted by a governance body within an organization. Policies can assist in both subjective and objective decision making. Policies to assist in subjective decision making usually assist senior management with decisions that must be based on the relative merits of a number of factors, and as a result are often hard to test objectively, e.g. work-life balance _____ . In contrast policies to assist in objective decision making are usually operational in nature and can be objectively tested, e.g. password _____ .

Exam Probability: **High**

49. *Answer choices:*
(see index for correct answer)

- a. ELECTRE
- b. Homothetic preferences
- c. Utility
- d. Taleb distribution

Guidance: level 1

:: Shareholders ::

A _____ is a payment made by a corporation to its shareholders, usually as a distribution of profits. When a corporation earns a profit or surplus, the corporation is able to re-invest the profit in the business and pay a proportion of the profit as a _____ to shareholders. Distribution to shareholders may be in cash or, if the corporation has a _____ reinvestment plan, the amount can be paid by the issue of further shares or share repurchase. When _____ s are paid, shareholders typically must pay income taxes, and the corporation does not receive a corporate income tax deduction for the _____ payments.

Exam Probability: **Medium**

50. *Answer choices:*
(see index for correct answer)

- a. Shareholder ownership value
- b. Dividend
- c. Majority interest
- d. Proxy fight

Guidance: level 1

:: Financial accounting ::

_____ is a financial metric which represents operating liquidity available to a business, organisation or other entity, including governmental entities. Along with fixed assets such as plant and equipment, _____ is considered a part of operating capital. Gross _____ is equal to current assets. _____ is calculated as current assets minus current liabilities. If current assets are less than current liabilities, an entity has a _____ deficiency, also called a _____ deficit.

Exam Probability: **Low**

51. *Answer choices:*
(see index for correct answer)

- a. Working capital
- b. Advance payment
- c. Intangibles
- d. Asset swap

Guidance: level 1

:: Generally Accepted Accounting Principles ::

In accounting, _____ , gross margin, sales profit, or credit sales is the difference between revenue and the cost of making a product or providing a service, before deducting overheads, payroll, taxation, and interest payments. This is different from operating profit . Gross margin is the term normally used in the U.S., while _____ is the more common usage in the UK and Australia.

Exam Probability: **Low**

52. *Answer choices:*
(see index for correct answer)

- a. Normal balance
- b. Income statement
- c. Earnings before interest, taxes and depreciation
- d. Petty cash

Guidance: level 1

:: Costs ::

In microeconomic theory, the _____ , or alternative cost, of making a particular choice is the value of the most valuable choice out of those that were not taken. In other words, opportunity that will require sacrifices.

Exam Probability: **Low**

53. *Answer choices:*
(see index for correct answer)

- a. Khozraschyot
- b. Cost of products sold
- c. Flyaway cost
- d. Cost per paper

Guidance: level 1

:: Stock market ::

_____ is freedom from, or resilience against, potential harm caused by others. Beneficiaries of _____ may be of persons and social groups, objects and institutions, ecosystems or any other entity or phenomenon vulnerable to unwanted change by its environment.

Exam Probability: **Low**

54. *Answer choices:*

- a. Central securities depository
- b. Wash sale
- c. Concentrated stock
- d. Mosaic theory

Guidance: level 1

:: ::

_____ Corporation was an American energy, commodities, and services company based in Houston, Texas. It was founded in 1985 as a merger between Houston Natural Gas and InterNorth, both relatively small regional companies. Before its bankruptcy on December 3, 2001, _____ employed approximately 29,000 staff and was a major electricity, natural gas, communications and pulp and paper company, with claimed revenues of nearly $101 billion during 2000. Fortune named _____ "America's Most Innovative Company" for six consecutive years.

Exam Probability: **Medium**

55. *Answer choices:*

- a. deep-level diversity
- b. Enron
- c. information systems assessment
- d. surface-level diversity

Guidance: level 1

:: Business economics ::

In finance, _____ is the risk of losses caused by interest rate changes. The prices of most financial instruments, such as stocks and bonds move inversely with interest rates, so investors are subject to capital loss when rates rise.

Exam Probability: **Medium**

56. *Answer choices:*
(see index for correct answer)

- a. Overnight cost
- b. Rate risk
- c. European embedded value
- d. Incremental operating margin

Guidance: level 1

:: Stock market ::

A share price is the price of a single share of a number of saleable stocks of a company, derivative or other financial asset.In layman`s terms, the _____ is the highest amount someone is willing to pay for the stock, or the lowest amount that it can be bought for.

Exam Probability: **High**

57. *Answer choices:*
(see index for correct answer)

- a. Stock price
- b. Stock Catalyst
- c. Accelerated Return Note
- d. Wealth management

Guidance: level 1

:: ::

MCI, Inc. was an American telecommunication corporation, currently a subsidiary of Verizon Communications, with its main office in Ashburn, Virginia. The corporation was formed originally as a result of the merger of _____ and MCI Communications corporations, and used the name MCI _____ , succeeded by _____ , before changing its name to the present version on April 12, 2003, as part of the corporation's ending of its bankruptcy status. The company traded on NASDAQ as WCOM and MCIP . The corporation was purchased by Verizon Communications with the deal finalizing on January 6, 2006, and is now identified as that company's Verizon Enterprise Solutions division with the local residential divisions being integrated slowly into local Verizon subsidiaries.

Exam Probability: **Medium**

58. *Answer choices:*
(see index for correct answer)

- a. WorldCom
- b. personal values
- c. process perspective
- d. co-culture

Guidance: level 1

:: Real estate valuation ::

_____ or OMV is the price at which an asset would trade in a competitive auction setting. _____ is often used interchangeably with open _____ , fair value or fair _____ , although these terms have distinct definitions in different standards, and may or may not differ in some circumstances.

Exam Probability: **High**

59. *Answer choices:*
(see index for correct answer)

- a. Market value
- b. Zoopla
- c. Appraisal Standards Board
- d. Extraordinary assumptions and hypothetical conditions

Guidance: level 1

Human resource management

Human resource (HR) management is the strategic approach to the effective management of organization workers so that they help the business gain a competitive advantage. It is designed to maximize employee performance in service of an employer's strategic objectives. HR is primarily concerned with the management of people within organizations, focusing on policies and on systems. HR departments are responsible for overseeing employee-benefits design, employee recruitment, training and development, performance appraisal, and rewarding (e.g., managing pay and benefit systems). HR also concerns itself with organizational change and industrial relations, that is, the balancing of organizational practices with requirements arising from collective bargaining and from governmental laws.

:: Organizational behavior ::

_____ is the act of matching attitudes, beliefs, and behaviors to group norms or politics. Norms are implicit, specific rules, shared by a group of individuals, that guide their interactions with others. People often choose to conform to society rather than to pursue personal desires because it is often easier to follow the path others have made already, rather than creating a new one. This tendency to conform occurs in small groups and/or society as a whole, and may result from subtle unconscious influences , or direct and overt social pressure. _____ can occur in the presence of others, or when an individual is alone. For example, people tend to follow social norms when eating or watching television, even when alone.

Exam Probability: **High**

1. *Answer choices:*
(see index for correct answer)

- a. Organizational commitment
- b. Organizational retaliatory behavior
- c. Burnout
- d. Positive organizational behavior

Guidance: level 1

A _____ usually refers to a group of individuals who work together from different geographic locations and rely on communication technology such as email, FAX, and video or voice conferencing services in order to collaborate. The term can also refer to groups or teams that work together asynchronously or across organizational levels. Powell, Piccoli and Ives define _____ s as "groups of geographically, organizationally and/or time dispersed workers brought together by information and telecommunication technologies to accomplish one or more organizational tasks." According to Ale Ebrahim et. al. , _____ s can also be defined as "small temporary groups of geographically, organizationally and/or time dispersed knowledge workers who coordinate their work predominantly with electronic information and communication technologies in order to accomplish one or more organization tasks."

Exam Probability: **Medium**

2. *Answer choices:*
(see index for correct answer)

- a. Virtual team
- b. Team-building

Guidance: level 1

_____ is the extraction of valuable minerals or other geological materials from the earth, usually from an ore body, lode, vein, seam, reef or placer deposit. These deposits form a mineralized package that is of economic interest to the miner.

Exam Probability: **Low**

3. *Answer choices:*
(see index for correct answer)

- a. imperative
- b. interpersonal communication
- c. co-culture
- d. Mining

:: Fundamental analysis ::

_____ , also known as letter stock or restricted securities, is stock of a company that is not fully transferable until certain conditions have been met. Upon satisfaction of those conditions, the stock is no longer restricted, and becomes transferable to the person holding the award. _____ is often used as a form of employee compensation, in which case it typically becomes transferrable upon the satisfaction of certain conditions, such as continued employment for a period of time or the achievement of particular product-development milestones, earnings per share goals or other financial targets. _____ is a popular alternative to stock options, particularly for executives, due to favorable accounting rules and income tax treatment.

Exam Probability: **Low**

4. *Answer choices:*
(see index for correct answer)

- a. Restricted stock
- b. Growth stock
- c. economic Value Added
- d. Public float

:: ::

_____ is an enduring pattern of romantic or sexual attraction to persons of the opposite sex or gender, the same sex or gender, or to both sexes or more than one gender. These attractions are generally subsumed under heterosexuality, homosexuality, and bisexuality, while asexuality is sometimes identified as the fourth category.

Exam Probability: **High**

5. *Answer choices:*
(see index for correct answer)

- a. Sexual orientation
- b. Character
- c. open system
- d. imperative

:: Behaviorism ::

In behavioral psychology, _____ is a consequence applied that will strengthen an organism's future behavior whenever that behavior is preceded by a specific antecedent stimulus. This strengthening effect may be measured as a higher frequency of behavior , longer duration , greater magnitude , or shorter latency . There are two types of _____ , known as positive _____ and negative _____ ; positive is where by a reward is offered on expression of the wanted behaviour and negative is taking away an undesirable element in the persons environment whenever the desired behaviour is achieved.

Exam Probability: **Medium**

6. *Answer choices:*
(see index for correct answer)

- a. Reinforcement
- b. chaining
- c. Systematic desensitization
- d. Matching Law

:: Trade union legislation ::

The _____ is the name for several legislative bills on US labor law which have been proposed and sometimes introduced into one or both chambers of the U.S. Congress.

Exam Probability: **High**

7. *Answer choices:*
(see index for correct answer)

- a. Trade Union and Labour Relations Act 1974
- b. Employee Free Choice Act
- c. Trade Disputes and Trade Unions Act 1927
- d. Employment Act 1980

:: Employment compensation ::

Employee stock ownership, or employee share ownership, is an ownership interest in a company held by the company's workforce. The ownership interest may be facilitated by the company as part of employees' remuneration or incentive compensation for work performed, or the company itself may be employee owned.

Exam Probability: **Medium**

8. *Answer choices:*
(see index for correct answer)

- a. Employee stock ownership plan
- b. Employees%27 Compensation Appeals Board
- c. Severance package
- d. Explanation of benefits

Guidance: level 1

:: Management ::

_____ or executive pay is composed of the financial compensation and other non-financial awards received by an executive from their firm for their service to the organization. It is typically a mixture of salary, bonuses, shares of or call options on the company stock, benefits, and perquisites, ideally configured to take into account government regulations, tax law, the desires of the organization and the executive, and rewards for performance.

Exam Probability: **High**

9. *Answer choices:*
(see index for correct answer)

- a. Business plan
- b. Scenario planning
- c. Executive compensation
- d. Distributed management

Guidance: level 1

:: Psychometrics ::

Electronic assessment, also known as e-assessment, _____ , computer assisted/mediated assessment and computer-based assessment, is the use of information technology in various forms of assessment such as educational assessment, health assessment, psychiatric assessment, and psychological assessment. This may utilize an online computer connected to a network. This definition embraces a wide range of student activity ranging from the use of a word processor to on-screen testing. Specific types of e-assessment include multiple choice, online/electronic submission, computerized adaptive testing and computerized classification testing.

Exam Probability: **High**

10. *Answer choices:*
(see index for correct answer)

- a. Bipolar spectrum diagnostic scale
- b. Jenkins activity survey
- c. Polytomous Rasch model
- d. Online assessment

Guidance: level 1

:: ::

An _____ is a period of work experience offered by an organization for a limited period of time. Once confined to medical graduates, the term is now used for a wide range of placements in businesses, non-profit organizations and government agencies. They are typically undertaken by students and graduates looking to gain relevant skills and experience in a particular field. Employers benefit from these placements because they often recruit employees from their best interns, who have known capabilities, thus saving time and money in the long run. _____ s are usually arranged by third-party organizations which recruit interns on behalf of industry groups. Rules vary from country to country about when interns should be regarded as employees. The system can be open to exploitation by unscrupulous employers.

Exam Probability: **High**

11. *Answer choices:*
(see index for correct answer)

- a. Internship
- b. deep-level diversity

- c. empathy
- d. personal values

Guidance: level 1

:: Free market ::

Piece work is any type of employment in which a worker is paid a fixed _____ for each unit produced or action performed regardless of time.

Exam Probability: **Low**

12. *Answer choices:*
(see index for correct answer)

- a. Piece rate
- b. Free market

Guidance: level 1

:: Social psychology ::

In social psychology, _____ is the phenomenon of a person exerting less effort to achieve a goal when he or she works in a group than when working alone. This is seen as one of the main reasons groups are sometimes less productive than the combined performance of their members working as individuals, but should be distinguished from the accidental coordination problems that groups sometimes experience.

Exam Probability: **Medium**

13. *Answer choices:*
(see index for correct answer)

- a. Social loafing
- b. co-optation
- c. sociometer
- d. thought control

Guidance: level 1

:: ::

_____ is the process of collecting, analyzing and/or reporting information regarding the performance of an individual, group, organization, system or component. _____ is not a new concept, some of the earliest records of human activity relate to the counting or recording of activities.

Exam Probability: **Low**

14. *Answer choices:*
(see index for correct answer)

- a. co-culture
- b. imperative
- c. Performance measurement
- d. interpersonal communication

Guidance: level 1

:: Foreign workers ::

A _____ or guest worker is a human who works in a country other than the one of which he or she is a citizen. Some _____ s are using a guest worker program in a country with more preferred job prospects than their home country. Guest workers are often either sent or invited to work outside their home country, or have acquired a job before they left their home country, whereas migrant workers often leave their home country without having a specific job at hand.

Exam Probability: **High**

15. *Answer choices:*
(see index for correct answer)

- a. Gastarbeiter
- b. Foreign worker
- c. Migrant domestic workers
- d. Union of Italian Migrant Workers

Guidance: level 1

:: Organizational structure ::

An _____ defines how activities such as task allocation, coordination, and supervision are directed toward the achievement of organizational aims.

Exam Probability: **High**

16. *Answer choices:*
(see index for correct answer)

- a. Automated Bureaucracy
- b. Organization of the New York City Police Department
- c. Organizational structure
- d. Blessed Unrest

Guidance: level 1

:: Human resource management ::

_____ or work sharing is an employment arrangement where typically two people are retained on a part-time or reduced-time basis to perform a job normally fulfilled by one person working full-time. Since all positions are shared thus leads to a net reduction in per-employee income. The people sharing the job work as a team to complete the job task and are equally responsible for the job workload. Compensation is apportioned between the workers. Working hours, pay and holidays are divided equally. The pay as you go system helps make deductions for national insurance and superannuations are made as a straightforward percentage.

Exam Probability: **Low**

17. *Answer choices:*
(see index for correct answer)

- a. At-will employment
- b. Contextual performance
- c. Job sharing
- d. Organizational behavior and human resources

Guidance: level 1

:: Human resource management ::

_____ is a continual process used to align the needs and priorities of the organization with those of its workforce to ensure it can meet its legislative, regulatory, service and production requirements and organizational objectives. _____ enables evidence based workforce development strategies.

Exam Probability: **High**

18. *Answer choices:*
(see index for correct answer)

- a. Workforce planning
- b. Idea portal
- c. Job description management
- d. Up or out

Guidance: level 1

:: Systems thinking ::

In business management, a _____ is a company that facilitates the learning of its members and continuously transforms itself. The concept was coined through the work and research of Peter Senge and his colleagues.

Exam Probability: **High**

19. *Answer choices:*
(see index for correct answer)

- a. World Future Society
- b. Delphi method
- c. Learning organization
- d. The Energy and Resources Institute

Guidance: level 1

:: Unemployment ::

The _____ is the negative relationship between the levels of unemployment and wages that arises when these variables are expressed in local terms. According to David Blanchflower and Andrew Oswald , the _____ summarizes the fact that "A worker who is employed in an area of high unemployment earns less than an identical individual who works in a region with low joblessness."

Exam Probability: **Low**

20. *Answer choices:*
(see index for correct answer)

- a. Youth unemployment
- b. Frictional unemployment
- c. Phillips curve
- d. Wage curve

Guidance: level 1

:: Self ::

_____ is a conscious or subconscious process in which people attempt to influence the perceptions of other people about a person, object or event. They do so by regulating and controlling information in social interaction. It was first conceptualized by Erving Goffman in 1959 in The Presentation of Self in Everyday Life, and then was expanded upon in 1967. An example of _____ theory in play is in sports such as soccer. At an important game, a player would want to showcase themselves in the best light possible, because there are college recruiters watching. This person would have the flashiest pair of cleats and try and perform their best to show off their skills. Their main goal may be to impress the college recruiters in a way that maximizes their chances of being chosen for a college team rather than winning the game.

Exam Probability: **Medium**

21. *Answer choices:*
(see index for correct answer)

- a. Impression management
- b. Egocentrism
- c. Narcissism
- d. Generalized other

Guidance: level 1

In psychometrics, _____ refers to the extent to which a measure represents all facets of a given construct. For example, a depression scale may lack _____ if it only assesses the affective dimension of depression but fails to take into account the behavioral dimension. An element of subjectivity exists in relation to determining _____ , which requires a degree of agreement about what a particular personality trait such as extraversion represents. A disagreement about a personality trait will prevent the gain of a high _____ .

Exam Probability: **High**

22. *Answer choices:*
(see index for correct answer)

- a. Criterion validity
- b. Predictive validity
- c. Internal validity
- d. Verification and validation

Guidance: level 1

_____ refers to the overall process of attracting, shortlisting, selecting and appointing suitable candidates for jobs within an organization. _____ can also refer to processes involved in choosing individuals for unpaid roles. Managers, human resource generalists and _____ specialists may be tasked with carrying out _____ , but in some cases public-sector employment agencies, commercial _____ agencies, or specialist search consultancies are used to undertake parts of the process. Internet-based technologies which support all aspects of _____ have become widespread.

Exam Probability: **Medium**

23. *Answer choices:*
(see index for correct answer)

- a. deep-level diversity
- b. interpersonal communication
- c. personal values
- d. Sarbanes-Oxley act of 2002

:: ::

_____ is the combination of structured planning and the active management choice of one's own professional career. _____ was first defined in a social work doctoral thesis by Mary Valentich as the implementation of a career strategy through application of career tactics in relation to chosen career orientation . Career orientation referred to the overall design or pattern of one's career, shaped by particular goals and interests and identifiable by particular positions that embody these goals and interests. Career strategy pertains to the individual's general approach to the realization of career goals, and to the specificity of the goals themselves. Two general strategy approaches are adaptive and planned. Career tactics are actions to maintain oneself in a satisfactory employment situation. Tactics may be more or less assertive, with assertiveness in the work situation referring to actions taken to advance one's career interests or to exercise one's legitimate rights while respecting the rights of others.

Exam Probability: **Low**

24. *Answer choices:*
(see index for correct answer)

- a. imperative
- b. deep-level diversity
- c. Career management
- d. Sarbanes-Oxley act of 2002

:: Lean manufacturing ::

_____ is the Sino-Japanese word for "improvement". In business, _____ refers to activities that continuously improve all functions and involve all employees from the CEO to the assembly line workers. It also applies to processes, such as purchasing and logistics, that cross organizational boundaries into the supply chain. It has been applied in healthcare, psychotherapy, life-coaching, government, and banking.

Exam Probability: **Low**

25. *Answer choices:*
(see index for correct answer)

- a. Continual improvement process
- b. Supply chain responsiveness matrix
- c. Visual control
- d. Lean product development

Guidance: level 1

:: United States federal labor legislation ::

The _____ of 1988 is a United States federal law that generally prevents employers from using polygraph tests, either for pre-employment screening or during the course of employment, with certain exemptions.

Exam Probability: **Low**

26. *Answer choices:*
(see index for correct answer)

- a. Anti-Pinkerton Act
- b. Employee Polygraph Protection Act
- c. Federal Emergency Relief Administration
- d. Employment Act of 1946

Guidance: level 1

:: Business terms ::

A _____ is a short statement of why an organization exists, what its overall goal is, identifying the goal of its operations: what kind of product or service it provides, its primary customers or market, and its geographical region of operation. It may include a short statement of such fundamental matters as the organization's values or philosophies, a business's main competitive advantages, or a desired future state—the "vision".

Exam Probability: **High**

27. *Answer choices:*
(see index for correct answer)

- a. customer base
- b. Mission statement
- c. Strategic partner
- d. front office

:: ::

_____ is a labor union representing almost 1.9 million workers in over 100 occupations in the United States and Canada. SEIU is focused on organizing workers in three sectors: health care , including hospital, home care and nursing home workers; public services ; and property services .

Exam Probability: **High**

28. *Answer choices:*

(see index for correct answer)

- a. Service Employees International Union
- b. similarity-attraction theory
- c. empathy
- d. hierarchical

:: Human resource management ::

_____ is the application of information technology for both networking and supporting at least two individual or collective actors in their shared performing of HR activities.

Exam Probability: **Low**

29. *Answer choices:*

(see index for correct answer)

- a. Talent management
- b. human resource
- c. Herrmann Brain Dominance Instrument
- d. Selection ratio

:: Employment compensation ::

A _____ is a type of employee benefit plan offered in the United States pursuant to Section 125 of the Internal Revenue Code. Its name comes from the earliest such plans that allowed employees to choose between different types of benefits, similar to the ability of a customer to choose among available items in a cafeteria. Qualified _____ s are excluded from gross income. To qualify, a _____ must allow employees to choose from two or more benefits consisting of cash or qualified benefit plans. The Internal Revenue Code explicitly excludes deferred compensation plans from qualifying as a _____ subject to a gross income exemption. Section 125 also provides two exceptions.

Exam Probability: **High**

30. *Answer choices:*
(see index for correct answer)

- a. Take-home vehicle
- b. Duvet day
- c. Non-wage labour costs
- d. Cafeteria plan

Guidance: level 1

:: Meetings ::

A _____ is a body of one or more persons that is subordinate to a deliberative assembly. Usually, the assembly sends matters into a _____ as a way to explore them more fully than would be possible if the assembly itself were considering them. _____ s may have different functions and their type of work differ depending on the type of the organization and its needs.

Exam Probability: **High**

31. *Answer choices:*
(see index for correct answer)

- a. Coffeehouse
- b. Convention
- c. Town hall meeting
- d. Committee

Guidance: level 1

A _____ describes the rationale of how an organization creates, delivers, and captures value, in economic, social, cultural or other contexts. The process of _____ construction and modification is also called _____ innovation and forms a part of business strategy.

Exam Probability: **Low**

32. *Answer choices:*
(see index for correct answer)

- a. Certified Project Management Professional
- b. Place management
- c. Supervisory board
- d. Certified management consultant

Guidance: level 1

:: ::

_____ involves the development of an action plan designed to motivate and guide a person or group toward a goal. _____ can be guided by goal-setting criteria such as SMART criteria. _____ is a major component of personal-development and management literature.

Exam Probability: **High**

33. *Answer choices:*
(see index for correct answer)

- a. open system
- b. surface-level diversity
- c. Sarbanes-Oxley act of 2002
- d. imperative

Guidance: level 1

:: ::

_____ is the formal act of giving up or quitting one's office or position. A _____ can occur when a person holding a position gained by election or appointment steps down, but leaving a position upon the expiration of a term, or choosing not to seek an additional term, is not considered _____ .

34. *Answer choices:*
(see index for correct answer)

- a. co-culture
- b. Resignation
- c. surface-level diversity
- d. functional perspective

Guidance: level 1

:: Problem solving ::

In other words, _____ is a situation where a group of people meet to generate new ideas and solutions around a specific domain of interest by removing inhibitions. People are able to think more freely and they suggest as many spontaneous new ideas as possible. All the ideas are noted down and those ideas are not criticized and after _____ session the ideas are evaluated. The term was popularized by Alex Faickney Osborn in the 1953 book Applied Imagination.

35. *Answer choices:*
(see index for correct answer)

- a. Encyclopedia of World Problems and Human Potential
- b. Brainstorming
- c. Trial and error
- d. Curiosity

Guidance: level 1

:: Unemployment in the United States ::

The _____ is a unit of the United States Department of Labor. It is the principal fact-finding agency for the U.S. government in the broad field of labor economics and statistics and serves as a principal agency of the U.S. Federal Statistical System. The BLS is a governmental statistical agency that collects, processes, analyzes, and disseminates essential statistical data to the American public, the U.S. Congress, other Federal agencies, State and local governments, business, and labor representatives. The BLS also serves as a statistical resource to the United States Department of Labor, and conducts research into how much families need to earn to be able to enjoy a decent standard of living.

Exam Probability: **Medium**

36. *Answer choices:*
(see index for correct answer)

- a. Unemployment extension
- b. Federal Unemployment Tax Act
- c. Bureau of Labor Statistics
- d. Ford Hunger March

Guidance: level 1

:: United States employment discrimination case law ::

_____ , 557 U.S. 557 , is a US labor law case of the United States Supreme Court on unlawful discrimination through disparate impact under the Civil Rights Act of 1964.

Exam Probability: **Low**

37. *Answer choices:*
(see index for correct answer)

- a. Executive Order 11375
- b. Hosanna-Tabor Evangelical Lutheran Church and School v. Equal Employment Opportunity Commission
- c. Vance v. Ball State University
- d. Gross v. FBL Financial Services, Inc.

Guidance: level 1

:: Legal terms ::

_____ , a form of alternative dispute resolution , is a way to resolve disputes outside the courts. The dispute will be decided by one or more persons , which renders the " _____ award". An _____ award is legally binding on both sides and enforceable in the courts.

Exam Probability: **Medium**

38. *Answer choices:*
(see index for correct answer)

- a. Legal doublet
- b. Pupil master
- c. Impunity
- d. Fundamental justice

Guidance: level 1

:: Employment discrimination ::

A _____ is a metaphor used to represent an invisible barrier that keeps a given demographic from rising beyond a certain level in a hierarchy.

Exam Probability: **Low**

39. *Answer choices:*
(see index for correct answer)

- a. Glass ceiling
- b. Employment discrimination
- c. MacBride Principles
- d. Employment discrimination law in the European Union

Guidance: level 1

:: Trade unions ::

A _____ , in North America, or union branch , in the United Kingdom and other countries, is a local branch of a usually national trade union. The terms used for sub-branches of _____ s vary from country to country and include "shop committee", "shop floor committee", "board of control", "chapel", and others.

40. *Answer choices:*

(see index for correct answer)

- a. Ghent system
- b. TU
- c. Local union
- d. Recognition strike

Guidance: level 1

:: ::

_____ is overt or covert, often harmful, social interaction with the intention of inflicting damage or other unpleasantness upon another individual. It may occur either reactively or without provocation. In humans, frustration due to blocked goals can cause _____ . Human _____ can be classified into direct and indirect _____ ; whilst the former is characterized by physical or verbal behavior intended to cause harm to someone, the latter is characterized by behavior intended to harm the social relations of an individual or group.

41. *Answer choices:*

(see index for correct answer)

- a. Aggression
- b. corporate values
- c. levels of analysis
- d. interpersonal communication

Guidance: level 1

:: Human resource management ::

_____ is the strategic approach to the effective management of people in an organization so that they help the business to gain a competitive advantage. It is designed to maximize employee performance in service of an employer's strategic objectives. HR is primarily concerned with the management of people within organizations, focusing on policies and on systems. HR departments are responsible for overseeing employee-benefits design, employee recruitment, training and development, performance appraisal, and Reward management . HR also concerns itself with organizational change and industrial relations, that is, the balancing of organizational practices with requirements arising from collective bargaining and from governmental laws.

Exam Probability: **High**

42. *Answer choices:*

(see index for correct answer)

- a. Cross-training
- b. Health human resources
- c. Human resource accounting
- d. Human resource management

Guidance: level 1

:: ::

Refresher/ _____ is the process of learning a new or the same old skill or trade for the same group of personnel. Refresher/ _____ is required to be provided on regular basis to avoid personnel obsolescence due to technological changes & the individuals memory capacity. This short term instruction course shall serve to re-acquaint personnel with skills previously learnt or to bring one's knowledge or skills up-to-date so that skills stay sharp. This kind of training could be provided annually or more frequently as maybe required, based on the importance of consistency of the task of which the skill is involved. Examples of refreshers are cGMP, GDP, HSE trainings.
_____ shall also be conducted for an employee, when the employee is rated as 'not qualified' for a skill or knowledge, as determined based on the assessment of answers in the training questionnaire of the employee.

Exam Probability: **High**

43. *Answer choices:*

(see index for correct answer)

- a. Retraining
- b. open system
- c. functional perspective
- d. co-culture

Guidance: level 1

:: Industrial relations ::

_____ or employee satisfaction is a measure of workers` contentedness with their job, whether or not they like the job or individual aspects or facets of jobs, such as nature of work or supervision. _____ can be measured in cognitive , affective , and behavioral components. Researchers have also noted that _____ measures vary in the extent to which they measure feelings about the job , or cognitions about the job .

Exam Probability: **Medium**

44. *Answer choices:*
(see index for correct answer)

- a. Job satisfaction
- b. Injury prevention
- c. European Journal of Industrial Relations
- d. Industrial violence

Guidance: level 1

:: Income ::

A _____ is a unit in systems of monetary compensation for employment. It is commonly used in public service, both civil and military, but also for companies of the private sector. _____ s facilitate the employment process by providing a fixed framework of salary ranges, as opposed to a free negotiation. Typically, _____ s encompass two dimensions: a "vertical" range where each level corresponds to the responsibility of, and requirements needed for a certain position; and a "horizontal" range within this scale to allow for monetary incentives rewarding the employee`s quality of performance or length of service. Thus, an employee progresses within the horizontal and vertical ranges upon achieving positive appraisal on a regular basis. In most cases, evaluation is done annually and encompasses more than one method.

Exam Probability: **Low**

- a. Return of investment
- b. bottom line
- c. Implied level of government service
- d. Pay grade

Guidance: level 1

:: Management ::

A _____ is a method or technique that has been generally accepted as superior to any alternatives because it produces results that are superior to those achieved by other means or because it has become a standard way of doing things, e.g., a standard way of complying with legal or ethical requirements.

Exam Probability: **Low**

- a. Best practice
- b. Maryland StateStat
- c. Resource management
- d. Document automation

Guidance: level 1

:: Labor terms ::

_____ , often called DI or disability income insurance, or income protection, is a form of insurance that insures the beneficiary's earned income against the risk that a disability creates a barrier for a worker to complete the core functions of their work. For example, the worker may suffer from an inability to maintain composure in the case of psychological disorders or an injury, illness or condition that causes physical impairment or incapacity to work. It encompasses paid sick leave, short-term disability benefits , and long-term disability benefits . Statistics show that in the US a disabling accident occurs, on average, once every second. In fact, nearly 18.5% of Americans are currently living with a disability, and 1 out of every 4 persons in the US workforce will suffer a disabling injury before retirement.

47. *Answer choices:*

- a. Capital services
- b. Strike action
- c. Disability insurance
- d. Deflator

Guidance: level 1

:: Management ::

In organizational studies, _____ is the efficient and effective development of an organization's resources when they are needed. Such resources may include financial resources, inventory, human skills, production resources, or information technology and natural resources.

Exam Probability: **Low**

48. *Answer choices:*

- a. Economic production quantity
- b. Resource management
- c. Matrix management
- d. Risk management

Guidance: level 1

:: Cognitive biases ::

In personality psychology, _____ is the degree to which people believe that they have control over the outcome of events in their lives, as opposed to external forces beyond their control. Understanding of the concept was developed by Julian B. Rotter in 1954, and has since become an aspect of personality studies. A person's "locus" is conceptualized as internal or external .

Exam Probability: **Low**

49. *Answer choices:*

- a. Locus of control
- b. Rhyme-as-reason effect
- c. Barnum effect
- d. Illusion of asymmetric insight

Guidance: level 1

:: Training ::

A _____ is commonly known as an individual taking part in a _____ program or a graduate program within a company after having graduated from university or college.

Exam Probability: **High**

50. *Answer choices:*
(see index for correct answer)

- a. Effective safety training
- b. ISpring Suite
- c. National Occupational Standards
- d. Simulation game

Guidance: level 1

:: ::

_____ is defined by sociologist John R. Schermerhorn as the "...degree to which the people affected by decision are treated by dignity and respect. The theory focuses on the interpersonal treatment people receive when procedures are implemented.

Exam Probability: **Low**

51. *Answer choices:*
(see index for correct answer)

- a. process perspective
- b. Interactional justice
- c. hierarchical perspective
- d. interpersonal communication

Guidance: level 1

:: Sociological theories ::

A _____ is a systematic process for determining and addressing needs, or "gaps" between current conditions and desired conditions or "wants". The discrepancy between the current condition and wanted condition must be measured to appropriately identify the need. The need can be a desire to improve current performance or to correct a deficiency.

Exam Probability: **Medium**

52. *Answer choices:*
(see index for correct answer)

- a. Needs assessment
- b. social constructionism
- c. comfort zone
- d. resource mobilization

Guidance: level 1

:: Industrial agreements ::

A _____ , in labor relations, is a group of employees with a clear and identifiable community of interests who are represented by a single labor union in collective bargaining and other dealings with management. Examples would be non-management professors, law enforcement professionals, blue-collar workers, clerical and administrative employees, etc. Geographic location as well as the number of facilities included in _____ s can be at issue during representation cases.

Exam Probability: **Low**

53. *Answer choices:*
(see index for correct answer)

- a. Bargaining unit
- b. Industrial Disputes Act 1947
- c. Conciliation and Arbitration Act 1904
- d. Court of Arbitration

Guidance: level 1

:: Working time ::

The shift plan, rota or roster is the central component of a shift schedule in shift work. The schedule includes considerations of shift overlap, shift change times and alignment with the clock, vacation, training, shift differentials, holidays, etc. The shift plan determines the sequence of work and free days within a shift system.

Exam Probability: **Medium**

54. *Answer choices:*
(see index for correct answer)

- a. Presenteeism
- b. Graveyard shift
- c. Shift work
- d. Blue laws in the United States

Guidance: level 1

:: Occupational safety and health law ::

The _____ of 1970 is a US labor law governing the federal law of occupational health and safety in the private sector and federal government in the United States. It was enacted by Congress in 1970 and was signed by President Richard Nixon on December 29, 1970. Its main goal is to ensure that employers provide employees with an environment free from recognized hazards, such as exposure to toxic chemicals, excessive noise levels, mechanical dangers, heat or cold stress, or unsanitary conditions. The Act created the Occupational Safety and Health Administration and the National Institute for Occupational Safety and Health .

Exam Probability: **Low**

55. *Answer choices:*
(see index for correct answer)

- a. Occupational Safety and Health Act
- b. Occupational Safety and Health Act 1994
- c. Factories Act 1961
- d. Offices, Shops and Railway Premises Act 1963

Guidance: level 1

:: Belief ::

_____ is an umbrella term of influence. _____ can attempt to influence a person's beliefs, attitudes, intentions, motivations, or behaviors. In business, _____ is a process aimed at changing a person's attitude or behavior toward some event, idea, object, or other person, by using written, spoken words or visual tools to convey information, feelings, or reasoning, or a combination thereof. _____ is also an often used tool in the pursuit of personal gain, such as election campaigning, giving a sales pitch, or in trial advocacy. _____ can also be interpreted as using one's personal or positional resources to change people's behaviors or attitudes. Systematic _____ is the process through which attitudes or beliefs are leveraged by appeals to logic and reason. Heuristic _____ on the other hand is the process through which attitudes or beliefs are leveraged by appeals to habit or emotion.

Exam Probability: **High**

56. *Answer choices:*
(see index for correct answer)

- a. Alief
- b. Doctrine
- c. Popular belief
- d. Ignorance

Guidance: level 1

:: Unemployment ::

_____ is the support service provided by responsible organizations, keen to support individuals who are exiting the business – to help former employees transition to new jobs and help them re-orient themselves in the job market. A consultancy firm usually provides the _____ services which are paid for by the former employer and are achieved usually through practical advice, training materials and workshops. Some companies may offer psychological support.

Exam Probability: **High**

57. *Answer choices:*
(see index for correct answer)

- a. Unemployment Provision Convention, 1934
- b. Phillips curve

- c. Employment-to-population ratio
- d. Outplacement

Guidance: level 1

:: ::

A _____ is a technical analysis of a biological specimen, for example urine, hair, blood, breath, sweat, and/or oral fluid/saliva—to determine the presence or absence of specified parent drugs or their metabolites. Major applications of _____ ing include detection of the presence of performance enhancing steroids in sport, employers and parole/probation officers screening for drugs prohibited by law and police officers testing for the presence and concentration of alcohol in the blood commonly referred to as BAC . BAC tests are typically administered via a breathalyzer while urinalysis is used for the vast majority of _____ ing in sports and the workplace. Numerous other methods with varying degrees of accuracy, sensitivity , and detection periods exist.

Exam Probability: **Low**

58. *Answer choices:*
(see index for correct answer)

- a. Drug test
- b. hierarchical perspective
- c. empathy
- d. open system

Guidance: level 1

:: Unemployment benefits ::

_____ are payments made by back authorized bodies to unemployed people. In the United States, benefits are funded by a compulsory governmental insurance system, not taxes on individual citizens. Depending on the jurisdiction and the status of the person, those sums may be small, covering only basic needs, or may compensate the lost time proportionally to the previous earned salary.

Exam Probability: **High**

59. *Answer choices:*

(see index for correct answer)

- a. National Insurance Act 1911
- b. Kela
- c. Unemployment benefits in Spain
- d. Unemployment benefits

Guidance: level 1

Information systems

Information systems (IS) are formal, sociotechnical, organizational systems designed to collect, process, store, and distribute information. In a sociotechnical perspective Information Systems are composed by four components: technology, process, people and organizational structure.

:: Data management ::

An _____ is any kind of information system which improves the functions of enterprise business processes by integration. This means typically offering high quality of service, dealing with large volumes of data and capable of supporting some large and possibly complex organization or enterprise. An EIS must be able to be used by all parts and all levels of an enterprise.

Exam Probability: **Low**

1. *Answer choices:*

(see index for correct answer)

- a. Secure electronic delivery service
- b. Online complex processing
- c. Operational historian
- d. Enterprise information system

Guidance: level 1

:: Marketing by medium ::

_____ or viral advertising is a business strategy that uses existing social networks to promote a product. Its name refers to how consumers spread information about a product with other people in their social networks, much in the same way that a virus spreads from one person to another. It can be delivered by word of mouth or enhanced by the network effects of the Internet and mobile networks.

Exam Probability: **Medium**

2. *Answer choices:*
(see index for correct answer)

- a. Direct Text Marketing
- b. Digital marketing
- c. Viral marketing
- d. Social marketing intelligence

Guidance: level 1

:: Supply chain management terms ::

In business and finance, _____ is a system of organizations, people, activities, information, and resources involved in moving a product or service from supplier to customer. _____ activities involve the transformation of natural resources, raw materials, and components into a finished product that is delivered to the end customer. In sophisticated _____ systems, used products may re-enter the _____ at any point where residual value is recyclable. _____ s link value chains.

Exam Probability: **High**

3. *Answer choices:*
(see index for correct answer)

- a. Consumables
- b. Cool Chain Quality Indicator
- c. Supply chain
- d. Work in process

Guidance: level 1

:: Information technology ::

_____ is the reorientation of product and service designs to focus on the end user as an individual consumer, in contrast with an earlier era of only organization-oriented offerings . Technologies whose first commercialization was at the inter-organization level thus have potential for later _____ . The emergence of the individual consumer as the primary driver of product and service design is most commonly associated with the IT industry, as large business and government organizations dominated the early decades of computer usage and development. Thus the microcomputer revolution, in which electronic computing moved from exclusively enterprise and government use to include personal computing, is a cardinal example of _____ . But many technology-based products, such as calculators and mobile phones, have also had their origins in business markets, and only over time did they become dominated by high-volume consumer usage, as these products commoditized and prices fell. An example of enterprise software that became consumer software is optical character recognition software, which originated with banks and postal systems but eventually became personal productivity software.

Exam Probability: **High**

4. *Answer choices:*
(see index for correct answer)

- a. Localization Industry Standards Association
- b. Consumerization
- c. Qualitest Group
- d. Software-defined storage

Guidance: level 1

:: Information science ::

_____ has been defined as "the branch of ethics that focuses on the relationship between the creation, organization, dissemination, and use of information, and the ethical standards and moral codes governing human conduct in society". It examines the morality that comes from information as a resource, a product, or as a target. It provides a critical framework for considering moral issues concerning informational privacy, moral agency , new environmental issues , problems arising from the life-cycle of information . It is very vital to understand that librarians, archivists, information professionals among others, really understand the importance of knowing how to disseminate proper information as well as being responsible with their actions when addressing information.

Exam Probability: **Low**

5. *Answer choices:*

(see index for correct answer)

- a. Retrievability
- b. Information ethics
- c. EJB QL
- d. Memory institution

Guidance: level 1

:: ::

_____ is a set of documents provided on paper, or online, or on digital or analog media, such as audio tape or CDs. Examples are user guides, white papers, on-line help, quick-reference guides. It is becoming less common to see paper _____ . _____ is distributed via websites, software products, and other on-line applications.

Exam Probability: **Medium**

6. *Answer choices:*

(see index for correct answer)

- a. interpersonal communication
- b. Documentation
- c. levels of analysis
- d. open system

Guidance: level 1

:: History of human–computer interaction ::

A _____ , plural mice, is a small rodent characteristically having a pointed snout, small rounded ears, a body-length scaly tail and a high breeding rate. The best known _____ species is the common house _____ . It is also a popular pet. In some places, certain kinds of field mice are locally common. They are known to invade homes for food and shelter.

Exam Probability: **Low**

7. *Answer choices:*
(see index for correct answer)

- a. IBM 2741
- b. Mouse
- c. Apple Mouse
- d. Command-line interface

Guidance: level 1

:: Information systems ::

A _____ manages the creation and modification of digital content. It typically supports multiple users in a collaborative environment.

Exam Probability: **High**

8. *Answer choices:*
(see index for correct answer)

- a. Dataspaces
- b. Intelligent decision support system
- c. FAO Country Profiles
- d. Content management system

Guidance: level 1

:: Production and manufacturing ::

_____ is the manufacturing approach of using computers to control entire production process. This integration allows individual processes to exchange information with each other and initiate actions. Although manufacturing can be faster and less error-prone by the integration of computers, the main advantage is the ability to create automated manufacturing processes. Typically CIM relies of closed-loop control processes, based on real-time input from sensors. It is also known as flexible design and manufacturing.

Exam Probability: **Medium**

9. *Answer choices:*
(see index for correct answer)

- a. Mockup
- b. Computer-integrated manufacturing
- c. Zero Defects
- d. Business Planning and Control System

Guidance: level 1

:: Confidence tricks ::

_____ is the fraudulent attempt to obtain sensitive information such as usernames, passwords and credit card details by disguising oneself as a trustworthy entity in an electronic communication. Typically carried out by email spoofing or instant messaging, it often directs users to enter personal information at a fake website which matches the look and feel of the legitimate site.

Exam Probability: **High**

10. *Answer choices:*
(see index for correct answer)

- a. Kansas City Shuffle
- b. Green goods scam
- c. Hokkani boro
- d. Phishing

Guidance: level 1

:: Information and communication technologies for development ::

_____ is a non-profit initiative established with the goal of transforming education for children around the world; this goal was to be achieved by creating and distributing educational devices for the developing world, and by creating software and content for those devices.

Exam Probability: **High**

11. *Answer choices:*
(see index for correct answer)

- a. Lemote
- b. PlayPower
- c. One Laptop per Child
- d. Asia-Pacific Development Information Programme

Guidance: level 1

:: Credit cards ::

A _____ is a payment card issued to users to enable the cardholder to pay a merchant for goods and services based on the cardholder's promise to the card issuer to pay them for the amounts plus the other agreed charges. The card issuer creates a revolving account and grants a line of credit to the cardholder, from which the cardholder can borrow money for payment to a merchant or as a cash advance.

Exam Probability: **High**

12. *Answer choices:*
(see index for correct answer)

- a. Credit Saison
- b. Card scheme
- c. Credit card
- d. TaiwanMoney Card

Guidance: level 1

:: IT risk management ::

_____ involves a set of policies, tools and procedures to enable the recovery or continuation of vital technology infrastructure and systems following a natural or human-induced disaster. _____ focuses on the IT or technology systems supporting critical business functions, as opposed to business continuity, which involves keeping all essential aspects of a business functioning despite significant disruptive events. _____ can therefore be considered as a subset of business continuity.

Exam Probability: **Medium**

13. *Answer choices:*
(see index for correct answer)

- a. Business continuity
- b. Information assurance
- c. Incident response team

Guidance: level 1

:: ::

_____ is an American video-sharing website headquartered in San Bruno, California. Three former PayPal employees—Chad Hurley, Steve Chen, and Jawed Karim—created the service in February 2005. Google bought the site in November 2006 for US$1.65 billion; _____ now operates as one of Google's subsidiaries.

Exam Probability: **Medium**

14. *Answer choices:*
(see index for correct answer)

- a. YouTube
- b. corporate values
- c. open system
- d. functional perspective

Guidance: level 1

:: Business models ::

_____ , a portmanteau of the words "free" and "premium", is a pricing strategy by which a product or service is provided free of charge, but money is charged for additional features, services, or virtual or physical goods. The business model has been in use by the software industry since the 1980s as a licensing scheme. A subset of this model used by the video game industry is called free-to-play.

Exam Probability: **Medium**

15. *Answer choices:*
(see index for correct answer)

- a. Pay to play
- b. Parent company
- c. Lawyers on Demand
- d. Very small business

Guidance: level 1

:: Management ::

Porter's Five Forces Framework is a tool for analyzing competition of a business. It draws from industrial organization economics to derive five forces that determine the competitive intensity and, therefore, the attractiveness of an industry in terms of its profitability. An "unattractive" industry is one in which the effect of these five forces reduces overall profitability. The most unattractive industry would be one approaching "pure competition", in which available profits for all firms are driven to normal profit levels. The five-forces perspective is associated with its originator, Michael E. Porter of Harvard University. This framework was first published in Harvard Business Review in 1979.

Exam Probability: **Low**

16. *Answer choices:*
(see index for correct answer)

- a. Board of governors
- b. Concept of operations
- c. Porter five forces analysis
- d. Main Street Manager

Guidance: level 1

:: E-commerce ::

_____ generally refer to payment services operated under financial regulation and performed from or via a mobile device. Instead of paying with cash, cheque, or credit cards, a consumer can use a mobile to pay for a wide range of services and digital or hard goods. Although the concept of using non-coin-based currency systems has a long history, it is only recently that the technology to support such systems has become widely available.

Exam Probability: **Low**

17. *Answer choices:*
(see index for correct answer)

- a. Helpling
- b. Mobile payment
- c. Virtual enterprise
- d. Coinye

Guidance: level 1

:: Management ::

In business, a _____ is the attribute that allows an organization to outperform its competitors. A _____ may include access to natural resources, such as high-grade ores or a low-cost power source, highly skilled labor, geographic location, high entry barriers, and access to new technology.

Exam Probability: **Medium**

18. *Answer choices:*
(see index for correct answer)

- a. Competitive advantage
- b. Control limits
- c. Omnex
- d. Top development

Guidance: level 1

:: Outsourcing ::

A service-level agreement is a commitment between a service provider and a client. Particular aspects of the service – quality, availability, responsibilities – are agreed between the service provider and the service user. The most common component of SLA is that the services should be provided to the customer as agreed upon in the contract. As an example, Internet service providers and telcos will commonly include _____ s within the terms of their contracts with customers to define the level of service being sold in plain language terms. In this case the SLA will typically have a technical definition in mean time between failures , mean time to repair or mean time to recovery ; identifying which party is responsible for reporting faults or paying fees; responsibility for various data rates; throughput; jitter; or similar measurable details.

Exam Probability: **Low**

19. *Answer choices:*
(see index for correct answer)

- a. Talentica Software
- b. LEO
- c. Print and mail outsourcing
- d. Service level agreement

Guidance: level 1

:: Fault tolerance ::

_____ is the property that enables a system to continue operating properly in the event of the failure of some of its components. If its operating quality decreases at all, the decrease is proportional to the severity of the failure, as compared to a naively designed system, in which even a small failure can cause total breakdown. _____ is particularly sought after in high-availability or life-critical systems. The ability of maintaining functionality when portions of a system break down is referred to as graceful degradation.

Exam Probability: **High**

20. *Answer choices:*
(see index for correct answer)

- a. Amplitude-shift keying
- b. Operational availability

- c. Degradation
- d. Fault tolerance

Guidance: level 1

:: Business process ::

Business process re-engineering is a business management strategy, originally pioneered in the early 1990s, focusing on the analysis and design of workflows and business processes within an organization. BPR aimed to help organizations fundamentally rethink how they do their work in order to improve customer service, cut operational costs, and become world-class competitors.

Exam Probability: **Medium**

21. *Answer choices:*
(see index for correct answer)

- a. PNMsoft
- b. Business process reengineering
- c. Steering committee
- d. Process capital

Guidance: level 1

:: Data management ::

An _____ is a term used in data warehousing to refer to a system that is used to process the day-to-day transactions of an organization. These systems are designed in a manner that processing of day-to-day transactions is performed efficiently and the integrity of the transactional data is preserved.

Exam Probability: **High**

22. *Answer choices:*
(see index for correct answer)

- a. Operational system
- b. Log trigger
- c. Data processing system
- d. Grid-oriented storage

Guidance: level 1

:: Marketing ::

_____ is a business model in which consumers create value and businesses consume that value. For example, when a consumer writes reviews or when a consumer gives a useful idea for new product development then that consumer is creating value for the business if the business adopts the input.
In the C2B model, a reverse auction or demand collection model, enables buyers to name or demand their own price, which is often binding, for a specific good or service. Inside of a consumer to business market the roles involved in the transaction must be established and the consumer must offer something of value to the business.

Exam Probability: **Medium**

23. *Answer choices:*
(see index for correct answer)

- a. Business stature
- b. Corporate capabilities package
- c. Product lining
- d. Mobile marketing research

Guidance: level 1

:: Data transmission ::

In telecommunications and computing, _____ is the number of bits that are conveyed or processed per unit of time.

Exam Probability: **High**

24. *Answer choices:*
(see index for correct answer)

- a. Bit rate
- b. Data link
- c. SDI-12
- d. Digital call quality

Guidance: level 1

:: Management ::

In organizational studies, _____ is the efficient and effective development of an organization's resources when they are needed. Such resources may include financial resources, inventory, human skills, production resources, or information technology and natural resources.

Exam Probability: **High**

25. *Answer choices:*
(see index for correct answer)

- a. Enterprise decision management
- b. Managerial economics
- c. Resource management
- d. Corporate foresight

Guidance: level 1

:: Internet marketing ::

_____ is the process of increasing the quality and quantity of website traffic, increasing visibility of a website or a web page to users of a web search engine.SEO refers to the improvement of unpaid results , and excludes the purchase of paid placement.

Exam Probability: **Medium**

26. *Answer choices:*
(see index for correct answer)

- a. SocialFlow
- b. Content farm
- c. Search engine optimization
- d. In-text advertising

Guidance: level 1

:: Google services ::

_____ is a word processor included as part of a free, web-based software office suite offered by Google within its Google Drive service. This service also includes Google Sheets and Google Slides, a spreadsheet and presentation program respectively. _____ is available as a web application, mobile app for Android, iOS, Windows, BlackBerry, and as a desktop application on Google's ChromeOS. The app is compatible with Microsoft Office file formats.The application allows users to create and edit files online while collaborating with other users in real-time. Edits are tracked by user with a revision history presenting changes. An editor's position is highlighted with an editor-specific color and cursor. A permissions system regulates what users can do. Updates have introduced features using machine learning, including "Explore", offering search results based on the contents of a document, and "Action items", allowing users to assign tasks to other users.

Exam Probability: **High**

27. *Answer choices:*
(see index for correct answer)

- a. Google Cloud Messaging
- b. WDYL
- c. Google Plugin for Eclipse
- d. Google Images

Guidance: level 1

:: Security compliance ::

A _____ is a communicated intent to inflict harm or loss on another person. A _____ is considered an act of coercion. _____ s are widely observed in animal behavior, particularly in a ritualized form, chiefly in order to avoid the unnecessary physical violence that can lead to physical damage or the death of both conflicting parties.

Exam Probability: **Medium**

28. *Answer choices:*
(see index for correct answer)

- a. Nikto Web Scanner
- b. Information assurance vulnerability alert
- c. Threat
- d. Security Content Automation Protocol

:: Computing output devices ::

An _____ is any piece of computer hardware equipment which converts information into human-readable form.

Exam Probability: **Medium**

29. *Answer choices:*
(see index for correct answer)

- a. Output device
- b. LongPen
- c. Powerwall
- d. Flicker fixer

:: ::

A _____ is a knowledge base website on which users collaboratively modify content and structure directly from the web browser. In a typical _____ , text is written using a simplified markup language and often edited with the help of a rich-text editor.

Exam Probability: **High**

30. *Answer choices:*
(see index for correct answer)

- a. surface-level diversity
- b. personal values
- c. hierarchical
- d. Sarbanes-Oxley act of 2002

:: ::

Collaborative software or _____ is application software designed to help people involved in a common task to achieve their goals. One of the earliest definitions of collaborative software is "intentional group processes plus software to support them".

Exam Probability: **High**

31. *Answer choices:*
(see index for correct answer)

- a. similarity-attraction theory
- b. imperative
- c. process perspective
- d. cultural

Guidance: level 1

:: E-commerce ::

_____ is a subset of electronic commerce that involves social media, online media that supports social interaction, and user contributions to assist online buying and selling of products and services.

Exam Probability: **High**

32. *Answer choices:*
(see index for correct answer)

- a. Social commerce
- b. DigiCash
- c. PayXpert
- d. Donna Hoffman

Guidance: level 1

:: ::

A _____ is a telecommunications network that extends over a large geographical distance for the primary purpose of computer networking. _____ s are often established with leased telecommunication circuits.

Exam Probability: **High**

33. *Answer choices:*

(see index for correct answer)

- a. levels of analysis
- b. co-culture
- c. Wide Area Network
- d. interpersonal communication

Guidance: level 1

:: Commerce ::

_____ , Inc. is an American media-services provider headquartered in Los Gatos, California, founded in 1997 by Reed Hastings and Marc Randolph in Scotts Valley, California. The company's primary business is its subscription-based streaming OTT service which offers online streaming of a library of films and television programs, including those produced in-house. As of April 2019, _____ had over 148 million paid subscriptions worldwide, including 60 million in the United States, and over 154 million subscriptions total including free trials. It is available almost worldwide except in mainland China as well as Syria, North Korea, and Crimea . The company also has offices in the Netherlands, Brazil, India, Japan, and South Korea.
_____ is a member of the Motion Picture Association of America .

Exam Probability: **Low**

34. *Answer choices:*

(see index for correct answer)

- a. Agio
- b. Mail order
- c. Issuing bank
- d. European Retail Round Table

Guidance: level 1

:: Information technology management ::

The term _____ is used to refer to periods when a system is unavailable. _____ or outage duration refers to a period of time that a system fails to provide or perform its primary function. Reliability, availability, recovery, and unavailability are related concepts. The unavailability is the proportion of a time-span that a system is unavailable or offline. This is usually a result of the system failing to function because of an unplanned event, or because of routine maintenance .

Exam Probability: **High**

35. *Answer choices:*

- a. Downtime
- b. IT baseline protection
- c. Document management system
- d. Information Technology Infrastructure Library

Guidance: level 1

:: Google services ::

_____ is a discontinued image organizer and image viewer for organizing and editing digital photos, plus an integrated photo-sharing website, originally created by a company named Lifescape in 2002. In July 2004, Google acquired _____ from Lifescape and began offering it as freeware. " _____ " is a blend of the name of Spanish painter Pablo Picasso, the phrase mi casa and "pic" for pictures.

Exam Probability: **Low**

36. *Answer choices:*

- a. Google IME
- b. Google Calendar
- c. Google Sky
- d. Picasa

Guidance: level 1

:: Payment systems ::

_____ s are part of a payment system issued by financial institutions, such as a bank, to a customer that enables its owner to access the funds in the customer's designated bank accounts, or through a credit account and make payments by electronic funds transfer and access automated teller machines . Such cards are known by a variety of names including bank cards, ATM cards, MAC , client cards, key cards or cash cards.

Exam Probability: **Medium**

37. *Answer choices:*
(see index for correct answer)

- a. Automated teller
- b. NetSpend
- c. Payment systems in India
- d. Cruise ship ID card

Guidance: level 1

:: E-commerce ::

Electronic governance or e-governance is the application of information and communication technology for delivering government services, exchange of information, communication transactions, integration of various stand-alone systems and services between government-to-citizen , government-to-business , _____ , government-to-employees as well as back-office processes and interactions within the entire government framework. Through e-governance, government services are made available to citizens in a convenient, efficient, and transparent manner. The three main target groups that can be distinguished in governance concepts are government, citizens, andbusinesses/interest groups. In e-governance, there are no distinct boundaries.

Exam Probability: **High**

38. *Answer choices:*
(see index for correct answer)

- a. Steam
- b. Authorize.Net
- c. DVD-by-mail
- d. Ven

Guidance: level 1

:: Ergonomics ::

_____ is the design of products, devices, services, or environments for people with disabilities. The concept of accessible design and practice of accessible development ensures both "direct access" and "indirect access" meaning compatibility with a person's assistive technology .

Exam Probability: **Medium**

39. *Answer choices:*
(see index for correct answer)

- a. Accessibility
- b. Back belt
- c. Treadmill desk
- d. Engineering psychology

Guidance: level 1

:: ::

A _____ is a research instrument consisting of a series of questions for the purpose of gathering information from respondents. The _____ was invented by the Statistical Society of London in 1838.

Exam Probability: **High**

40. *Answer choices:*
(see index for correct answer)

- a. Character
- b. Questionnaire
- c. information systems assessment
- d. similarity-attraction theory

Guidance: level 1

:: Service-oriented (business computing) ::

_____ is a style of software design where services are provided to the other components by application components, through a communication protocol over a network. The basic principles of _____ are independent of vendors, products and technologies.A service is a discrete unit of functionality that can be accessed remotely and acted upon and updated independently, such as retrieving a credit card statement online.

Exam Probability: **Medium**

41. *Answer choices:*

- a. Service-oriented architecture
- b. Service abstraction
- c. Service-oriented programming
- d. Enterprise service bus

Guidance: level 1

:: Virtual reality ::

A _____ is a computer-based simulated environment which may be populated by many users who can create a personal avatar, and simultaneously and independently explore the _____ , participate in its activities and communicate with others. These avatars can be textual, two or three-dimensional graphical representations, or live video avatars with auditory and touch sensations. In general, _____ s allow for multiple users but single player computer games, such as Skyrim, can also be considered a type of _____ .

Exam Probability: **High**

42. *Answer choices:*

- a. Virtual world
- b. Telepointer
- c. XVRML
- d. Simulation hypothesis

Guidance: level 1

:: Industrial automation ::

_____ is the technology by which a process or procedure is performed with minimal human assistance. _____ or automatic control is the use of various control systems for operating equipment such as machinery, processes in factories, boilers and heat treating ovens, switching on telephone networks, steering and stabilization of ships, aircraft and other applications and vehicles with minimal or reduced human intervention.

Exam Probability: **Medium**

43. *Answer choices:*
(see index for correct answer)

- a. Automation
- b. Automation surprise
- c. IODD
- d. Collaborative process automation systems

Guidance: level 1

:: History of human–computer interaction ::

_____ is a line of motion sensing input devices produced by Microsoft. Initially, the _____ was developed as a gaming accessory for Xbox 360 and Xbox One video game consoles and Microsoft Windows PCs. Based around a webcam-style add-on peripheral, it enabled users to control and interact with their console/computer without the need for a game controller, through a natural user interface using gestures and spoken commands. While the gaming line did not gain much traction and eventually discontinued, third-party developers and researches found several after-market uses for _____ 's advanced low-cost sensor features, leading Microsoft to drive the product line towards more application-neutral uses, including integrating the device with Microsoft's cloud computing platform Azure.

Exam Probability: **Medium**

44. *Answer choices:*
(see index for correct answer)

- a. Kinect
- b. Hypertext Editing System
- c. IRCF360
- d. Apple Mouse

Guidance: level 1

:: Product testing ::

_____ is a characteristic of a product or system, whose interfaces are completely understood, to work with other products or systems, at present or in the future, in either implementation or access, without any restrictions.

Exam Probability: **High**

45. *Answer choices:*
(see index for correct answer)

- a. Product testing
- b. Coffee cupping
- c. Interoperability
- d. Testing reliability

Guidance: level 1

:: Google services ::

Google Ads is an online advertising platform developed by Google, where advertisers pay to display brief advertisements, service offerings, product listings, video content, and generate mobile application installs within the Google ad network to web users.

Exam Probability: **High**

46. *Answer choices:*
(see index for correct answer)

- a. AdWords
- b. Google WiFi
- c. Picasa
- d. Nymwars

Guidance: level 1

:: Business ::

_____ is a sourcing model in which individuals or organizations obtain goods and services, including ideas and finances, from a large, relatively open and often rapidly-evolving group of internet users; it divides work between participants to achieve a cumulative result. The word _____ itself is a portmanteau of crowd and outsourcing, and was coined in 2005. As a mode of sourcing, _____ existed prior to the digital age .

Exam Probability: **High**

47. *Answer choices:*
(see index for correct answer)

- a. Business partnering
- b. Professional services
- c. Relationship Science
- d. Equality impact assessment

Guidance: level 1

:: Process management ::

When used in the context of communication networks, such as Ethernet or packet radio, _____ or network _____ is the rate of successful message delivery over a communication channel. The data these messages belong to may be delivered over a physical or logical link, or it can pass through a certain network node. _____ is usually measured in bits per second , and sometimes in data packets per second or data packets per time slot.

Exam Probability: **Medium**

48. *Answer choices:*
(see index for correct answer)

- a. Business process discovery
- b. Stock clearance
- c. Throughput
- d. Process specification

Guidance: level 1

:: ::

A _____ is a computer file which stores data to be used by a computer application or system, including input and output data. A _____ usually does not contain instructions or code to be executed .

Exam Probability: **Low**

49. *Answer choices:*
(see index for correct answer)

- a. Data file
- b. hierarchical
- c. co-culture
- d. interpersonal communication

Guidance: level 1

:: Metadata ::

_____ s usage can be discovered by inspection of software applications or application data files through a process of manual or automated Application Discovery and Understanding. Once _____ s are discovered they can be registered in a metadata registry.

Exam Probability: **Low**

50. *Answer choices:*
(see index for correct answer)

- a. Application profile
- b. Data element definition
- c. Data element
- d. CEPIC

Guidance: level 1

:: Computer memory ::

_____ is an electronic non-volatile computer storage medium that can be electrically erased and reprogrammed.

Exam Probability: **High**

51. *Answer choices:*

(see index for correct answer)

- a. Drum memory
- b. FWord
- c. Internal RAM
- d. Content Addressable Parallel Processor

Guidance: level 1

:: Distribution, retailing, and wholesaling ::

_____ measures the performance of a system. Certain goals are defined and the _____ gives the percentage to which those goals should be achieved. Fill rate is different from _____ .

Exam Probability: **Medium**

52. *Answer choices:*
(see index for correct answer)

- a. New Leaf Distributing Company
- b. Bridgewater House, Manchester
- c. Wholesale list
- d. Cash and carry

Guidance: level 1

:: Telecommunication theory ::

In reliability theory and reliability engineering, the term _____ has the following meanings.

Exam Probability: **High**

53. *Answer choices:*
(see index for correct answer)

- a. Availability
- b. Articulation score
- c. Transactive communication
- d. Exformation

Guidance: level 1

:: Stochastic processes ::

_____ in its modern meaning is a "new idea, creative thoughts, new imaginations in form of device or method". _____ is often also viewed as the application of better solutions that meet new requirements, unarticulated needs, or existing market needs. Such _____ takes place through the provision of more-effective products, processes, services, technologies, or business models that are made available to markets, governments and society. An _____ is something original and more effective and, as a consequence, new, that "breaks into" the market or society. _____ is related to, but not the same as, invention, as _____ is more apt to involve the practical implementation of an invention to make a meaningful impact in the market or society, and not all _____ s require an invention. _____ often manifests itself via the engineering process, when the problem being solved is of a technical or scientific nature. The opposite of _____ is exnovation.

Exam Probability: **Medium**

54. *Answer choices:*
(see index for correct answer)

- a. Kolmogorov extension theorem
- b. Sigma-martingale
- c. Traffic equations
- d. Disorder problem

Guidance: level 1

:: Internet governance ::

A _____ is one of the domains at the highest level in the hierarchical Domain Name System of the Internet. The _____ names are installed in the root zone of the name space. For all domains in lower levels, it is the last part of the domain name, that is, the last label of a fully qualified domain name. For example, in the domain name www.example.com, the _____ is com. Responsibility for management of most _____ s is delegated to specific organizations by the Internet Corporation for Assigned Names and Numbers , which operates the Internet Assigned Numbers Authority , and is in charge of maintaining the DNS root zone.

Exam Probability: **High**

55. *Answer choices:*
(see index for correct answer)

- a. Pathetic dot theory
- b. Global Multistakeholder Meeting on the Future of Internet Governance
- c. Top-level domain
- d. Local Internet registry

Guidance: level 1

:: Mereology ::

_____ , in the abstract, is what belongs to or with something, whether as an attribute or as a component of said thing. In the context of this article, it is one or more components , whether physical or incorporeal, of a person's estate; or so belonging to, as in being owned by, a person or jointly a group of people or a legal entity like a corporation or even a society. Depending on the nature of the _____ , an owner of _____ has the right to consume, alter, share, redefine, rent, mortgage, pawn, sell, exchange, transfer, give away or destroy it, or to exclude others from doing these things, as well as to perhaps abandon it; whereas regardless of the nature of the _____ , the owner thereof has the right to properly use it , or at the very least exclusively keep it.

Exam Probability: **Medium**

56. *Answer choices:*
(see index for correct answer)

- a. Gunk
- b. Property
- c. Mereology
- d. Mereotopology

Guidance: level 1

:: Infographics ::

A _____ is a symbolic representation of information according to visualization technique. _____ s have been used since ancient times, but became more prevalent during the Enlightenment. Sometimes, the technique uses a three-dimensional visualization which is then projected onto a two-dimensional surface. The word graph is sometimes used as a synonym for _____ .

Exam Probability: **High**

57. *Answer choices:*

- a. Coat of arms
- b. Diagram
- c. Information sign
- d. Previsualization

Guidance: level 1

:: Transaction processing ::

In _____ , information systems typically facilitate and manage transaction-oriented applications.

Exam Probability: **High**

58. *Answer choices:*

- a. Extreme Transaction Processing
- b. Online transaction processing
- c. CloudTran
- d. Memory semantics

Guidance: level 1

:: Information technology management ::

In information technology to _____ means to move from one place to another, information to detailed data by focusing in on something. In a GUI-environment, "drilling-down" may involve clicking on some representation in order to reveal more detail.

Exam Probability: **Medium**

59. *Answer choices:*

- a. Website promotion
- b. Autonomic networking
- c. Soluto
- d. Performance engineering

Guidance: level 1

Marketing

Marketing is the study and management of exchange relationships. Marketing is the business process of creating relationships with and satisfying customers. With its focus on the customer, marketing is one of the premier components of business management.

Marketing is defined by the American Marketing Association as "the activity, set of institutions, and processes for creating, communicating, delivering, and exchanging offerings that have value for customers, clients, partners, and society at large."

:: Investment ::

In finance, the benefit from an _____ is called a return. The return may consist of a gain realised from the sale of property or an _____, unrealised capital appreciation , or _____ income such as dividends, interest, rental income etc., or a combination of capital gain and income. The return may also include currency gains or losses due to changes in foreign currency exchange rates.

Exam Probability: **Low**

1. *Answer choices:*
(see index for correct answer)

- a. Dollar cost averaging
- b. Fed model
- c. Insurance bond
- d. Capital budgeting

Guidance: level 1

:: ::

_____ is the act of conveying meanings from one entity or group to another through the use of mutually understood signs, symbols, and semiotic rules.

Exam Probability: **High**

2. *Answer choices:*

(see index for correct answer)

- a. corporate values
- b. Communication
- c. surface-level diversity
- d. co-culture

Guidance: level 1

:: Mereology ::

_____ , in the abstract, is what belongs to or with something, whether as an attribute or as a component of said thing. In the context of this article, it is one or more components , whether physical or incorporeal, of a person's estate; or so belonging to, as in being owned by, a person or jointly a group of people or a legal entity like a corporation or even a society. Depending on the nature of the _____ , an owner of _____ has the right to consume, alter, share, redefine, rent, mortgage, pawn, sell, exchange, transfer, give away or destroy it, or to exclude others from doing these things, as well as to perhaps abandon it; whereas regardless of the nature of the _____ , the owner thereof has the right to properly use it , or at the very least exclusively keep it.

Exam Probability: **Medium**

3. *Answer choices:*

(see index for correct answer)

- a. Gunk
- b. Mereology
- c. Mereological essentialism
- d. Property

Guidance: level 1

:: Business models ::

A _____ , _____ company or daughter company is a company that is owned or controlled by another company, which is called the parent company, parent, or holding company. The _____ can be a company, corporation, or limited liability company. In some cases it is a government or state-owned enterprise. In some cases, particularly in the music and book publishing industries, subsidiaries are referred to as imprints.

Exam Probability: **High**

4. *Answer choices:*
(see index for correct answer)

- a. The Community Company
- b. Co-operative Wholesale Society
- c. Entreship
- d. Brainsworking

Guidance: level 1

:: Project management ::

A _____ is a source or supply from which a benefit is produced and it has some utility. _____ s can broadly be classified upon their availability—they are classified into renewable and non-renewable _____ s.Examples of non renewable _____ s are coal ,crude oil natural gas nuclear energy etc. Examples of renewable _____ s are air,water,wind,solar energy etc. They can also be classified as actual and potential on the basis of level of development and use, on the basis of origin they can be classified as biotic and abiotic, and on the basis of their distribution, as ubiquitous and localized . An item becomes a _____ with time and developing technology. Typically, _____ s are materials, energy, services, staff, knowledge, or other assets that are transformed to produce benefit and in the process may be consumed or made unavailable. Benefits of _____ utilization may include increased wealth, proper functioning of a system, or enhanced well-being. From a human perspective a natural _____ is anything obtained from the environment to satisfy human needs and wants. From a broader biological or ecological perspective a _____ satisfies the needs of a living organism .

Exam Probability: **Low**

5. *Answer choices:*
(see index for correct answer)

- a. Work package
- b. Resource
- c. Project plan
- d. Resource leveling

Guidance: level 1

:: ::

A _____ is the process of presenting a topic to an audience. It is typically a demonstration, introduction, lecture, or speech meant to inform, persuade, inspire, motivate, or to build good will or to present a new idea or product. The term can also be used for a formal or ritualized introduction or offering, as with the _____ of a debutante. _____ s in certain formats are also known as keynote address.

Exam Probability: **High**

6. *Answer choices:*

(see index for correct answer)

- a. functional perspective
- b. hierarchical
- c. Presentation
- d. empathy

Guidance: level 1

:: Product management ::

A _____ is a professional role which is responsible for the development of products for an organization, known as the practice of product management. _____ s own the business strategy behind a product , specify its functional requirements and generally manage the launch of features. They coordinate work done by many other functions and are ultimately responsible for the business success of the product.

Exam Probability: **Medium**

7. *Answer choices:*

(see index for correct answer)

- a. Product information management
- b. Product manager
- c. Swing tag

- d. Service life

Guidance: level 1

:: Marketing ::

_____ is a pricing strategy where the price of a product is initially set low to rapidly reach a wide fraction of the market and initiate word of mouth. The strategy works on the expectation that customers will switch to the new brand because of the lower price. _____ is most commonly associated with marketing objectives of enlarging market share and exploiting economies of scale or experience.

Exam Probability: **High**

8. *Answer choices:*
(see index for correct answer)

- a. Distributed presence
- b. Product category volume
- c. Discounting
- d. Interactive collateral management

Guidance: level 1

:: Supply chain management ::

_____ is the removal of intermediaries in economics from a supply chain, or cutting out the middlemen in connection with a transaction or a series of transactions. Instead of going through traditional distribution channels, which had some type of intermediary , companies may now deal with customers directly, for example via the Internet. Hence, the use of factory direct and direct from the factory to mean the same thing.

Exam Probability: **Medium**

9. *Answer choices:*
(see index for correct answer)

- a. Disintermediation
- b. Enterprise resource planning
- c. Entry visibility
- d. CSCMP Supply Chain Process Standards

Guidance: level 1

_____ is the process of selling consumer goods or services to customers through multiple channels of distribution to earn a profit. _____ ers satisfy demand identified through a supply chain. The term " _____ er" is typically applied where a service provider fills the small orders of a large number of individuals, who are end-users, rather than large orders of a small number of wholesale, corporate or government clientele. Shopping generally refers to the act of buying products. Sometimes this is done to obtain final goods, including necessities such as food and clothing; sometimes it takes place as a recreational activity. Recreational shopping often involves window shopping and browsing: it does not always result in a purchase.

Exam Probability: **High**

10. *Answer choices:*
(see index for correct answer)

- a. People counter
- b. Showroom
- c. Motorized shopping cart
- d. Diffusion line

Guidance: level 1

:: Data interchange standards ::

_____ is the concept of businesses electronically communicating information that was traditionally communicated on paper, such as purchase orders and invoices. Technical standards for EDI exist to facilitate parties transacting such instruments without having to make special arrangements.

Exam Probability: **High**

11. *Answer choices:*
(see index for correct answer)

- a. Data Interchange Standards Association
- b. Domain Application Protocol
- c. Electronic data interchange
- d. ASC X12

Guidance: level 1

In _____ relations and communication science, _____ s are groups of individual people, and the _____ is the totality of such groupings. This is a different concept to the sociological concept of the Öffentlichkeit or _____ sphere. The concept of a _____ has also been defined in political science, psychology, marketing, and advertising. In _____ relations and communication science, it is one of the more ambiguous concepts in the field. Although it has definitions in the theory of the field that have been formulated from the early 20th century onwards, it has suffered in more recent years from being blurred, as a result of conflation of the idea of a _____ with the notions of audience, market segment, community, constituency, and stakeholder.

Exam Probability: **High**

12. *Answer choices:*
(see index for correct answer)

- a. personal values
- b. corporate values
- c. deep-level diversity
- d. Public

Guidance: level 1

:: Advertising by type ::

_____ or advertising war is an advertisement in which a particular product, or service, specifically mentions a competitor by name for the express purpose of showing why the competitor is inferior to the product naming it. Also referred to as "knocking copy", it is loosely defined as advertising where "the advertised brand is explicitly compared with one or more competing brands and the comparison is obvious to the audience."

Exam Probability: **Low**

13. *Answer choices:*
(see index for correct answer)

- a. Virtual advertising
- b. Parody advertisement
- c. Aerial advertising
- d. Comparative advertising

:: Information technology management ::

B2B is often contrasted with business-to-consumer . In B2B commerce, it is often the case that the parties to the relationship have comparable negotiating power, and even when they do not, each party typically involves professional staff and legal counsel in the negotiation of terms, whereas B2C is shaped to a far greater degree by economic implications of information asymmetry. However, within a B2B context, large companies may have many commercial, resource and information advantages over smaller businesses. The United Kingdom government, for example, created the post of Small Business Commissioner under the Enterprise Act 2016 to "enable small businesses to resolve disputes" and "consider complaints by small business suppliers about payment issues with larger businesses that they supply."

Exam Probability: **Low**

14. *Answer choices:*
(see index for correct answer)

- a. Web operations
- b. Intelligent device management
- c. Information technology planning
- d. Ubiquitous commerce

:: Marketing ::

A _____ is the quantity of payment or compensation given by one party to another in return for one unit of goods or services.. A _____ is influenced by both production costs and demand for the product. A _____ may be determined by a monopolist or may be imposed on the firm by market conditions.

Exam Probability: **Medium**

15. *Answer choices:*
(see index for correct answer)

- a. Carrying cost
- b. Earned media

- c. Price
- d. Product marketing

Guidance: level 1

:: Data management ::

_____ is a form of intellectual property that grants the creator of an original creative work an exclusive legal right to determine whether and under what conditions this original work may be copied and used by others, usually for a limited term of years. The exclusive rights are not absolute but limited by limitations and exceptions to _____ law, including fair use. A major limitation on _____ on ideas is that _____ protects only the original expression of ideas, and not the underlying ideas themselves.

Exam Probability: **Low**

16. *Answer choices:*
(see index for correct answer)

- a. Copyright
- b. Data monetization
- c. Database engine
- d. Government Performance Management

Guidance: level 1

:: ::

_____ refers to a diverse array of media technologies that reach a large audience via mass communication. The technologies through which this communication takes place include a variety of outlets.

Exam Probability: **Low**

17. *Answer choices:*
(see index for correct answer)

- a. functional perspective
- b. Mass media
- c. surface-level diversity
- d. corporate values

Guidance: level 1

:: Marketing ::

_____ comes from the Latin neg and otsia referring to businessmen who, unlike the patricians, had no leisure time in their industriousness; it held the meaning of business until the 17th century when it took on the diplomatic connotation as a dialogue between two or more people or parties intended to reach a beneficial outcome over one or more issues where a conflict exists with respect to at least one of these issues. Thus, _____ is a process of combining divergent positions into a joint agreement under a decision rule of unanimity.

Exam Probability: **Medium**

18. *Answer choices:*
(see index for correct answer)

- a. Negotiation
- b. Corporate anniversary
- c. All-commodity volume
- d. Kidification

Guidance: level 1

:: Belief ::

_____ is an umbrella term of influence. _____ can attempt to influence a person's beliefs, attitudes, intentions, motivations, or behaviors. In business, _____ is a process aimed at changing a person's attitude or behavior toward some event, idea, object, or other person, by using written, spoken words or visual tools to convey information, feelings, or reasoning, or a combination thereof. _____ is also an often used tool in the pursuit of personal gain, such as election campaigning, giving a sales pitch, or in trial advocacy. _____ can also be interpreted as using one's personal or positional resources to change people's behaviors or attitudes.Systematic _____ is the process through which attitudes or beliefs are leveraged by appeals to logic and reason. Heuristic _____ on the other hand is the process through which attitudes or beliefs are leveraged by appeals to habit or emotion.

Exam Probability: **Low**

19. *Answer choices:*

(see index for correct answer)

- a. Disquotational principle
- b. Ideological assumption
- c. Faith
- d. Persuasion

Guidance: level 1

:: ::

_____ , also referred to as orthostasis, is a human position in which the body is held in an upright position and supported only by the feet.

Exam Probability: **Medium**

20. *Answer choices:*
(see index for correct answer)

- a. Standing
- b. imperative
- c. Sarbanes-Oxley act of 2002
- d. hierarchical perspective

Guidance: level 1

:: Marketing ::

A _____ is an overall experience of a customer that distinguishes an organization or product from its rivals in the eyes of the customer. _____ s are used in business, marketing, and advertising. Name _____ s are sometimes distinguished from generic or store _____ s.

Exam Probability: **Medium**

21. *Answer choices:*
(see index for correct answer)

- a. Movement marketing
- b. Optimal discriminant analysis
- c. Brand
- d. Porter hypothesis

Guidance: level 1

:: Product management ::

_____ ` is a phrase used in the marketing industry which describes the value of having a well-known brand name, based on the idea that the owner of a well-known brand name can generate more revenue simply from brand recognition; that is from products with that brand name than from products with a less well known name, as consumers believe that a product with a well-known name is better than products with less well-known names.

Exam Probability: **Medium**

22. *Answer choices:*
(see index for correct answer)

- a. Product family engineering
- b. Product information
- c. Requirement prioritization
- d. Brand equity

Guidance: level 1

:: Debt ::

_____ , in finance and economics, is payment from a borrower or deposit-taking financial institution to a lender or depositor of an amount above repayment of the principal sum , at a particular rate. It is distinct from a fee which the borrower may pay the lender or some third party. It is also distinct from dividend which is paid by a company to its shareholders from its profit or reserve, but not at a particular rate decided beforehand, rather on a pro rata basis as a share in the reward gained by risk taking entrepreneurs when the revenue earned exceeds the total costs.

Exam Probability: **Low**

23. *Answer choices:*
(see index for correct answer)

- a. Museum of Foreign Debt
- b. Extendible bond
- c. Debt compliance
- d. Credit cycle

Guidance: level 1

:: Summary statistics ::

_____ is the number of occurrences of a repeating event per unit of time. It is also referred to as temporal _____ , which emphasizes the contrast to spatial _____ and angular _____ . The period is the duration of time of one cycle in a repeating event, so the period is the reciprocal of the _____ . For example: if a newborn baby's heart beats at a _____ of 120 times a minute, its period—the time interval between beats—is half a second . _____ is an important parameter used in science and engineering to specify the rate of oscillatory and vibratory phenomena, such as mechanical vibrations, audio signals , radio waves, and light.

Exam Probability: **High**

24. *Answer choices:*
(see index for correct answer)

- a. Mean percentage error
- b. Frequency
- c. Five-number summary
- d. Scan statistic

Guidance: level 1

:: ::

Management is the administration of an organization, whether it is a business, a not-for-profit organization, or government body. Management includes the activities of setting the strategy of an organization and coordinating the efforts of its employees to accomplish its objectives through the application of available resources, such as financial, natural, technological, and human resources. The term "management" may also refer to those people who manage an organization.

Exam Probability: **High**

25. *Answer choices:*
(see index for correct answer)

- a. surface-level diversity
- b. co-culture
- c. deep-level diversity
- d. Manager

Guidance: level 1

_____ s are formal, sociotechnical, organizational systems designed to collect, process, store, and distribute information. In a sociotechnical perspective, _____ s are composed by four components: task, people, structure , and technology.

Exam Probability: **Medium**

26. *Answer choices:*

(see index for correct answer)

- a. Information system
- b. Character
- c. imperative
- d. functional perspective

Guidance: level 1

:: Human resource management ::

_____ encompasses values and behaviors that contribute to the unique social and psychological environment of a business. The _____ influences the way people interact, the context within which knowledge is created, the resistance they will have towards certain changes, and ultimately the way they share knowledge. _____ represents the collective values, beliefs and principles of organizational members and is a product of factors such as history, product, market, technology, strategy, type of employees, management style, and national culture; culture includes the organization's vision, values, norms, systems, symbols, language, assumptions, environment, location, beliefs and habits.

Exam Probability: **Low**

27. *Answer choices:*

(see index for correct answer)

- a. Emotional labor
- b. Behavioral Competencies
- c. Organizational culture
- d. Applicant tracking system

Guidance: level 1

A _____ , also known as an industry trade group, business association, sector association or industry body, is an organization founded and funded by businesses that operate in a specific industry. An industry _____ participates in public relations activities such as advertising, education, political donations, lobbying and publishing, but its focus is collaboration between companies. Associations may offer other services, such as producing conferences, networking or charitable events or offering classes or educational materials. Many associations are non-profit organizations governed by bylaws and directed by officers who are also members.

Exam Probability: **Medium**

28. *Answer choices:*
(see index for correct answer)

- a. Trade association
- b. Property Care Association
- c. Lighting Association
- d. IPC

Guidance: level 1

:: ::

_____ Corporation is an American multinational technology company with headquarters in Redmond, Washington. It develops, manufactures, licenses, supports and sells computer software, consumer electronics, personal computers, and related services. Its best known software products are the _____ Windows line of operating systems, the _____ Office suite, and the Internet Explorer and Edge Web browsers. Its flagship hardware products are the Xbox video game consoles and the _____ Surface lineup of touchscreen personal computers. As of 2016, it is the world's largest software maker by revenue, and one of the world's most valuable companies. The word "_____ " is a portmanteau of "microcomputer" and "software". _____ is ranked No. 30 in the 2018 Fortune 500 rankings of the largest United States corporations by total revenue.

Exam Probability: **Medium**

29. *Answer choices:*

- a. surface-level diversity
- b. hierarchical
- c. Microsoft
- d. levels of analysis

Guidance: level 1

:: International trade ::

In finance, an _____ is the rate at which one currency will be exchanged for another. It is also regarded as the value of one country's currency in relation to another currency. For example, an interbank _____ of 114 Japanese yen to the United States dollar means that ¥114 will be exchanged for each US$1 or that US$1 will be exchanged for each ¥114. In this case it is said that the price of a dollar in relation to yen is ¥114, or equivalently that the price of a yen in relation to dollars is $1/114.

Exam Probability: **High**

30. *Answer choices:*

- a. North American Competitiveness Council
- b. Re-exportation
- c. Ocean freight differential
- d. Exchange rate

Guidance: level 1

:: Industry ::

_____ describes various measures of the efficiency of production. Often , a _____ measure is expressed as the ratio of an aggregate output to a single input or an aggregate input used in a production process, i.e. output per unit of input. Most common example is the labour _____ measure, e.g., such as GDP per worker. There are many different definitions of _____ and the choice among them depends on the purpose of the _____ measurement and/or data availability. The key source of difference between various _____ measures is also usually related to how the outputs and the inputs are aggregated into scalars to obtain such a ratio-type measure of _____ .

31. *Answer choices:*

(see index for correct answer)

- a. Economic importance of bacteria
- b. Industrial region
- c. Tube and clamp scaffold
- d. Low carbon leakage

Guidance: level 1

:: ::

In sales, commerce and economics, a _____ is the recipient of a good, service, product or an idea - obtained from a seller, vendor, or supplier via a financial transaction or exchange for money or some other valuable consideration.

Exam Probability: **Medium**

32. *Answer choices:*

(see index for correct answer)

- a. Customer
- b. co-culture
- c. hierarchical
- d. open system

Guidance: level 1

:: Reputation management ::

A _____ is an astronomical object consisting of a luminous spheroid of plasma held together by its own gravity. The nearest _____ to Earth is the Sun. Many other _____ s are visible to the naked eye from Earth during the night, appearing as a multitude of fixed luminous points in the sky due to their immense distance from Earth. Historically, the most prominent _____ s were grouped into constellations and asterisms, the brightest of which gained proper names. Astronomers have assembled _____ catalogues that identify the known _____ s and provide standardized stellar designations. However, most of the estimated 300 sextillion _____ s in the Universe are invisible to the naked eye from Earth, including all _____ s outside our galaxy, the Milky Way.

Exam Probability: **Medium**

33. *Answer choices:*
(see index for correct answer)

- a. Reputation
- b. Hilltop algorithm
- c. The Economy of Esteem
- d. Meta-moderation system

Guidance: level 1

:: ::

An _____ is the production of goods or related services within an economy. The major source of revenue of a group or company is the indicator of its relevant _____ . When a large group has multiple sources of revenue generation, it is considered to be working in different industries. Manufacturing _____ became a key sector of production and labour in European and North American countries during the Industrial Revolution, upsetting previous mercantile and feudal economies. This came through many successive rapid advances in technology, such as the production of steel and coal.

Exam Probability: **High**

34. *Answer choices:*
(see index for correct answer)

- a. Industry
- b. similarity-attraction theory

- c. cultural
- d. process perspective

Guidance: level 1

:: Business ::

The seller, or the provider of the goods or services, completes a sale in response to an acquisition, appropriation, requisition or a direct interaction with the buyer at the point of sale. There is a passing of title of the item, and the settlement of a price, in which agreement is reached on a price for which transfer of ownership of the item will occur. The seller, not the purchaser typically executes the sale and it may be completed prior to the obligation of payment. In the case of indirect interaction, a person who sells goods or service on behalf of the owner is known as a _____ man or _____ woman or _____ person, but this often refers to someone selling goods in a store/shop, in which case other terms are also common, including _____ clerk, shop assistant, and retail clerk.

Exam Probability: **Low**

35. *Answer choices:*
(see index for correct answer)

- a. Sales
- b. Service recovery
- c. Ian McLeod
- d. CyberAlert, Inc.

Guidance: level 1

:: Public relations ::

_____ is the public visibility or awareness for any product, service or company. It may also refer to the movement of information from its source to the general public, often but not always via the media. The subjects of _____ include people , goods and services, organizations, and works of art or entertainment.

Exam Probability: **Low**

36. *Answer choices:*
(see index for correct answer)

- a. Flaunt
- b. Public Relations Institute of Australia
- c. Media contacts database
- d. Ice block expedition of 1959

Guidance: level 1

:: ::

A _____ is any person who contracts to acquire an asset in return for some form of consideration.

Exam Probability: **Low**

37. *Answer choices:*
(see index for correct answer)

- a. Buyer
- b. corporate values
- c. interpersonal communication
- d. deep-level diversity

Guidance: level 1

:: Product development ::

In business and engineering, _____ covers the complete process of bringing a new product to market. A central aspect of NPD is product design, along with various business considerations. _____ is described broadly as the transformation of a market opportunity into a product available for sale. The product can be tangible or intangible , though sometimes services and other processes are distinguished from "products." NPD requires an understanding of customer needs and wants, the competitive environment, and the nature of the market.Cost, time and quality are the main variables that drive customer needs. Aiming at these three variables, innovative companies develop continuous practices and strategies to better satisfy customer requirements and to increase their own market share by a regular development of new products. There are many uncertainties and challenges which companies must face throughout the process. The use of best practices and the elimination of barriers to communication are the main concerns for the management of the NPD .

Exam Probability: **Low**

38. *Answer choices:*
(see index for correct answer)

- a. Product optimization
- b. Design brief
- c. Design specification
- d. Product line extension

Guidance: level 1

:: ::

_____ is the process whereby a business sets the price at which it will sell its products and services, and may be part of the business's marketing plan. In setting prices, the business will take into account the price at which it could acquire the goods, the manufacturing cost, the market place, competition, market condition, brand, and quality of product.

Exam Probability: **High**

39. *Answer choices:*
(see index for correct answer)

- a. cultural
- b. interpersonal communication
- c. imperative
- d. Sarbanes-Oxley act of 2002

Guidance: level 1

:: Services management and marketing ::

_____ is a specialised branch of marketing. _____ emerged as a separate field of study in the early 1980s, following the recognition that the unique characteristics of services required different strategies compared with the marketing of physical goods.

Exam Probability: **Low**

40. *Answer choices:*
(see index for correct answer)

- a. Viable systems approach
- b. Business service provider
- c. Industrialization of services business model
- d. Services marketing

:: Advertising ::

A _____ is a document used by creative professionals and agencies to develop creative deliverables: visual design, copy, advertising, web sites, etc. The document is usually developed by the requestor and approved by the creative team of designers, writers, and project managers. In some cases, the project's _____ may need creative director approval before work will commence.

Exam Probability: **Medium**

41. *Answer choices:*
(see index for correct answer)

- a. Bumvertising
- b. Creative brief
- c. Frequency capping
- d. Criteo

:: Marketing ::

_____ is a growth strategy that identifies and develops new market segments for current products. A _____ strategy targets non-buying customers in currently targeted segments. It also targets new customers in new segments.

Exam Probability: **High**

42. *Answer choices:*
(see index for correct answer)

- a. Market development
- b. Nano-campaigning
- c. Pitching engine
- d. Hakan Okay

:: ::

A _____ service is an online platform which people use to build social networks or social relationship with other people who share similar personal or career interests, activities, backgrounds or real-life connections.

Exam Probability: **Low**

43. *Answer choices:*
(see index for correct answer)

- a. empathy
- b. process perspective
- c. personal values
- d. deep-level diversity

Guidance: level 1

:: ::

Advertising is a marketing communication that employs an openly sponsored, non-personal message to promote or sell a product, service or idea. Sponsors of advertising are typically businesses wishing to promote their products or services. Advertising is differentiated from public relations in that an advertiser pays for and has control over the message. It differs from personal selling in that the message is non-personal, i.e., not directed to a particular individual. Advertising is communicated through various mass media, including traditional media such as newspapers, magazines, television, radio, outdoor advertising or direct mail; and new media such as search results, blogs, social media, websites or text messages. The actual presentation of the message in a medium is referred to as an _____ , or "ad" or advert for short.

Exam Probability: **High**

44. *Answer choices:*
(see index for correct answer)

- a. interpersonal communication
- b. Character
- c. Advertisement
- d. personal values

Guidance: level 1

:: ::

_____ consists of using generic or ad hoc methods in an orderly manner to find solutions to problems. Some of the problem-solving techniques developed and used in philosophy, artificial intelligence, computer science, engineering, mathematics, or medicine are related to mental problem-solving techniques studied in psychology.

Exam Probability: **Medium**

45. *Answer choices:*
(see index for correct answer)

- a. Problem Solving
- b. hierarchical
- c. personal values
- d. levels of analysis

Guidance: level 1

:: Promotion and marketing communications ::

_____ is one of the elements of the promotional mix. . _____ uses both media and non-media marketing communications for a pre-determined, limited time to increase consumer demand, stimulate market demand or improve product availability. Examples include contests, coupons, freebies, loss leaders, point of purchase displays, premiums, prizes, product samples, and rebates.

Exam Probability: **Low**

46. *Answer choices:*
(see index for correct answer)

- a. PR NewsChannel
- b. news release
- c. Sales promotion
- d. Slogan

Guidance: level 1

:: ::

_____ is a marketing communication that employs an openly sponsored, non-personal message to promote or sell a product, service or idea. Sponsors of _____ are typically businesses wishing to promote their products or services. _____ is differentiated from public relations in that an advertiser pays for and has control over the message. It differs from personal selling in that the message is non-personal, i.e., not directed to a particular individual. _____ is communicated through various mass media, including traditional media such as newspapers, magazines, television, radio, outdoor _____ or direct mail; and new media such as search results, blogs, social media, websites or text messages. The actual presentation of the message in a medium is referred to as an advertisement, or "ad" or advert for short.

Exam Probability: **Medium**

47. *Answer choices:*
(see index for correct answer)

- a. hierarchical
- b. Advertising
- c. process perspective
- d. imperative

Guidance: level 1

:: Data ::

Data has two ways of being created or generated. The first is what is called `captured data`, and is found through purposeful investigation or analysis. The second is called `exhaust data`, and is gathered usually by machines or terminals as a secondary function. For example, cash registers, smartphones, and speedometers serve a main function but may collect data as a secondary task. Exhaustive data is usually too large or of little use to process and becomes `transient` or thrown away.

Exam Probability: **High**

48. *Answer choices:*
(see index for correct answer)

- a. DataSplice
- b. Humanities Indicators
- c. Primary data
- d. Biological data

:: Planning ::

_____ is a high level plan to achieve one or more goals under conditions of uncertainty. In the sense of the "art of the general," which included several subsets of skills including tactics, siegecraft, logistics etc., the term came into use in the 6th century C.E. in East Roman terminology, and was translated into Western vernacular languages only in the 18th century. From then until the 20th century, the word "_____ " came to denote "a comprehensive way to try to pursue political ends, including the threat or actual use of force, in a dialectic of wills" in a military conflict, in which both adversaries interact.

Exam Probability: **Medium**

49. *Answer choices:*
(see index for correct answer)

- a. Counterplan
- b. Strategy
- c. Parish plan
- d. Strategic communication

:: Packaging ::

In work place, _____ or job _____ means good ranking with the hypothesized conception of requirements of a role. There are two types of job _____ s: contextual and task. Task _____ is related to cognitive ability while contextual _____ is dependent upon personality. Task _____ are behavioral roles that are recognized in job descriptions and by remuneration systems, they are directly related to organizational _____ , whereas, contextual _____ are value based and additional behavioral roles that are not recognized in job descriptions and covered by compensation; they are extra roles that are indirectly related to organizational _____ . Citizenship _____ like contextual _____ means a set of individual activity/contribution that supports the organizational culture.

Exam Probability: **Medium**

50. *Answer choices:*
(see index for correct answer)

- a. Dangerous Preparations Directive
- b. Performance
- c. Tin box
- d. Permeation

Guidance: level 1

:: Television commercials ::

_____ is a phenomenon whereby something new and somehow valuable is formed. The created item may be intangible or a physical object .

Exam Probability: **High**

51. *Answer choices:*
(see index for correct answer)

- a. Mountain
- b. The Program Exchange
- c. An American Revolution
- d. Creativity

Guidance: level 1

:: Management ::

The term _____ refers to measures designed to increase the degree of autonomy and self-determination in people and in communities in order to enable them to represent their interests in a responsible and self-determined way, acting on their own authority. It is the process of becoming stronger and more confident, especially in controlling one's life and claiming one's rights. _____ as action refers both to the process of self-_____ and to professional support of people, which enables them to overcome their sense of powerlessness and lack of influence, and to recognize and use their resources. To do work with power.

Exam Probability: **Low**

52. *Answer choices:*
(see index for correct answer)

- a. Empowerment

- b. Document automation
- c. Tata Management Training Centre
- d. Balanced scorecard

:: Project management ::

_____ is the right to exercise power, which can be formalized by a state and exercised by way of judges, appointed executives of government, or the ecclesiastical or priestly appointed representatives of a God or other deities.

Exam Probability: **Low**

53. *Answer choices:*
(see index for correct answer)

- a. Lean project management
- b. Bottleneck
- c. Gantt chart
- d. Authority

:: Stochastic processes ::

_____ in its modern meaning is a "new idea, creative thoughts, new imaginations in form of device or method". _____ is often also viewed as the application of better solutions that meet new requirements, unarticulated needs, or existing market needs. Such _____ takes place through the provision of more-effective products, processes, services, technologies, or business models that are made available to markets, governments and society. An _____ is something original and more effective and, as a consequence, new, that "breaks into" the market or society. _____ is related to, but not the same as, invention, as _____ is more apt to involve the practical implementation of an invention to make a meaningful impact in the market or society, and not all _____ s require an invention. _____ often manifests itself via the engineering process, when the problem being solved is of a technical or scientific nature. The opposite of _____ is exnovation.

Exam Probability: **Low**

54. *Answer choices:*

(see index for correct answer)

- a. Increasing process
- b. Discrete-time stochastic process
- c. Law of the iterated logarithm
- d. Innovation

Guidance: level 1

:: Management accounting ::

_____ s are costs that change as the quantity of the good or service that a business produces changes. _____ s are the sum of marginal costs over all units produced. They can also be considered normal costs. Fixed costs and _____ s make up the two components of total cost. Direct costs are costs that can easily be associated with a particular cost object. However, not all _____ s are direct costs. For example, variable manufacturing overhead costs are _____ s that are indirect costs, not direct costs. _____ s are sometimes called unit-level costs as they vary with the number of units produced.

Exam Probability: **Medium**

55. *Answer choices:*

(see index for correct answer)

- a. Variable cost
- b. Institute of Certified Management Accountants
- c. Relevant cost
- d. Responsibility center

Guidance: level 1

:: Brokered programming ::

An _____ is a form of television commercial, which generally includes a toll-free telephone number or website. Most often used as a form of direct response television , long-form _____ s are typically 28:30 or 58:30 minutes in length. _____ s are also known as paid programming . This phenomenon started in the United States, where _____ s were typically shown overnight , outside peak prime time hours for commercial broadcasters. Some television stations chose to air _____ s as an alternative to the former practice of signing off. Some channels air _____ s 24 hours. Some stations also choose to air _____ s during the daytime hours mostly on weekends to fill in for unscheduled network or syndicated programming. By 2009, most _____ spending in the U.S. occurred during the early morning, daytime and evening hours, or in the afternoon. Stations in most countries around the world have instituted similar media structures. The _____ industry is worth over $200 billion.

56. *Answer choices:*
(see index for correct answer)

- a. Leased access
- b. Brokered programming
- c. Infomercial
- d. Toonzai

Guidance: level 1

:: Consumer behaviour ::

_____ is an activity in which a customer browses the available goods or services presented by one or more retailers with the potential intent to purchase a suitable selection of them. A typology of shopper types has been developed by scholars which identifies one group of shoppers as recreational shoppers, that is, those who enjoy _____ and view it as a leisure activity.

57. *Answer choices:*
(see index for correct answer)

- a. Consumption smoothing
- b. Shopping

- c. Shopping while black
- d. Visual merchandising

Guidance: level 1

:: ::

_____ is a concept of English common law and is a necessity for simple contracts but not for special contracts . The concept has been adopted by other common law jurisdictions, including the US.

Exam Probability: **Low**

58. *Answer choices:*
(see index for correct answer)

- a. Sarbanes-Oxley act of 2002
- b. corporate values
- c. empathy
- d. interpersonal communication

Guidance: level 1

:: E-commerce ::

_____ is the activity of buying or selling of products on online services or over the Internet. Electronic commerce draws on technologies such as mobile commerce, electronic funds transfer, supply chain management, Internet marketing, online transaction processing, electronic data interchange , inventory management systems, and automated data collection systems.

Exam Probability: **Medium**

59. *Answer choices:*
(see index for correct answer)

- a. E-commerce
- b. Demandware
- c. Bill2phone
- d. AdsML

Guidance: level 1

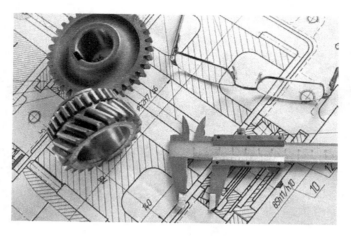

Manufacturing

Manufacturing is the production of merchandise for use or sale using labor and machines, tools, chemical and biological processing, or formulation. The term may refer to a range of human activity, from handicraft to high tech, but is most commonly applied to industrial design , in which raw materials are transformed into finished goods on a large scale. Such finished goods may be sold to other manufacturers for the production of other, more complex products, such as aircraft, household appliances, furniture, sports equipment or automobiles, or sold to wholesalers, who in turn sell them to retailers, who then sell them to end users and consumers.

:: Management ::

_____ is the identification, evaluation, and prioritization of risks followed by coordinated and economical application of resources to minimize, monitor, and control the probability or impact of unfortunate events or to maximize the realization of opportunities.

Exam Probability: **Medium**

1. *Answer choices:*
(see index for correct answer)

- a. Adhocracy
- b. Risk management
- c. Duality
- d. U-procedure and Theory U

Guidance: level 1

:: Product management ::

_____ s, also known as Shewhart charts or process-behavior charts, are a statistical process control tool used to determine if a manufacturing or business process is in a state of control.

Exam Probability: **Low**

2. *Answer choices:*

(see index for correct answer)

- a. Crossing the Chasm
- b. Dwinell-Wright Company
- c. Technology acceptance model
- d. Control chart

Guidance: level 1

:: Commercial item transport and distribution ::

In commerce, supply-chain management , the management of the flow of goods and services, involves the movement and storage of raw materials, of work-in-process inventory, and of finished goods from point of origin to point of consumption. Interconnected or interlinked networks, channels and node businesses combine in the provision of products and services required by end customers in a supply chain. Supply-chain management has been defined as the "design, planning, execution, control, and monitoring of supply-chain activities with the objective of creating net value, building a competitive infrastructure, leveraging worldwide logistics, synchronizing supply with demand and measuring performance globally."SCM practice draws heavily from the areas of industrial engineering, systems engineering, operations management, logistics, procurement, information technology, and marketing and strives for an integrated approach. Marketing channels play an important role in supply-chain management. Current research in supply-chain management is concerned with topics related to sustainability and risk management, among others. Some suggest that the "people dimension" of SCM, ethical issues, internal integration, transparency/visibility, and human capital/talent management are topics that have, so far, been underrepresented on the research agenda.

Exam Probability: **High**

3. *Answer choices:*

(see index for correct answer)

- a. Supply chain management
- b. Stillage
- c. Duty
- d. Air cargo

Guidance: level 1

:: Costs ::

In microeconomic theory, the _____ , or alternative cost, of making a particular choice is the value of the most valuable choice out of those that were not taken. In other words, opportunity that will require sacrifices.

Exam Probability: **Medium**

4. *Answer choices:*
(see index for correct answer)

- a. Flyaway cost
- b. Manufacturing cost
- c. Sliding scale
- d. Psychic cost

Guidance: level 1

:: Outsourcing ::

A _____ is a document that solicits proposal, often made through a bidding process, by an agency or company interested in procurement of a commodity, service, or valuable asset, to potential suppliers to submit business proposals. It is submitted early in the procurement cycle, either at the preliminary study, or procurement stage.

Exam Probability: **High**

5. *Answer choices:*
(see index for correct answer)

- a. Chris Ducker
- b. Request for proposal
- c. Managed VoIP Service
- d. Regional insourcing

Guidance: level 1

A _____ is an employee within a company, business or other organization who is responsible at some level for buying or approving the acquisition of goods and services needed by the company. Responsible for buying the best quality products, goods and services for their company at the most competitive prices, _____ s work in a wide range of sectors for many different organizations. The position responsibilities may be the same as that of a buyer or purchasing agent, or may include wider supervisory or managerial responsibilities. A _____ may oversee the acquisition of materials needed for production, general supplies for offices and facilities, equipment, or construction contracts. A _____ often supervises purchasing agents and buyers, but in small companies the _____ may also be the purchasing agent or buyer. The _____ position may also carry the title "Procurement Manager" or in the public sector, "Procurement Officer". He or she can come from both an Engineering or Economics background.

Exam Probability: **Low**

6. *Answer choices:*
(see index for correct answer)

- a. Too cheap to meter
- b. Contingent payment sales
- c. Coincidence of wants
- d. Purchasing manager

Guidance: level 1

:: Production and manufacturing ::

_____ is a systematic method to improve the "value" of goods or products and services by using an examination of function. Value, as defined, is the ratio of function to cost. Value can therefore be manipulated by either improving the function or reducing the cost. It is a primary tenet of _____ that basic functions be preserved and not be reduced as a consequence of pursuing value improvements.

Exam Probability: **Medium**

7. *Answer choices:*
(see index for correct answer)

- a. Agricultural cooperative
- b. Reverse engineering
- c. Technological theory of social production
- d. SafetyBUS p

Guidance: level 1

:: ::

_____ is a kind of action that occur as two or more objects have an effect upon one another. The idea of a two-way effect is essential in the concept of _____ , as opposed to a one-way causal effect. A closely related term is interconnectivity, which deals with the _____ s of _____ s within systems: combinations of many simple _____ s can lead to surprising emergent phenomena. _____ has different tailored meanings in various sciences. Changes can also involve _____ .

Exam Probability: **Low**

8. *Answer choices:*
(see index for correct answer)

- a. empathy
- b. process perspective
- c. interpersonal communication
- d. Character

Guidance: level 1

:: Information technology management ::

_____ is the discipline of engineering concerned with the principles and practice of product and service quality assurance and control. In the software development, it is the management, development, operation and maintenance of IT systems and enterprise architectures with a high quality standard.

Exam Probability: **Low**

9. *Answer choices:*
(see index for correct answer)

- a. Quality Engineering
- b. Knowledge management software
- c. Problem management

- d. Digital Fuel

Guidance: level 1

:: Management ::

A supply-chain network is an evolution of the basic supply chain. Due to rapid technological advancement, organisations with a basic supply chain can develop this chain into a more complex structure involving a higher level of interdependence and connectivity between more organisations, this constitutes a supply-chain network.

Exam Probability: **Low**

10. *Answer choices:*
(see index for correct answer)

- a. Lead scoring
- b. Supply chain network
- c. Voice of the customer
- d. Double linking

Guidance: level 1

:: Project management ::

A _____ is a professional in the field of project management. _____ s have the responsibility of the planning, procurement and execution of a project, in any undertaking that has a defined scope, defined start and a defined finish; regardless of industry. _____ s are first point of contact for any issues or discrepancies arising from within the heads of various departments in an organization before the problem escalates to higher authorities. Project management is the responsibility of a _____ . This individual seldom participates directly in the activities that produce the end result, but rather strives to maintain the progress, mutual interaction and tasks of various parties in such a way that reduces the risk of overall failure, maximizes benefits, and minimizes costs.

Exam Probability: **Medium**

11. *Answer choices:*
(see index for correct answer)

- a. Project planning
- b. Level of Effort
- c. Project manager
- d. Product description

Guidance: level 1

:: Distribution, retailing, and wholesaling ::

The _____ is a distribution channel phenomenon in which forecasts yield supply chain inefficiencies. It refers to increasing swings in inventory in response to shifts in customer demand as one moves further up the supply chain. The concept first appeared in Jay Forrester's Industrial Dynamics and thus it is also known as the Forrester effect. The _____ was named for the way the amplitude of a whip increases down its length. The further from the originating signal, the greater the distortion of the wave pattern. In a similar manner, forecast accuracy decreases as one moves upstream along the supply chain. For example, many consumer goods have fairly consistent consumption at retail but this signal becomes more chaotic and unpredictable as the focus moves away from consumer purchasing behavior.

Exam Probability: **High**

12. *Answer choices:*
(see index for correct answer)

- a. Free box
- b. Concession
- c. Physical inventory
- d. Bullwhip effect

Guidance: level 1

:: Gas technologies ::

A _____ is a rotary mechanical device that extracts energy from a fluid flow and converts it into useful work. The work produced by a _____ can be used for generating electrical power when combined with a generator. A _____ is a turbomachine with at least one moving part called a rotor assembly, which is a shaft or drum with blades attached. Moving fluid acts on the blades so that they move and impart rotational energy to the rotor. Early _____ examples are windmills and waterwheels.

13. *Answer choices:*

- a. Turbine
- b. Air pump
- c. Deutsche Vereinigung des Gas- und Wasserfaches
- d. Positive pressure

Guidance: level 1

:: Lean manufacturing ::

_____ is a scheduling system for lean manufacturing and just-in-time manufacturing . Taiichi Ohno, an industrial engineer at Toyota, developed _____ to improve manufacturing efficiency. _____ is one method to achieve JIT. The system takes its name from the cards that track production within a factory. For many in the automotive sector, _____ is known as the "Toyota nameplate system" and as such the term is not used by some other automakers.

14. *Answer choices:*

- a. Overall Labor Effectiveness
- b. Kanban
- c. JobShopLean
- d. Manufacturing supermarket

Guidance: level 1

:: Building materials ::

_____ is an alloy of iron and carbon, and sometimes other elements. Because of its high tensile strength and low cost, it is a major component used in buildings, infrastructure, tools, ships, automobiles, machines, appliances, and weapons.

15. *Answer choices:*

- a. Geomembrane
- b. Reed mat
- c. Turbo seal
- d. IS 456

:: Packaging materials ::

_____ is a non-crystalline, amorphous solid that is often transparent and has widespread practical, technological, and decorative uses in, for example, window panes, tableware, and optoelectronics. The most familiar, and historically the oldest, types of manufactured _____ are "silicate _____ es" based on the chemical compound silica , the primary constituent of sand. The term _____ , in popular usage, is often used to refer only to this type of material, which is familiar from use as window _____ and in _____ bottles. Of the many silica-based _____ es that exist, ordinary glazing and container _____ is formed from a specific type called soda-lime _____ , composed of approximately 75% silicon dioxide , sodium oxide from sodium carbonate , calcium oxide , also called lime, and several minor additives.

Exam Probability: **Low**

16. *Answer choices:*
(see index for correct answer)

- a. Paper
- b. Glass
- c. Soilon
- d. Jute

:: Chemical reactions ::

A _____ is a process that leads to the chemical transformation of one set of chemical substances to another. Classically, _____ s encompass changes that only involve the positions of electrons in the forming and breaking of chemical bonds between atoms, with no change to the nuclei , and can often be described by a chemical equation. Nuclear chemistry is a sub-discipline of chemistry that involves the _____ s of unstable and radioactive elements where both electronic and nuclear changes can occur.

Exam Probability: **High**

17. *Answer choices:*
(see index for correct answer)

- a. Work-up
- b. Chemical reaction
- c. Product-determining step
- d. Ionic hydrogenation

Guidance: level 1

:: Materials ::

A _____ , also known as a feedstock, unprocessed material, or primary commodity, is a basic material that is used to produce goods, finished products, energy, or intermediate materials which are feedstock for future finished products. As feedstock, the term connotes these materials are bottleneck assets and are highly important with regard to producing other products. An example of this is crude oil, which is a _____ and a feedstock used in the production of industrial chemicals, fuels, plastics, and pharmaceutical goods; lumber is a _____ used to produce a variety of products including all types of furniture. The term " _____ " denotes materials in minimally processed or unprocessed in states; e.g., raw latex, crude oil, cotton, coal, raw biomass, iron ore, air, logs, or water i.e. "...any product of agriculture, forestry, fishing and any other mineral that is in its natural form or which has undergone the transformation required to prepare it for internationally marketing in substantial volumes."

Exam Probability: **High**

18. *Answer choices:*
(see index for correct answer)

- a. Auxetics
- b. Ion Gel
- c. Nordic Institute of Dental Materials
- d. Raw material

Guidance: level 1

:: ::

An _____ is, most an organized examination or formal evaluation exercise. In engineering activities _____ involves the measurements, tests, and gauges applied to certain characteristics in regard to an object or activity. The results are usually compared to specified requirements and standards for determining whether the item or activity is in line with these targets, often with a Standard _____ Procedure in place to ensure consistent checking. _____ s are usually non-destructive.

Exam Probability: **High**

19. *Answer choices:*
(see index for correct answer)

- a. corporate values
- b. similarity-attraction theory
- c. empathy
- d. functional perspective

Guidance: level 1

:: Supply chain management terms ::

In business and finance, _____ is a system of organizations, people, activities, information, and resources involved inmoving a product or service from supplier to customer. _____ activities involve the transformation of natural resources, raw materials, and components into a finished product that is delivered to the end customer. In sophisticated _____ systems, used products may re-enter the _____ at any point where residual value is recyclable. _____ s link value chains.

Exam Probability: **Low**

20. *Answer choices:*
(see index for correct answer)

- a. Capital spare
- b. Work in process
- c. Supply chain
- d. Price look-up code

Guidance: level 1

:: ::

In sales, commerce and economics, a _____ is the recipient of a good, service, product or an idea - obtained from a seller, vendor, or supplier via a financial transaction or exchange for money or some other valuable consideration.

Exam Probability: **Medium**

21. *Answer choices:*

(see index for correct answer)

- a. interpersonal communication
- b. surface-level diversity
- c. information systems assessment
- d. Customer

Guidance: level 1

:: Industrial organization ::

In economics, specifically general equilibrium theory, a perfect market is defined by several idealizing conditions, collectively called _____ . In theoretical models where conditions of _____ hold, it has been theoretically demonstrated that a market will reach an equilibrium in which the quantity supplied for every product or service, including labor, equals the quantity demanded at the current price. This equilibrium would be a Pareto optimum.

Exam Probability: **Medium**

22. *Answer choices:*

(see index for correct answer)

- a. Theory of the firm
- b. Hold-up problem
- c. Perfect competition
- d. Switching barriers

:: Business process ::

A committee is a body of one or more persons that is subordinate to a deliberative assembly. Usually, the assembly sends matters into a committee as a way to explore them more fully than would be possible if the assembly itself were considering them. Committees may have different functions and their type of work differ depending on the type of the organization and its needs.

Exam Probability: **Medium**

23. *Answer choices:*
(see index for correct answer)

- a. Business process management
- b. Software Ideas Modeler
- c. Signavio
- d. Steering committee

:: Project management ::

In political science, an _____ is a means by which a petition signed by a certain minimum number of registered voters can force a government to choose to either enact a law or hold a public vote in parliament in what is called indirect _____ , or under direct _____ , the proposition is immediately put to a plebiscite or referendum, in what is called a Popular initiated Referendum or citizen-initiated referendum).

Exam Probability: **Medium**

24. *Answer choices:*
(see index for correct answer)

- a. Initiative
- b. P3M3
- c. Goodwerp
- d. Hammock activity

:: Asset ::

In financial accounting, an _____ is any resource owned by the business. Anything tangible or intangible that can be owned or controlled to produce value and that is held by a company to produce positive economic value is an _____ . Simply stated, _____ s represent value of ownership that can be converted into cash . The balance sheet of a firm records the monetary value of the _____ s owned by that firm. It covers money and other valuables belonging to an individual or to a business.

Exam Probability: **Medium**

25. *Answer choices:*
(see index for correct answer)

- a. Fixed asset
- b. Asset

Guidance: level 1

:: Data management ::

_____ is the ability of a physical product to remain functional, without requiring excessive maintenance or repair, when faced with the challenges of normal operation over its design lifetime. There are several measures of _____ in use, including years of life, hours of use, and number of operational cycles. In economics, goods with a long usable life are referred to as durable goods.

Exam Probability: **Low**

26. *Answer choices:*
(see index for correct answer)

- a. XLDB
- b. Ontology merging
- c. ISO 8000
- d. Durability

Guidance: level 1

:: Occupational safety and health ::

_____ is a chemical element with symbol Pb and atomic number 82. It is a heavy metal that is denser than most common materials. _____ is soft and malleable, and also has a relatively low melting point. When freshly cut, _____ is silvery with a hint of blue; it tarnishes to a dull gray color when exposed to air. _____ has the highest atomic number of any stable element and three of its isotopes are endpoints of major nuclear decay chains of heavier elements.

Exam Probability: **Low**

27. *Answer choices:*
(see index for correct answer)

- a. National Fire Fighter Near-Miss Reporting System
- b. Robens Report
- c. Safety school
- d. Asbestos

Guidance: level 1

:: Decision theory ::

_____ is a method developed in Japan beginning in 1966 to help transform the voice of the customer into engineering characteristics for a product. Yoji Akao, the original developer, described QFD as a "method to transform qualitative user demands into quantitative parameters, to deploy the functions forming quality, and to deploy methods for achieving the design quality into subsystems and component parts, and ultimately to specific elements of the manufacturing process." The author combined his work in quality assurance and quality control points with function deployment used in value engineering.

Exam Probability: **Low**

28. *Answer choices:*
(see index for correct answer)

- a. Kepner-Tregoe
- b. Homothetic preferences
- c. Stochastic dominance
- d. Trade study

Guidance: level 1

:: Industrial equipment ::

_____ s are heat exchangers typically used to provide heat to the bottom of industrial distillation columns. They boil the liquid from the bottom of a distillation column to generate vapors which are returned to the column to drive the distillation separation. The heat supplied to the column by the _____ at the bottom of the column is removed by the condenser at the top of the column.

Exam Probability: **Low**

29. *Answer choices:*
(see index for correct answer)

- a. Glass crusher
- b. Whirlwind mill
- c. Rolling bed dryer
- d. Reboiler

Guidance: level 1

:: Project management ::

Rolling-wave planning is the process of project planning in waves as the project proceeds and later details become clearer; similar to the techniques used in agile software development approaches like Scrum..

Exam Probability: **High**

30. *Answer choices:*
(see index for correct answer)

- a. Product-based planning
- b. Basis of estimate
- c. Rolling Wave planning
- d. Mandated lead arranger

Guidance: level 1

:: Quality control tools ::

A _____ is a type of diagram that represents an algorithm, workflow or process. _____ can also be defined as a diagramatic representation of an algorithm .

Exam Probability: **Low**

31. *Answer choices:*
(see index for correct answer)

- a. Scatter plot
- b. C-chart
- c. Flowchart
- d. Robustness validation

Guidance: level 1

:: Costs ::

In process improvement efforts, _____ or cost of quality is a means to quantify the total cost of quality-related efforts and deficiencies. It was first described by Armand V. Feigenbaum in a 1956 Harvard Business Review article.

Exam Probability: **Low**

32. *Answer choices:*
(see index for correct answer)

- a. Cost reduction
- b. Quality costs
- c. Opportunity cost
- d. Khozraschyot

Guidance: level 1

:: ::

The _____ is a project plan of how the production budget will be spent over a given timescale, for every phase of a business project.

Exam Probability: **Medium**

33. *Answer choices:*

(see index for correct answer)

- a. corporate values
- b. deep-level diversity
- c. empathy
- d. Production schedule

Guidance: level 1

:: ::

Catalysis is the process of increasing the rate of a chemical reaction by adding a substance known as a _____ , which is not consumed in the catalyzed reaction and can continue to act repeatedly. Because of this, only very small amounts of _____ are required to alter the reaction rate in principle.

Exam Probability: **High**

34. *Answer choices:*
(see index for correct answer)

- a. Character
- b. surface-level diversity
- c. information systems assessment
- d. Catalyst

Guidance: level 1

:: Sensitivity analysis ::

_____ is the study of how the uncertainty in the output of a mathematical model or system can be divided and allocated to different sources of uncertainty in its inputs. A related practice is uncertainty analysis, which has a greater focus on uncertainty quantification and propagation of uncertainty; ideally, uncertainty and _____ should be run in tandem.

Exam Probability: **Medium**

35. *Answer choices:*
(see index for correct answer)

- a. Tornado diagram
- b. Fourier amplitude sensitivity testing
- c. Sensitivity analysis

- d. Elementary effects method

Guidance: level 1

:: Quality ::

A _____ is an initiating cause of either a condition or a causal chain that leads to an outcome or effect of interest. The term denotes the earliest, most basic, 'deepest', cause for a given behavior; most often a fault. The idea is that you can only see an error by its manifest signs. Those signs can be widespread, multitudinous, and convoluted, whereas the _____ leading to them often is a lot simpler.

Exam Probability: **High**

36. *Answer choices:*
(see index for correct answer)

- a. Dualistic Petri nets
- b. American Society for Quality
- c. Root cause
- d. OptiY

Guidance: level 1

:: E-commerce ::

_____ is the business-to-business or business-to-consumer or business-to-government purchase and sale of supplies, work, and services through the Internet as well as other information and networking systems, such as electronic data interchange and enterprise resource planning.

Exam Probability: **Medium**

37. *Answer choices:*
(see index for correct answer)

- a. MonkeySports
- b. Online Shopping in Bangladesh
- c. E-procurement
- d. Webstore

Guidance: level 1

:: Management ::

_____ is the practice of initiating, planning, executing, controlling, and closing the work of a team to achieve specific goals and meet specific success criteria at the specified time.

Exam Probability: **Low**

38. *Answer choices:*
(see index for correct answer)

- a. Project management
- b. Value migration
- c. Quality
- d. Quick response manufacturing

Guidance: level 1

:: Commercial item transport and distribution ::

_____ in logistics and supply chain management is an organization's use of third-party businesses to outsource elements of its distribution, warehousing, and fulfillment services.

Exam Probability: **High**

39. *Answer choices:*
(see index for correct answer)

- a. Duty
- b. Third-party logistics
- c. Break bulk cargo
- d. Human mail

Guidance: level 1

:: Software testing ::

_____ 1 was the first artificial Earth satellite. The Soviet Union launched it into an elliptical low Earth orbit on 4 October 1957, orbiting for three weeks before its batteries died, then silently for two more months before falling back into the atmosphere. It was a 58 cm diameter polished metal sphere, with four external radio antennas to broadcast radio pulses. Its radio signal was easily detectable even by radio amateurs, and the 65° inclination and duration of its orbit made its flight path cover virtually the entire inhabited Earth. This surprise success precipitated the American _____ crisis and triggered the Space Race, a part of the Cold War. The launch was the beginning of a new era of political, military, technological, and scientific developments.

Exam Probability: **High**

40. *Answer choices:*

(see index for correct answer)

- a. Test plan
- b. Test data generation
- c. Heisenbug
- d. Compatibility testing

Guidance: level 1

:: Product management ::

_____ is the state of being which occurs when an object, service, or practice is no longer wanted even though it may still be in good working order; however, the international standard EN62402 _____ Management - Application Guide defines _____ as being the "transition from availability of products by the original manufacturer or supplier to unavailability". _____ frequently occurs because a replacement has become available that has, in sum, more advantages compared to the disadvantages incurred by maintaining or repairing the original. Obsolete also refers to something that is already disused or discarded, or antiquated. Typically, _____ is preceded by a gradual decline in popularity.

Exam Probability: **Low**

41. *Answer choices:*

(see index for correct answer)

- a. Coolanol
- b. Obsolescence
- c. Consumer adoption of technological innovations
- d. Tipping point

Guidance: level 1

:: Management ::

_____ is a category of business activity made possible by software tools that aim to provide customers with both independence from vendors and better means for engaging with vendors. These same tools can also apply to individuals` relations with other institutions and organizations.

Exam Probability: **High**

42. *Answer choices:*
(see index for correct answer)

- a. Preventive action
- b. Vendor relationship management
- c. Outrage constraint
- d. Reval

Guidance: level 1

:: Product development ::

In business and engineering, _____ covers the complete process of bringing a new product to market. A central aspect of NPD is product design, along with various business considerations. _____ is described broadly as the transformation of a market opportunity into a product available for sale. The product can be tangible or intangible , though sometimes services and other processes are distinguished from "products." NPD requires an understanding of customer needs and wants, the competitive environment, and the nature of the market.Cost, time and quality are the main variables that drive customer needs. Aiming at these three variables, innovative companies develop continuous practices and strategies to better satisfy customer requirements and to increase their own market share by a regular development of new products. There are many uncertainties and challenges which companies must face throughout the process. The use of best practices and the elimination of barriers to communication are the main concerns for the management of the NPD .

43. *Answer choices:*

- a. Design brief
- b. Product design specification
- c. EXtreme Manufacturing
- d. New product development

Guidance: level 1

:: Industrial engineering ::

_____ , in its contemporary conceptualisation, is a comparison of perceived expectations of a service with perceived performance , giving rise to the equation SQ=P-E. This conceptualistion of _____ has its origins in the expectancy-disconfirmation paradigm.

Exam Probability: **Low**

44. *Answer choices:*

- a. Society of Industrial Engineering
- b. Institute of Industrial Engineers
- c. Service quality
- d. Worker-machine activity chart

Guidance: level 1

:: Metals ::

A _____ is a material that, when freshly prepared, polished, or fractured, shows a lustrous appearance, and conducts electricity and heat relatively well. _____ s are typically malleable or ductile . A _____ may be a chemical element such as iron, or an alloy such as stainless steel.

Exam Probability: **Medium**

45. *Answer choices:*

- a. Metal
- b. Metals of antiquity

- c. Polymetal
- d. Depleted uranium

Guidance: level 1

:: ::

A _____ or till is a mechanical or electronic device for registering and calculating transactions at a point of sale. It is usually attached to a drawer for storing cash and other valuables. A modern _____ is usually attached to a printer that can print out receipts for record-keeping purposes.

Exam Probability: **High**

46. *Answer choices:*
(see index for correct answer)

- a. interpersonal communication
- b. levels of analysis
- c. Cash register
- d. hierarchical perspective

Guidance: level 1

:: ::

_____ is the process of finding an estimate, or approximation, which is a value that is usable for some purpose even if input data may be incomplete, uncertain, or unstable. The value is nonetheless usable because it is derived from the best information available. Typically, _____ involves "using the value of a statistic derived from a sample to estimate the value of a corresponding population parameter". The sample provides information that can be projected, through various formal or informal processes, to determine a range most likely to describe the missing information. An estimate that turns out to be incorrect will be an overestimate if the estimate exceeded the actual result, and an underestimate if the estimate fell short of the actual result.

Exam Probability: **Low**

47. *Answer choices:*
(see index for correct answer)

- a. co-culture
- b. empathy

- c. imperative
- d. similarity-attraction theory

Guidance: level 1

:: Marketing techniques ::

A _____ is an award to be given to a person, a group of people like a sports team, or organization to recognise and reward actions or achievements. Official _____ s often involve monetary rewards as well as the fame that comes with them. Some _____ s are also associated with extravagant awarding ceremonies, such as the Academy Awards.

Exam Probability: **Medium**

48. *Answer choices:*
(see index for correct answer)

- a. Not sold in stores
- b. Smarketing
- c. Prize
- d. Freebie marketing

Guidance: level 1

:: Management ::

_____ , also known as natural process limits, are horizontal lines drawn on a statistical process control chart, usually at a distance of ±3 standard deviations of the plotted statistic from the statistic's mean.

Exam Probability: **Low**

49. *Answer choices:*
(see index for correct answer)

- a. Law practice management
- b. Crisis plan
- c. Intopia
- d. Managerial prerogative

Guidance: level 1

:: Information technology management ::

_____ within quality management systems and information technology systems is a process—either formal or informal—used to ensure that changes to a product or system are introduced in a controlled and coordinated manner. It reduces the possibility that unnecessary changes will be introduced to a system without forethought, introducing faults into the system or undoing changes made by other users of software. The goals of a _____ procedure usually include minimal disruption to services, reduction in back-out activities, and cost-effective utilization of resources involved in implementing change.

Exam Probability: **Medium**

50. *Answer choices:*
(see index for correct answer)

- a. Granular configuration automation
- b. One-to-one marketing
- c. Change control
- d. Acceptable use policy

Guidance: level 1

:: Process management ::

A _____ is a diagram commonly used in chemical and process engineering to indicate the general flow of plant processes and equipment. The PFD displays the relationship between major equipment of a plant facility and does not show minor details such as piping details and designations. Another commonly used term for a PFD is a flowsheet.

Exam Probability: **Medium**

51. *Answer choices:*
(see index for correct answer)

- a. Process flow diagram
- b. business process re-engineering
- c. GROW model
- d. Process modeling

Guidance: level 1

:: Industrial processes ::

A _____ is a device used for high-temperature heating. The name derives from Latin word fornax, which means oven. The heat energy to fuel a _____ may be supplied directly by fuel combustion, by electricity such as the electric arc _____ , or through induction heating in induction _____ s.

Exam Probability: **Medium**

52. *Answer choices:*
(see index for correct answer)

- a. Furnace
- b. Fusion splicing
- c. Basic sediment and water
- d. Cryogenic oxygen plant

Guidance: level 1

:: Promotion and marketing communications ::

The _____ of American Manufacturers, now ThomasNet, is an online platform for supplier discovery and product sourcing in the US and Canada. It was once known as the "big green books" and "Thomas Registry", and was a multi-volume directory of industrial product information covering 650,000 distributors, manufacturers and service companies within 67,000-plus industrial categories that is now published on ThomasNet.

Exam Probability: **Low**

53. *Answer choices:*
(see index for correct answer)

- a. Cross-promotion
- b. The One Club
- c. Infoganda
- d. Sales promotion

Guidance: level 1

:: Infographics ::

The _____ is a form used to collect data in real time at the location where the data is generated. The data it captures can be quantitative or qualitative. When the information is quantitative, the _____ is sometimes called a tally sheet.

Exam Probability: **High**

54. *Answer choices:*
(see index for correct answer)

- a. Infographic
- b. Chart
- c. A New Chart of History
- d. Semiology of Graphics

Guidance: level 1

:: Industrial design ::

In physics and mathematics, the _____ of a mathematical space is informally defined as the minimum number of coordinates needed to specify any point within it. Thus a line has a _____ of one because only one coordinate is needed to specify a point on it for example, the point at 5 on a number line. A surface such as a plane or the surface of a cylinder or sphere has a _____ of two because two coordinates are needed to specify a point on it for example, both a latitude and longitude are required to locate a point on the surface of a sphere. The inside of a cube, a cylinder or a sphere is three- _____ al because three coordinates are needed to locate a point within these spaces.

Exam Probability: **Low**

55. *Answer choices:*
(see index for correct answer)

- a. Electronic packaging
- b. Chintz
- c. Dimension
- d. Electric guitar design

Guidance: level 1

:: Data interchange standards ::

_____ is the concept of businesses electronically communicating information that was traditionally communicated on paper, such as purchase orders and invoices. Technical standards for EDI exist to facilitate parties transacting such instruments without having to make special arrangements.

56. *Answer choices:*
(see index for correct answer)

- a. Domain Application Protocol
- b. Electronic data interchange
- c. Uniform Communication Standard
- d. Common Alerting Protocol

Guidance: level 1

:: Retailing ::

_____ is the process of selling consumer goods or services to customers through multiple channels of distribution to earn a profit. _____ ers satisfy demand identified through a supply chain. The term " _____ er" is typically applied where a service provider fills the small orders of a large number of individuals, who are end-users, rather than large orders of a small number of wholesale, corporate or government clientele. Shopping generally refers to the act of buying products. Sometimes this is done to obtain final goods, including necessities such as food and clothing; sometimes it takes place as a recreational activity. Recreational shopping often involves window shopping and browsing: it does not always result in a purchase.

57. *Answer choices:*
(see index for correct answer)

- a. Supermarket
- b. Planogram
- c. Shoppable Windows
- d. Warehouse club

Guidance: level 1

:: Direct marketing ::

_____ Inc. is an American privately owned multi-level marketing company. According to Direct Selling News, _____ was the sixth largest network marketing company in the world in 2018, with a wholesale volume of US$3.25 billion. _____ is based in Addison, Texas, outside Dallas. The company was founded by _____ Ash in 1963. Richard Rogers, _____ `s son, is the chairman, and David Holl is president and was named CEO in 2006.

Exam Probability: **Low**

58. *Answer choices:*
(see index for correct answer)

- a. Multi-level marketing
- b. Telebrands
- c. Synapse Group, Inc.
- d. Mary Kay

Guidance: level 1

:: Quality assurance ::

The _____ is a United States-based nonprofit tax-exempt 501 organization that accredits more than 21,000 US health care organizations and programs. The international branch accredits medical services from around the world. A majority of US state governments recognize _____ accreditation as a condition of licensure for the receipt of Medicaid and Medicare reimbursements.

Exam Probability: **Medium**

59. *Answer choices:*
(see index for correct answer)

- a. National Certification Corporation
- b. Health Information and Quality Authority
- c. United Kingdom Accreditation Service
- d. Healthcare Quality Association on Accreditation

Guidance: level 1

Commerce

Commerce relates to "the exchange of goods and services, especially on a large scale." It includes legal, economic, political, social, cultural and technological systems that operate in any country or internationally.

:: ::

In Western musical notation, the staff or stave is a set of five horizontal lines and four spaces that each represent a different musical pitch or in the case of a percussion staff, different percussion instruments. Appropriate music symbols, depending on the intended effect, are placed on the staff according to their corresponding pitch or function. Musical notes are placed by pitch, percussion notes are placed by instrument, and rests and other symbols are placed by convention.

Exam Probability: **High**

1. *Answer choices:*

(see index for correct answer)

- a. functional perspective
- b. Staff position
- c. corporate values
- d. interpersonal communication

Guidance: level 1

:: Commerce ::

_____ , also known as duty _____ is defined by the United States Customs and Border Protection as the refund of certain duties, internal and revenue taxes and certain fees collected upon the importation of goods. Such refunds are only allowed upon the exportation or destruction of goods under U.S. Customs and Border Protection supervision. Duty _____ is an export promotions program sanctioned by the World Trade Organization and allows the refund of certain duties taxes and fees paid upon importation which was established in 1789 in order to promote U.S. innovation and manufacturing across the global market.

Exam Probability: **Low**

2. *Answer choices:*
(see index for correct answer)

- a. Bargaining power
- b. Drawback
- c. Agio
- d. European Retail Round Table

Guidance: level 1

:: Globalization-related theories ::

_____ is the process in which a nation is being improved in the sector of the economic, political, and social well-being of its people. The term has been used frequently by economists, politicians, and others in the 20th and 21st centuries. The concept, however, has been in existence in the West for centuries. "Modernization, "westernization", and especially "industrialization" are other terms often used while discussing _____ . _____ has a direct relationship with the environment and environmental issues. _____ is very often confused with industrial development, even in some academic sources.

Exam Probability: **High**

3. *Answer choices:*
(see index for correct answer)

- a. Capitalism
- b. postmodernism
- c. post-industrial

:: ::

_____ is the production of products for use or sale using labour and machines, tools, chemical and biological processing, or formulation. The term may refer to a range of human activity, from handicraft to high tech, but is most commonly applied to industrial design, in which raw materials are transformed into finished goods on a large scale. Such finished goods may be sold to other manufacturers for the production of other, more complex products, such as aircraft, household appliances, furniture, sports equipment or automobiles, or sold to wholesalers, who in turn sell them to retailers, who then sell them to end users and consumers.

Exam Probability: **Low**

4. *Answer choices:*
(see index for correct answer)

- a. deep-level diversity
- b. empathy
- c. Manufacturing
- d. co-culture

:: ::

_____ is a term frequently used in marketing. It is a measure of how products and services supplied by a company meet or surpass customer expectation. _____ is defined as "the number of customers, or percentage of total customers, whose reported experience with a firm, its products, or its services exceeds specified satisfaction goals."

Exam Probability: **Medium**

5. *Answer choices:*
(see index for correct answer)

- a. hierarchical perspective
- b. information systems assessment
- c. surface-level diversity
- d. Customer satisfaction

:: ::

_____ is the extraction of valuable minerals or other geological materials from the earth, usually from an ore body, lode, vein, seam, reef or placer deposit. These deposits form a mineralized package that is of economic interest to the miner.

Exam Probability: **Medium**

6. *Answer choices:*

(see index for correct answer)

- a. deep-level diversity
- b. hierarchical
- c. Sarbanes-Oxley act of 2002
- d. open system

:: ::

A _____ is a graphic mark, emblem, or symbol used to aid and promote public identification and recognition. It may be of an abstract or figurative design or include the text of the name it represents as in a wordmark.

Exam Probability: **Medium**

7. *Answer choices:*

(see index for correct answer)

- a. Logo
- b. open system
- c. personal values
- d. co-culture

:: Packaging ::

In work place, _____ or job _____ means good ranking with the hypothesized conception of requirements of a role. There are two types of job _____ s: contextual and task. Task _____ is related to cognitive ability while contextual _____ is dependent upon personality. Task _____ are behavioral roles that are recognized in job descriptions and by remuneration systems, they are directly related to organizational _____, whereas, contextual _____ are value based and additional behavioral roles that are not recognized in job descriptions and covered by compensation; they are extra roles that are indirectly related to organizational _____. Citizenship _____ like contextual _____ means a set of individual activity/contribution that supports the organizational culture.

Exam Probability: **Low**

8. *Answer choices:*

(see index for correct answer)

- a. Phillumeny
- b. Performance
- c. Security seal
- d. Octabin

Guidance: level 1

:: Organizational structure ::

An _____ defines how activities such as task allocation, coordination, and supervision are directed toward the achievement of organizational aims.

Exam Probability: **Medium**

9. *Answer choices:*

(see index for correct answer)

- a. Automated Bureaucracy
- b. Organizational structure
- c. Followership
- d. Blessed Unrest

Guidance: level 1

:: Price fixing convictions ::

_____ is the flag carrier airline of the United Kingdom, headquartered at Waterside, Harmondsworth. It is the second largest airline in the United Kingdom, based on fleet size and passengers carried, behind easyJet. The airline is based in Waterside near its main hub at London Heathrow Airport. In January 2011 BA merged with Iberia, creating the International Airlines Group , a holding company registered in Madrid, Spain. IAG is the world's third-largest airline group in terms of annual revenue and the second-largest in Europe. It is listed on the London Stock Exchange and in the FTSE 100 Index. _____ is the first passenger airline to have generated more than $1 billion on a single air route in a year .

Exam Probability: **Medium**

10. *Answer choices:*

(see index for correct answer)

- a. High Noon Western Americana
- b. Siemens
- c. Grolsch Brewery
- d. British Airways

Guidance: level 1

:: ::

A _____ is monetary compensation paid by an employer to an employee in exchange for work done. Payment may be calculated as a fixed amount for each task completed , or at an hourly or daily rate , or based on an easily measured quantity of work done.

Exam Probability: **High**

11. *Answer choices:*

(see index for correct answer)

- a. open system
- b. interpersonal communication
- c. co-culture
- d. empathy

Guidance: level 1

:: Stochastic processes ::

_____ in its modern meaning is a "new idea, creative thoughts, new imaginations in form of device or method". _____ is often also viewed as the application of better solutions that meet new requirements, unarticulated needs, or existing market needs. Such _____ takes place through the provision of more-effective products, processes, services, technologies, or business models that are made available to markets, governments and society. An _____ is something original and more effective and, as a consequence, new, that "breaks into" the market or society. _____ is related to, but not the same as, invention, as _____ is more apt to involve the practical implementation of an invention to make a meaningful impact in the market or society, and not all _____ s require an invention. _____ often manifests itself via the engineering process, when the problem being solved is of a technical or scientific nature. The opposite of _____ is exnovation.

12. *Answer choices:*
(see index for correct answer)

- a. Brownian meander
- b. Innovation
- c. Progressively measurable process
- d. Master equation

Guidance: level 1

:: Computer access control ::

_____ is the act of confirming the truth of an attribute of a single piece of data claimed true by an entity. In contrast with identification, which refers to the act of stating or otherwise indicating a claim purportedly attesting to a person or thing's identity, _____ is the process of actually confirming that identity. It might involve confirming the identity of a person by validating their identity documents, verifying the authenticity of a website with a digital certificate, determining the age of an artifact by carbon dating, or ensuring that a product is what its packaging and labeling claim to be. In other words, _____ often involves verifying the validity of at least one form of identification.

13. *Answer choices:*
(see index for correct answer)

- a. Identity provider
- b. Mutual authentication
- c. EAuthentication
- d. Authentication

Guidance: level 1

:: ::

_____ is a means of protection from financial loss. It is a form of risk management, primarily used to hedge against the risk of a contingent or uncertain loss

Exam Probability: **High**

14. *Answer choices:*
(see index for correct answer)

- a. Character
- b. co-culture
- c. hierarchical
- d. Insurance

Guidance: level 1

:: ::

The _____ or just chief executive , is the most senior corporate, executive, or administrative officer in charge of managing an organization especially an independent legal entity such as a company or nonprofit institution. CEOs lead a range of organizations, including public and private corporations, non-profit organizations and even some government organizations . The CEO of a corporation or company typically reports to the board of directors and is charged with maximizing the value of the entity, which may include maximizing the share price, market share, revenues or another element. In the non-profit and government sector, CEOs typically aim at achieving outcomes related to the organization's mission, such as reducing poverty, increasing literacy, etc.

Exam Probability: **High**

15. *Answer choices:*

(see index for correct answer)

- a. functional perspective
- b. interpersonal communication
- c. corporate values
- d. Sarbanes-Oxley act of 2002

Guidance: level 1

:: Marketing by medium ::

_____ , also called online marketing or Internet advertising or web advertising, is a form of marketing and advertising which uses the Internet to deliver promotional marketing messages to consumers. Many consumers find _____ disruptive and have increasingly turned to ad blocking for a variety of reasons. When software is used to do the purchasing, it is known as programmatic advertising.

Exam Probability: **High**

16. *Answer choices:*

(see index for correct answer)

- a. New media marketing
- b. Viral marketing
- c. Online advertising
- d. Social marketing intelligence

Guidance: level 1

:: Goods ::

In most contexts, the concept of _____ denotes the conduct that should be preferred when posed with a choice between possible actions. _____ is generally considered to be the opposite of evil, and is of interest in the study of morality, ethics, religion and philosophy. The specific meaning and etymology of the term and its associated translations among ancient and contemporary languages show substantial variation in its inflection and meaning depending on circumstances of place, history, religious, or philosophical context.

Exam Probability: **Medium**

17. *Answer choices:*

(see index for correct answer)

- a. Substitute good
- b. Durable good
- c. Neutral good
- d. Good

Guidance: level 1

:: Market structure and pricing ::

_____ has historically emerged in two separate types of discussions in economics, that of Adam Smith on the one hand, and that of Karl Marx on the other hand. Adam Smith in his writing on economics stressed the importance of laissez-faire principles outlining the operation of the market in the absence of dominant political mechanisms of control, while Karl Marx discussed the working of the market in the presence of a controlled economy sometimes referred to as a command economy in the literature. Both types of _____ have been in historical evidence throughout the twentieth century and twenty-first century.

Exam Probability: **Low**

18. *Answer choices:*

(see index for correct answer)

- a. Open-source economics
- b. Open source
- c. Liberalization
- d. Market structure

Guidance: level 1

:: ::

_____ s and acquisitions are transactions in which the ownership of companies, other business organizations, or their operating units are transferred or consolidated with other entities. As an aspect of strategic management, M&A can allow enterprises to grow or downsize, and change the nature of their business or competitive position.

Exam Probability: **Medium**

19. *Answer choices:*

- a. corporate values
- b. open system
- c. Merger
- d. personal values

Guidance: level 1

:: ::

_____ is "property consisting of land and the buildings on it, along with its natural resources such as crops, minerals or water; immovable property of this nature; an interest vested in this an item of real property, buildings or housing in general. Also: the business of _____ ; the profession of buying, selling, or renting land, buildings, or housing." It is a legal term used in jurisdictions whose legal system is derived from English common law, such as India, England, Wales, Northern Ireland, United States, Canada, Pakistan, Australia, and New Zealand.

Exam Probability: **High**

20. *Answer choices:*

- a. Real estate
- b. hierarchical perspective
- c. cultural
- d. information systems assessment

Guidance: level 1

:: Auctioneering ::

A _____ is a type of sealed-bid auction. Bidders submit written bids without knowing the bid of the other people in the auction. The highest bidder wins but the price paid is the second-highest bid. This type of auction is strategically similar to an English auction and gives bidders an incentive to bid their true value. The auction was first described academically by Columbia University professor William Vickrey in 1961 though it had been used by stamp collectors since 1893. In 1797 Johann Wolfgang von Goethe sold a manuscript using a sealed-bid, second-price auction.

21. *Answer choices:*

- a. Dutch auction
- b. Bid shading
- c. Bidding fee auction
- d. Vickrey auction

Guidance: level 1

:: Real property law ::

A _____ is the grant of authority or rights, stating that the granter formally recognizes the prerogative of the recipient to exercise the rights specified. It is implicit that the granter retains superiority , and that the recipient admits a limited status within the relationship, and it is within that sense that _____ s were historically granted, and that sense is retained in modern usage of the term.

Exam Probability: **High**

22. *Answer choices:*

- a. Escheat
- b. Lesion beyond moiety
- c. NES Financial
- d. Charter

Guidance: level 1

:: E-commerce ::

_____ is the activity of buying or selling of products on online services or over the Internet. Electronic commerce draws on technologies such as mobile commerce, electronic funds transfer, supply chain management, Internet marketing, online transaction processing, electronic data interchange , inventory management systems, and automated data collection systems.

Exam Probability: **Low**

23. *Answer choices:*

- a. Cyberservices
- b. Friend-to-friend
- c. Bill2phone
- d. E-commerce

Guidance: level 1

:: Income ::

In business and accounting, net income is an entity's income minus cost of goods sold, expenses and taxes for an accounting period. It is computed as the residual of all revenues and gains over all expenses and losses for the period, and has also been defined as the net increase in shareholders' equity that results from a company's operations. In the context of the presentation of financial statements, the IFRS Foundation defines net income as synonymous with profit and loss. The difference between revenue and the cost of making a product or providing a service, before deducting overheads, payroll, taxation, and interest payments. This is different from operating income .

Exam Probability: **Medium**

24. *Answer choices:*
(see index for correct answer)

- a. Income Per User
- b. Trinity study
- c. Bottom line
- d. Creative real estate investing

Guidance: level 1

:: Theories ::

A _____ union is a type of multinational political union where negotiated power is delegated to an authority by governments of member states.

Exam Probability: **High**

25. *Answer choices:*
(see index for correct answer)

- a. incrementalism
- b. Supranational

Guidance: level 1

_____ involves the transfer of goods or services from one person or entity to another, often in exchange for money. A system or network that allows _____ is called a market.

Exam Probability: **High**

26. *Answer choices:*
(see index for correct answer)

- a. Trade
- b. Bilateral trade
- c. Third country dumping
- d. Omnibus Foreign Trade and Competitiveness Act

Guidance: level 1

:: ::

A _____ is a fund into which a sum of money is added during an employee's employment years, and from which payments are drawn to support the person's retirement from work in the form of periodic payments. A _____ may be a "defined benefit plan" where a fixed sum is paid regularly to a person, or a "defined contribution plan" under which a fixed sum is invested and then becomes available at retirement age. _____ s should not be confused with severance pay; the former is usually paid in regular installments for life after retirement, while the latter is typically paid as a fixed amount after involuntary termination of employment prior to retirement.

Exam Probability: **High**

27. *Answer choices:*
(see index for correct answer)

- a. levels of analysis
- b. Character
- c. Pension
- d. surface-level diversity

Guidance: level 1

A _____ is a hosted service offering that acts as an intermediary between business partners sharing standards based or proprietary data via shared business processes. The offered service is referred to as " _____ services".

Exam Probability: **High**

28. *Answer choices:*
(see index for correct answer)

- a. Value-added network
- b. Electronic billing
- c. Switchwise
- d. Transactional Link

Guidance: level 1

:: ::

_____ is getting a diploma or academic degree or the ceremony that is sometimes associated with it, in which students become graduates. The date of _____ is often called _____ day. The _____ ceremony itself is also called commencement, convocation or invocation.

Exam Probability: **High**

29. *Answer choices:*
(see index for correct answer)

- a. personal values
- b. co-culture
- c. hierarchical perspective
- d. open system

Guidance: level 1

:: ::

In financial markets, a share is a unit used as mutual funds, limited partnerships, and real estate investment trusts. The owner of _____ in the corporation/company is a shareholder of the corporation. A share is an indivisible unit of capital, expressing the ownership relationship between the company and the shareholder. The denominated value of a share is its face value, and the total of the face value of issued _____ represent the capital of a company, which may not reflect the market value of those _____ .

Exam Probability: **Low**

30. *Answer choices:*
(see index for correct answer)

- a. Shares
- b. information systems assessment
- c. cultural
- d. personal values

Guidance: level 1

:: ::

_____ is a qualitative measure used to relate the quality of motor vehicle traffic service. LOS is used to analyze roadways and intersections by categorizing traffic flow and assigning quality levels of traffic based on performance measure like vehicle speed, density, congestion, etc.

Exam Probability: **Low**

31. *Answer choices:*
(see index for correct answer)

- a. empathy
- b. Sarbanes-Oxley act of 2002
- c. hierarchical perspective
- d. Level of service

Guidance: level 1

:: Cryptography ::

In cryptography, _____ is the process of encoding a message or information in such a way that only authorized parties can access it and those who are not authorized cannot. _____ does not itself prevent interference, but denies the intelligible content to a would-be interceptor. In an _____ scheme, the intended information or message, referred to as plaintext, is encrypted using an _____ algorithm – a cipher – generating ciphertext that can be read only if decrypted. For technical reasons, an _____ scheme usually uses a pseudo-random _____ key generated by an algorithm. It is in principle possible to decrypt the message without possessing the key, but, for a well-designed _____ scheme, considerable computational resources and skills are required. An authorized recipient can easily decrypt the message with the key provided by the originator to recipients but not to unauthorized users.

Exam Probability: **High**

32. *Answer choices:*
(see index for correct answer)

- a. backdoor
- b. Encryption
- c. Anonymous matching
- d. Electronic Signature

Guidance: level 1

:: Business ethics ::

_____ is a type of harassment technique that relates to a sexual nature and the unwelcome or inappropriate promise of rewards in exchange for sexual favors. _____ includes a range of actions from mild transgressions to sexual abuse or assault. Harassment can occur in many different social settings such as the workplace, the home, school, churches, etc. Harassers or victims may be of any gender.

Exam Probability: **Low**

33. *Answer choices:*
(see index for correct answer)

- a. Institute for Business and Professional Ethics
- b. Resource Conservation and Recovery Act
- c. Conspiracy of Fools

- d. Accounting ethics

Guidance: level 1

:: ::

_____ is the exchange of capital, goods, and services across international borders or territories.

Exam Probability: **Medium**

34. *Answer choices:*
(see index for correct answer)

- a. empathy
- b. Sarbanes-Oxley act of 2002
- c. International trade
- d. interpersonal communication

Guidance: level 1

:: Industrial automation ::

_____ is the technology by which a process or procedure is performed with minimal human assistance. _____ or automatic control is the use of various control systems for operating equipment such as machinery, processes in factories, boilers and heat treating ovens, switching on telephone networks, steering and stabilization of ships, aircraft and other applications and vehicles with minimal or reduced human intervention.

Exam Probability: **High**

35. *Answer choices:*
(see index for correct answer)

- a. RAPIEnet
- b. IODD
- c. Automation
- d. Distributed control system

Guidance: level 1

:: ::

An _____ is the production of goods or related services within an economy. The major source of revenue of a group or company is the indicator of its relevant _____ . When a large group has multiple sources of revenue generation, it is considered to be working in different industries. Manufacturing _____ became a key sector of production and labour in European and North American countries during the Industrial Revolution, upsetting previous mercantile and feudal economies. This came through many successive rapid advances in technology, such as the production of steel and coal.

Exam Probability: **Medium**

36. *Answer choices:*

(see index for correct answer)

- a. similarity-attraction theory
- b. empathy
- c. Sarbanes-Oxley act of 2002
- d. personal values

Guidance: level 1

:: ::

Competition law is a law that promotes or seeks to maintain market competition by regulating anti-competitive conduct by companies. Competition law is implemented through public and private enforcement. Competition law is known as " _____ law" in the United States for historical reasons, and as "anti-monopoly law" in China and Russia. In previous years it has been known as trade practices law in the United Kingdom and Australia. In the European Union, it is referred to as both _____ and competition law.

Exam Probability: **Medium**

37. *Answer choices:*

(see index for correct answer)

- a. levels of analysis
- b. open system
- c. co-culture
- d. Antitrust

Guidance: level 1

:: Customs duties ::

A _____ is a tax on imports or exports between sovereign states. It is a form of regulation of foreign trade and a policy that taxes foreign products to encourage or safeguard domestic industry. _____ s are the simplest and oldest instrument of trade policy. Traditionally, states have used them as a source of income. Now, they are among the most widely used instruments of protection, along with import and export quotas.

Exam Probability: **Low**

38. *Answer choices:*
(see index for correct answer)

- a. Cochin Duty Free
- b. World Customs Organization
- c. You Are on Indian Land
- d. Customs bond

Guidance: level 1

:: Cash flow ::

_____ s are narrowly interconnected with the concepts of value, interest rate and liquidity. A _____ that shall happen on a future day tN can be transformed into a _____ of the same value in t0.

Exam Probability: **Medium**

39. *Answer choices:*
(see index for correct answer)

- a. Cash flow
- b. Cash flow statement
- c. Valuation using discounted cash flows
- d. Cash carrier

Guidance: level 1

:: Payment systems ::

Amazon Pay is an online payments processing service that is owned by Amazon. Launched in 2007, Amazon Pay uses the consumer base of Amazon.com and focuses on giving users the option to pay with their Amazon accounts on external merchant websites. As of January 2019 the service is available in Austria, Belgium, Cyprus, Germany, Denmark, Spain, France, Hungary, Luxembourg, Republic of Ireland, India, Italy, Japan, Netherlands, Portugal, Sweden, United Kingdom, United States.

Exam Probability: **Low**

40. *Answer choices:*
(see index for correct answer)

- a. QC Record Format
- b. Euronet Pakistan
- c. CCBill
- d. Amazon Payments

Guidance: level 1

:: Debt ::

_____ , in finance and economics, is payment from a borrower or deposit-taking financial institution to a lender or depositor of an amount above repayment of the principal sum , at a particular rate. It is distinct from a fee which the borrower may pay the lender or some third party. It is also distinct from dividend which is paid by a company to its shareholders from its profit or reserve, but not at a particular rate decided beforehand, rather on a pro rata basis as a share in the reward gained by risk taking entrepreneurs when the revenue earned exceeds the total costs.

Exam Probability: **Medium**

41. *Answer choices:*
(see index for correct answer)

- a. Cessio bonorum
- b. Interest
- c. Odious debt
- d. Debt-lag

Guidance: level 1

:: Credit cards ::

The _____ Company, also known as Amex, is an American multinational financial services corporation headquartered in Three World Financial Center in New York City. The company was founded in 1850 and is one of the 30 components of the Dow Jones Industrial Average. The company is best known for its charge card, credit card, and traveler`s cheque businesses.

Exam Probability: **Medium**

42. *Answer choices:*
(see index for correct answer)

- a. American Express
- b. Smiley v. Citibank
- c. Credit Saison
- d. Gravity Payments

Guidance: level 1

:: Management ::

_____ is the identification, evaluation, and prioritization of risks followed by coordinated and economical application of resources to minimize, monitor, and control the probability or impact of unfortunate events or to maximize the realization of opportunities.

Exam Probability: **High**

43. *Answer choices:*
(see index for correct answer)

- a. Dominant design
- b. Court of Assistants
- c. Risk management
- d. Project management

Guidance: level 1

:: Economic globalization ::

_____ is an agreement in which one company hires another company to be responsible for a planned or existing activity that is or could be done internally,and sometimes involves transferring employees and assets from one firm to another.

Exam Probability: **High**

44. *Answer choices:*
(see index for correct answer)

- a. Outsourcing
- b. reshoring

Guidance: level 1

:: Data interchange standards ::

_____ is the concept of businesses electronically communicating information that was traditionally communicated on paper, such as purchase orders and invoices. Technical standards for EDI exist to facilitate parties transacting such instruments without having to make special arrangements.

Exam Probability: **Medium**

45. *Answer choices:*
(see index for correct answer)

- a. Common Alerting Protocol
- b. Domain Application Protocol
- c. Data Interchange Standards Association
- d. Interaction protocol

Guidance: level 1

:: Market research ::

_____ is an organized effort to gather information about target markets or customers. It is a very important component of business strategy. The term is commonly interchanged with marketing research; however, expert practitioners may wish to draw a distinction, in that marketing research is concerned specifically about marketing processes, while _____ is concerned specifically with markets.

Exam Probability: **Medium**

46. *Answer choices:*

(see index for correct answer)

- a. Fuld-Gilad-Herring Academy of Competitive Intelligence
- b. Qualitative marketing research
- c. Market research
- d. Innovation game

Guidance: level 1

:: ::

In law, a _____ is a coming together of parties to a dispute, to present information in a tribunal, a formal setting with the authority to adjudicate claims or disputes. One form of tribunal is a court. The tribunal, which may occur before a judge, jury, or other designated trier of fact, aims to achieve a resolution to their dispute.

Exam Probability: **High**

47. *Answer choices:*

(see index for correct answer)

- a. hierarchical
- b. Character
- c. deep-level diversity
- d. Trial

Guidance: level 1

:: Budgets ::

A _____ is a financial plan for a defined period, often one year. It may also include planned sales volumes and revenues, resource quantities, costs and expenses, assets, liabilities and cash flows. Companies, governments, families and other organizations use it to express strategic plans of activities or events in measurable terms.

Exam Probability: **Medium**

48. *Answer choices:*
(see index for correct answer)

- a. Railway Budget
- b. Operating budget
- c. Participatory budgeting
- d. Zero budget

Guidance: level 1

:: E-commerce ::

IBM _____ also known as WCS is a software platform framework for e-commerce, including marketing, sales, customer and order processing functionality in a tailorable, integrated package. It is a single, unified platform which offers the ability to do business directly with consumers , with businesses , indirectly through channel partners , or all of these simultaneously. _____ is a customizable, scalable and high availability solution built on the Java - Java EE platform using open standards, such as XML, and Web services.

Exam Probability: **High**

49. *Answer choices:*
(see index for correct answer)

- a. Authorize.Net
- b. WebSphere Commerce
- c. Smscoin
- d. Centricom

Guidance: level 1

:: Stock market ::

_____ is freedom from, or resilience against, potential harm caused by others. Beneficiaries of _____ may be of persons and social groups, objects and institutions, ecosystems or any other entity or phenomenon vulnerable to unwanted change by its environment.

Exam Probability: **Low**

50. *Answer choices:*

(see index for correct answer)

- a. Trading halt
- b. Security
- c. Short-term trading
- d. Sector rotation

Guidance: level 1

:: Decision theory ::

Within economics the concept of _____ is used to model worth or value, but its usage has evolved significantly over time. The term was introduced initially as a measure of pleasure or satisfaction within the theory of utilitarianism by moral philosophers such as Jeremy Bentham and John Stuart Mill. But the term has been adapted and reapplied within neoclassical economics, which dominates modern economic theory, as a _____ function that represents a consumer's preference ordering over a choice set. As such, it is devoid of its original interpretation as a measurement of the pleasure or satisfaction obtained by the consumer from that choice.

Exam Probability: **High**

51. *Answer choices:*

(see index for correct answer)

- a. There are known knowns
- b. Decision-matrix method
- c. Kelly criterion
- d. Utility

Guidance: level 1

:: ::

A trade union is an association of workers forming a legal unit or legal personhood, usually called a "bargaining unit", which acts as bargaining agent and legal representative for a unit of employees in all matters of law or right arising from or in the administration of a collective agreement. Labour unions typically fund the formal organisation, head office, and legal team functions of the labour union through regular fees or union dues. The delegate staff of the labour union representation in the workforce are made up of workplace volunteers who are appointed by members in democratic elections.

Exam Probability: **Low**

52. *Answer choices:*
(see index for correct answer)

- a. Labor union
- b. co-culture
- c. functional perspective
- d. surface-level diversity

Guidance: level 1

:: Marketing techniques ::

_____ is the activity of dividing a broad consumer or business market, normally consisting of existing and potential customers, into sub-groups of consumers based on some type of shared characteristics. In dividing or segmenting markets, researchers typically look for common characteristics such as shared needs, common interests, similar lifestyles or even similar demographic profiles. The overall aim of segmentation is to identify high yield segments – that is, those segments that are likely to be the most profitable or that have growth potential – so that these can be selected for special attention .

Exam Probability: **Low**

53. *Answer choices:*
(see index for correct answer)

- a. Introductory rate
- b. Wait marketing
- c. Market segmentation
- d. Unique perceived benefit

Guidance: level 1

Logistics is generally the detailed organization and implementation of a complex operation. In a general business sense, logistics is the management of the flow of things between the point of origin and the point of consumption in order to meet requirements of customers or corporations. The resources managed in logistics may include tangible goods such as materials, equipment, and supplies, as well as food and other consumable items. The logistics of physical items usually involves the integration of information flow, materials handling, production, packaging, inventory, transportation, warehousing, and often security.

Exam Probability: **High**

54. *Answer choices:*

(see index for correct answer)

- a. Best current practice
- b. Operations research
- c. Wireless informatics
- d. Logistics Management

Guidance: level 1

The Walt _____ Company, commonly known as Walt _____ or simply _____ , is an American diversified multinational mass media and entertainment conglomerate headquartered at the Walt _____ Studios in Burbank, California.

Exam Probability: **Medium**

55. *Answer choices:*

(see index for correct answer)

- a. empathy
- b. surface-level diversity
- c. Disney
- d. co-culture

Guidance: level 1

:: Industry ::

A _____ is a set of sequential operations established in a factory where materials are put through a refining process to produce an end-product that is suitable for onward consumption; or components are assembled to make a finished article.

Exam Probability: **Low**

56. *Answer choices:*
(see index for correct answer)

- a. Industrial safety system
- b. Production line
- c. Industrialisation
- d. Private sector

Guidance: level 1

:: Production economics ::

In economics and related disciplines, a _____ is a cost in making any economic trade when participating in a market.

Exam Probability: **Low**

57. *Answer choices:*
(see index for correct answer)

- a. Foundations of Economic Analysis
- b. Choice of techniques
- c. Robinson Crusoe economy
- d. Transaction cost

Guidance: level 1

:: ::

_____ is both a research area and a practical skill encompassing the ability of an individual or organization to "lead" or guide other individuals, teams, or entire organizations. Specialist literature debates various viewpoints, contrasting Eastern and Western approaches to _____ , and also United States versus European approaches. U.S. academic environments define _____ as "a process of social influence in which a person can enlist the aid and support of others in the accomplishment of a common task".

Exam Probability: **Medium**

58. *Answer choices:*
(see index for correct answer)

- a. interpersonal communication
- b. Leadership
- c. similarity-attraction theory
- d. hierarchical

Guidance: level 1

:: Project management ::

A _____ is a source or supply from which a benefit is produced and it has some utility. _____ s can broadly be classified upon their availability—they are classified into renewable and non-renewable _____ s.Examples of non renewable _____ s are coal ,crude oil natural gas nuclear energy etc. Examples of renewable _____ s are air,water,wind,solar energy etc. They can also be classified as actual and potential on the basis of level of development and use, on the basis of origin they can be classified as biotic and abiotic, and on the basis of their distribution, as ubiquitous and localized . An item becomes a _____ with time and developing technology. Typically, _____ s are materials, energy, services, staff, knowledge, or other assets that are transformed to produce benefit and in the process may be consumed or made unavailable. Benefits of _____ utilization may include increased wealth, proper functioning of a system, or enhanced well-being. From a human perspective a natural _____ is anything obtained from the environment to satisfy human needs and wants. From a broader biological or ecological perspective a _____ satisfies the needs of a living organism .

Exam Probability: **Medium**

59. *Answer choices:*

(see index for correct answer)

- a. Resource
- b. Theory Z of Ouchi
- c. Resource allocation
- d. Project accounting

Guidance: level 1

Business ethics

Business ethics (also known as corporate ethics) is a form of applied ethics or professional ethics, that examines ethical principles and moral or ethical problems that can arise in a business environment. It applies to all aspects of business conduct and is relevant to the conduct of individuals and entire organizations. These ethics originate from individuals, organizational statements or from the legal system. These norms, values, ethical, and unethical practices are what is used to guide business. They help those businesses maintain a better connection with their stakeholders.

:: Auditing ::

_____ is a general term that can reflect various types of evaluations intended to identify environmental compliance and management system implementation gaps, along with related corrective actions. In this way they perform an analogous function to financial audits. There are generally two different types of _____ s: compliance audits and management systems audits. Compliance audits tend to be the primary type in the US or within US-based multinationals.

Exam Probability: **High**

1. *Answer choices:*
(see index for correct answer)

- a. Environmental audit
- b. Negative assurance
- c. Technical audit
- d. ISACA

Guidance: level 1

:: ::

The American Recovery and Reinvestment Act of 2009 , nicknamed the _____ , was a stimulus package enacted by the 111th U.S. Congress and signed into law by President Barack Obama in February 2009. Developed in response to the Great Recession, the ARRA`s primary objective was to save existing jobs and create new ones as soon as possible. Other objectives were to provide temporary relief programs for those most affected by the recession and invest in infrastructure, education, health, and renewable energy.

Exam Probability: **Medium**

2. *Answer choices:*
(see index for correct answer)

- a. open system
- b. hierarchical
- c. levels of analysis
- d. Recovery Act

Guidance: level 1

:: Culture ::

_____ is a society which is characterized by individualism, which is the prioritization or emphasis, of the individual over the entire group. _____ s are oriented around the self, being independent instead of identifying with a group mentality. They see each other as only loosely linked, and value personal goals over group interests. _____ s tend to have a more diverse population and are characterized with emphasis on personal achievements, and a rational assessment of both the beneficial and detrimental aspects of relationships with others. _____ s have such unique aspects of communication as being a low power-distance culture and having a low-context communication style. The United States, Australia, Great Britain, Canada, the Netherlands, and New Zealand have been identified as highly _____ s.

Exam Probability: **High**

3. *Answer choices:*
(see index for correct answer)

- a. cultural framework
- b. Low-context culture
- c. Intracultural
- d. High-context

:: ::

A _____ is a set of rules, often written, with regards to clothing. _____ s are created out of social perceptions and norms, and vary based on purpose, circumstances and occasions. Different societies and cultures are likely to have different _____ s.

Exam Probability: **Medium**

4. *Answer choices:*
(see index for correct answer)

- a. cultural
- b. information systems assessment
- c. Dress code
- d. hierarchical perspective

:: Occupational safety and health ::

_____ is a chemical element with symbol Pb and atomic number 82. It is a heavy metal that is denser than most common materials. _____ is soft and malleable, and also has a relatively low melting point. When freshly cut, _____ is silvery with a hint of blue; it tarnishes to a dull gray color when exposed to air. _____ has the highest atomic number of any stable element and three of its isotopes are endpoints of major nuclear decay chains of heavier elements.

Exam Probability: **Low**

5. *Answer choices:*
(see index for correct answer)

- a. Animal lead poisoning
- b. Confined space
- c. Lead
- d. Occupational rehabilitation

:: ::

_____ is the study and management of exchange relationships. _____ is the business process of creating relationships with and satisfying customers. With its focus on the customer, _____ is one of the premier components of business management.

6. *Answer choices:*

- a. process perspective
- b. hierarchical perspective
- c. co-culture
- d. surface-level diversity

Guidance: level 1

:: Social enterprise ::

Corporate social responsibility is a type of international private business self-regulation. While once it was possible to describe CSR as an internal organisational policy or a corporate ethic strategy, that time has passed as various international laws have been developed and various organisations have used their authority to push it beyond individual or even industry-wide initiatives. While it has been considered a form of corporate self-regulation for some time, over the last decade or so it has moved considerably from voluntary decisions at the level of individual organisations, to mandatory schemes at regional, national and even transnational levels.

7. *Answer choices:*

- a. Corporate citizenship
- b. Social enterprise

Guidance: level 1

:: Electronic waste ::

_____ or e-waste describes discarded electrical or electronic devices. Used electronics which are destined for refurbishment, reuse, resale, salvage, recycling through material recovery, or disposal are also considered e-waste. Informal processing of e-waste in developing countries can lead to adverse human health effects and environmental pollution.

Exam Probability: **Medium**

8. *Answer choices:*
(see index for correct answer)

- a. Solving the E-waste Problem
- b. Global waste trade
- c. Electronic waste
- d. ReGlobe

Guidance: level 1

:: Competition regulators ::

The _____ is an independent agency of the United States government, established in 1914 by the _____ Act. Its principal mission is the promotion of consumer protection and the elimination and prevention of anticompetitive business practices, such as coercive monopoly. It is headquartered in the _____ Building in Washington, D.C.

Exam Probability: **Medium**

9. *Answer choices:*
(see index for correct answer)

- a. Federal Trade Commission
- b. Competition Appeal Tribunal
- c. Jersey Competition Regulatory Authority
- d. Australian Competition and Consumer Commission

Guidance: level 1

:: ::

_____ is a private Dominican liberal arts college in Madison, Wisconsin. The college occupies a 55 acres campus overlooking the shores of Lake Wingra.

Exam Probability: **Low**

10. *Answer choices:*
(see index for correct answer)

- a. open system
- b. imperative
- c. Edgewood College
- d. Sarbanes-Oxley act of 2002

Guidance: level 1

:: Business ethics ::

_____ is a persistent pattern of mistreatment from others in the workplace that causes either physical or emotional harm. It can include such tactics as verbal, nonverbal, psychological, physical abuse and humiliation. This type of workplace aggression is particularly difficult because, unlike the typical school bully, workplace bullies often operate within the established rules and policies of their organization and their society. In the majority of cases, bullying in the workplace is reported as having been by someone who has authority over their victim. However, bullies can also be peers, and occasionally subordinates. Research has also investigated the impact of the larger organizational context on bullying as well as the group-level processes that impact on the incidence and maintenance of bullying behaviour. Bullying can be covert or overt. It may be missed by superiors; it may be known by many throughout the organization. Negative effects are not limited to the targeted individuals, and may lead to a decline in employee morale and a change in organizational culture. It can also take place as overbearing supervision, constant criticism, and blocking promotions.

Exam Probability: **Medium**

11. *Answer choices:*
(see index for correct answer)

- a. Corruption of Foreign Public Officials Act
- b. International Association for Business and Society
- c. Fair value

- d. Interfaith Center on Corporate Responsibility

Guidance: level 1

:: ::

The Catholic Church, also known as the Roman Catholic Church, is the largest Christian church, with approximately 1.3 billion baptised Catholics worldwide as of 2017. As the world's oldest continuously functioning international institution, it has played a prominent role in the history and development of Western civilisation. The church is headed by the Bishop of Rome, known as the pope. Its central administration, the Holy See, is in the Vatican City, an enclave within the city of Rome in Italy.

Exam Probability: **Medium**

12. *Answer choices:*
(see index for correct answer)

- a. Character
- b. cultural
- c. imperative
- d. personal values

Guidance: level 1

:: Auditing ::

_____ , as defined by accounting and auditing, is a process for assuring of an organization's objectives in operational effectiveness and efficiency, reliable financial reporting, and compliance with laws, regulations and policies. A broad concept, _____ involves everything that controls risks to an organization.

Exam Probability: **High**

13. *Answer choices:*
(see index for correct answer)

- a. Management representation
- b. Environmental audit
- c. Negative assurance
- d. RSM International

Guidance: level 1

A _____ is a proceeding by a party or parties against another in the civil court of law. The archaic term "suit in law" is found in only a small number of laws still in effect today. The term " _____ " is used in reference to a civil action brought in a court of law in which a plaintiff, a party who claims to have incurred loss as a result of a defendant's actions, demands a legal or equitable remedy. The defendant is required to respond to the plaintiff's complaint. If the plaintiff is successful, judgment is in the plaintiff's favor, and a variety of court orders may be issued to enforce a right, award damages, or impose a temporary or permanent injunction to prevent an act or compel an act. A declaratory judgment may be issued to prevent future legal disputes.

Exam Probability: **High**

14. *Answer choices:*
(see index for correct answer)

- a. similarity-attraction theory
- b. Lawsuit
- c. deep-level diversity
- d. hierarchical perspective

Guidance: level 1

:: Timber industry ::

The _____ is an international non-profit, multi-stakeholder organization established in 1993 to promote responsible management of the world's forests. The FSC does this by setting standards on forest products, along with certifying and labeling them as eco-friendly.

Exam Probability: **Low**

15. *Answer choices:*
(see index for correct answer)

- a. Naval stores
- b. Forest Stewardship Council
- c. Firewood processor
- d. West Coast lumber trade

:: Leadership ::

_____ is a theory of leadership where a leader works with teams to identify needed change, creating a vision to guide the change through inspiration, and executing the change in tandem with committed members of a group; it is an integral part of the Full Range Leadership Model. _____ serves to enhance the motivation, morale, and job performance of followers through a variety of mechanisms; these include connecting the follower's sense of identity and self to a project and to the collective identity of the organization; being a role model for followers in order to inspire them and to raise their interest in the project; challenging followers to take greater ownership for their work, and understanding the strengths and weaknesses of followers, allowing the leader to align followers with tasks that enhance their performance.

Exam Probability: **Medium**

16. *Answer choices:*
(see index for correct answer)

- a. The Saint, the Surfer, and the CEO
- b. Evolutionary leadership theory
- c. Three levels of leadership model
- d. Transformational leadership

:: ::

The _____ Group is a global financial investment management and insurance company headquartered in Des Moines, Iowa.

Exam Probability: **High**

17. *Answer choices:*
(see index for correct answer)

- a. corporate values
- b. Principal Financial
- c. open system
- d. deep-level diversity

:: ::

Sustainability is the process of people maintaining change in a balanced environment, in which the exploitation of resources, the direction of investments, the orientation of technological development and institutional change are all in harmony and enhance both current and future potential to meet human needs and aspirations. For many in the field, sustainability is defined through the following interconnected domains or pillars: environment, economic and social, which according to Fritjof Capra is based on the principles of Systems Thinking. Sub-domains of _____ development have been considered also: cultural, technological and political. While _____ development may be the organizing principle for sustainability for some, for others, the two terms are paradoxical . _____ development is the development that meets the needs of the present without compromising the ability of future generations to meet their own needs. Brundtland Report for the World Commission on Environment and Development introduced the term of _____ development.

Exam Probability: **High**

18. *Answer choices:*
(see index for correct answer)

- a. co-culture
- b. interpersonal communication
- c. surface-level diversity
- d. Sustainable

:: Leadership ::

_____ is leadership that is directed by respect for ethical beliefs and values and for the dignity and rights of others. It is thus related to concepts such as trust, honesty, consideration, charisma, and fairness.

Exam Probability: **Medium**

19. *Answer choices:*
(see index for correct answer)

- a. Situational leadership

- b. Complex adaptive leadership
- c. The Leadership Council
- d. Consideration and Initiating Structure

Guidance: level 1

:: Supply chain management terms ::

In business and finance, _____ is a system of organizations, people, activities, information, and resources involved in moving a product or service from supplier to customer. _____ activities involve the transformation of natural resources, raw materials, and components into a finished product that is delivered to the end customer. In sophisticated _____ systems, used products may re-enter the _____ at any point where residual value is recyclable. _____ s link value chains.

Exam Probability: **Low**

20. *Answer choices:*
(see index for correct answer)

- a. Supply Chain
- b. Most valuable customers
- c. Final assembly schedule
- d. Work in process

Guidance: level 1

:: Fraud ::

In the United States, _____ is the claiming of Medicare health care reimbursement to which the claimant is not entitled. There are many different types of _____ , all of which have the same goal: to collect money from the Medicare program illegitimately.

Exam Probability: **Low**

21. *Answer choices:*
(see index for correct answer)

- a. Pharma fraud
- b. Statute of frauds
- c. Virginity fraud
- d. Telemarketing fraud

:: Carbon finance ::

The _____ is an international treaty which extends the 1992 United Nations Framework Convention on Climate Change that commits state parties to reduce greenhouse gas emissions, based on the scientific consensus that global warming is occurring and it is extremely likely that human-made CO2 emissions have predominantly caused it. The _____ was adopted in Kyoto, Japan on 11 December 1997 and entered into force on 16 February 2005. There are currently 192 parties to the Protocol.

Exam Probability: **Medium**

22. *Answer choices:*
(see index for correct answer)

- a. FirstCarbon Solutions
- b. Kyoto Protocol
- c. Ecosecurities
- d. Renewable Energy Payments

:: ::

_____ is a naturally occurring, yellowish-black liquid found in geological formations beneath the Earth's surface. It is commonly refined into various types of fuels. Components of _____ are separated using a technique called fractional distillation, i.e. separation of a liquid mixture into fractions differing in boiling point by means of distillation, typically using a fractionating column.

Exam Probability: **Low**

23. *Answer choices:*
(see index for correct answer)

- a. Petroleum
- b. Character
- c. co-culture
- d. corporate values

In personality psychology, _____ is the degree to which people believe that they have control over the outcome of events in their lives, as opposed to external forces beyond their control. Understanding of the concept was developed by Julian B. Rotter in 1954, and has since become an aspect of personality studies. A person's "locus" is conceptualized as internal or external .

Exam Probability: **Low**

24. *Answer choices:*
(see index for correct answer)

- a. Fading affect bias
- b. Scarcity heuristic
- c. Positive illusions
- d. Locus of control

Guidance: level 1

_____ is an eight-block-long street running roughly northwest to southeast from Broadway to South Street, at the East River, in the Financial District of Lower Manhattan in New York City. Over time, the term has become a metonym for the financial markets of the United States as a whole, the American financial services industry , or New York–based financial interests.

Exam Probability: **Medium**

25. *Answer choices:*
(see index for correct answer)

- a. surface-level diversity
- b. cultural
- c. Wall Street
- d. functional perspective

Guidance: level 1

The _____ was a severe worldwide economic depression that took place mostly during the 1930s, beginning in the United States. The timing of the _____ varied across nations; in most countries it started in 1929 and lasted until the late-1930s. It was the longest, deepest, and most widespread depression of the 20th century. In the 21st century, the _____ is commonly used as an example of how intensely the world's economy can decline.

Exam Probability: **Low**

26. *Answer choices:*
(see index for correct answer)

- a. empathy
- b. Great Depression
- c. deep-level diversity
- d. functional perspective

Guidance: level 1

:: Hazard analysis ::

Broadly speaking, a _____ is the combined effort of 1. identifying and analyzing potential events that may negatively impact individuals, assets, and/or the environment ; and 2. making judgments "on the tolerability of the risk on the basis of a risk analysis" while considering influencing factors . Put in simpler terms, a _____ analyzes what can go wrong, how likely it is to happen, what the potential consequences are, and how tolerable the identified risk is. As part of this process, the resulting determination of risk may be expressed in a quantitative or qualitative fashion. The _____ is an inherent part of an overall risk management strategy, which attempts to, after a _____ , "introduce control measures to eliminate or reduce" any potential risk-related consequences.

Exam Probability: **Low**

27. *Answer choices:*
(see index for correct answer)

- a. Risk assessment
- b. Swiss cheese model
- c. Hazard identification
- d. Hazardous Materials Identification System

Guidance: level 1

Cannabis, also known as _____ among other names, is a psychoactive drug from the Cannabis plant used for medical or recreational purposes. The main psychoactive part of cannabis is tetrahydrocannabinol , one of 483 known compounds in the plant, including at least 65 other cannabinoids. Cannabis can be used by smoking, vaporizing, within food, or as an extract.

Exam Probability: **High**

28. *Answer choices:*
(see index for correct answer)

- a. interpersonal communication
- b. Marijuana
- c. deep-level diversity
- d. information systems assessment

Guidance: level 1

:: Workplace ::

In business management, _____ is a management style whereby a manager closely observes and/or controls the work of his/her subordinates or employees.

Exam Probability: **High**

29. *Answer choices:*
(see index for correct answer)

- a. Work etiquette
- b. 360-degree feedback
- c. Rat race
- d. Feminisation of the workplace

Guidance: level 1

:: Utilitarianism ::

_____ is a school of thought that argues that the pursuit of pleasure and intrinsic goods are the primary or most important goals of human life. A hedonist strives to maximize net pleasure . However upon finally gaining said pleasure, happiness may remain stationary.

Exam Probability: **Medium**

30. *Answer choices:*
(see index for correct answer)

- a. Utilitarianism
- b. Utility monster
- c. Hedonism
- d. Rule utilitarianism

Guidance: level 1

:: ::

The _____ is an agency of the United States Department of Labor. Congress established the agency under the Occupational Safety and Health Act , which President Richard M. Nixon signed into law on December 29, 1970. OSHA's mission is to "assure safe and healthy working conditions for working men and women by setting and enforcing standards and by providing training, outreach, education and assistance". The agency is also charged with enforcing a variety of whistleblower statutes and regulations. OSHA is currently headed by Acting Assistant Secretary of Labor Loren Sweatt. OSHA's workplace safety inspections have been shown to reduce injury rates and injury costs without adverse effects to employment, sales, credit ratings, or firm survival.

Exam Probability: **High**

31. *Answer choices:*
(see index for correct answer)

- a. functional perspective
- b. similarity-attraction theory
- c. Occupational Safety and Health Administration
- d. hierarchical perspective

Guidance: level 1

:: Separation of investment and commercial banking ::

The _____ refers to § 619 of the Dodd–Frank Wall Street Reform and Consumer Protection Act . The rule was originally proposed by American economist and former United States Federal Reserve Chairman Paul Volcker to restrict United States banks from making certain kinds of speculative investments that do not benefit their customers. Volcker argued that such speculative activity played a key role in the financial crisis of 2007–2008. The rule is often referred to as a ban on proprietary trading by commercial banks, whereby deposits are used to trade on the bank`s own accounts, although a number of exceptions to this ban were included in the Dodd-Frank law.

Exam Probability: **Medium**

32. *Answer choices:*
(see index for correct answer)

- a. Commercial bank
- b. Merchant bank
- c. Bancassurance
- d. Volcker Rule

Guidance: level 1

:: Power (social and political) ::

_____ is a form of reverence gained by a leader who has strong interpersonal relationship skills. _____ , as an aspect of personal power, becomes particularly important as organizational leadership becomes increasingly about collaboration and influence, rather than command and control.

Exam Probability: **Low**

33. *Answer choices:*
(see index for correct answer)

- a. Referent power
- b. Hard power
- c. need for power

Guidance: level 1

:: Confidence tricks ::

A _____ is a business model that recruits members via a promise of payments or services for enrolling others into the scheme, rather than supplying investments or sale of products. As recruiting multiplies, recruiting becomes quickly impossible, and most members are unable to profit; as such, _____ s are unsustainable and often illegal.

Exam Probability: **Low**

34. *Answer choices:*
(see index for correct answer)

- a. Pyramid scheme
- b. Phishing
- c. Pigeon drop
- d. Miracle cars scam

Guidance: level 1

:: Parental leave ::

_____ , or family leave, is an employee benefit available in almost all countries. The term " _____ " may include maternity, paternity, and adoption leave; or may be used distinctively from "maternity leave" and "paternity leave" to describe separate family leave available to either parent to care for small children. In some countries and jurisdictions, "family leave" also includes leave provided to care for ill family members. Often, the minimum benefits and eligibility requirements are stipulated by law.

Exam Probability: **High**

35. *Answer choices:*
(see index for correct answer)

- a. Pregnancy discrimination
- b. Pregnant Workers Directive
- c. Motherhood penalty
- d. Maternity and Parental Leave, etc Regulations 1999

Guidance: level 1

:: Euthenics ::

_____ is an ethical framework and suggests that an entity, be it an organization or individual, has an obligation to act for the benefit of society at large. _____ is a duty every individual has to perform so as to maintain a balance between the economy and the ecosystems. A trade-off may exist between economic development, in the material sense, and the welfare of the society and environment, though this has been challenged by many reports over the past decade. _____ means sustaining the equilibrium between the two. It pertains not only to business organizations but also to everyone whose any action impacts the environment. This responsibility can be passive, by avoiding engaging in socially harmful acts, or active, by performing activities that directly advance social goals. _____ must be intergenerational since the actions of one generation have consequences on those following.

Exam Probability: **Medium**

36. *Answer choices:*
(see index for correct answer)

- a. Euthenics
- b. Home economics
- c. Social responsibility
- d. Minnie Cumnock Blodgett

Guidance: level 1

:: ::

The _____ of 1973 serves as the enacting legislation to carry out the provisions outlined in The Convention on International Trade in Endangered Species of Wild Fauna and Flora . Designed to protect critically imperiled species from extinction as a "consequence of economic growth and development untempered by adequate concern and conservation", the ESA was signed into law by President Richard Nixon on December 28, 1973. The law requires federal agencies to consult with the Fish and Wildlife Service &/or the NOAA Fisheries Service to ensure their actions are not likely to jeopardize the continued existence of any listed species or result in the destruction or adverse modification of designated critical habitat of such species. The U.S. Supreme Court found that "the plain intent of Congress in enacting" the ESA "was to halt and reverse the trend toward species extinction, whatever the cost." The Act is administered by two federal agencies, the United States Fish and Wildlife Service and the National Marine Fisheries Service .

Exam Probability: **Medium**

37. *Answer choices:*
(see index for correct answer)

- a. co-culture
- b. deep-level diversity
- c. hierarchical
- d. Endangered Species Act

Guidance: level 1

:: ::

The _____ , founded in 1912, is a private, nonprofit organization whose self-described mission is to focus on advancing marketplace trust, consisting of 106 independently incorporated local BBB organizations in the United States and Canada, coordinated under the Council of _____ s in Arlington, Virginia.

Exam Probability: **Medium**

38. *Answer choices:*
(see index for correct answer)

- a. deep-level diversity
- b. empathy
- c. co-culture

- d. corporate values

Guidance: level 1

:: Private equity ::

In finance, a high-yield bond is a bond that is rated below investment grade. These bonds have a higher risk of default or other adverse credit events, but typically pay higher yields than better quality bonds in order to make them attractive to investors.

Exam Probability: **Medium**

39. *Answer choices:*
(see index for correct answer)

- a. History of private equity and venture capital
- b. Equity co-investment
- c. Junk bond
- d. Carried interest

Guidance: level 1

:: Offshoring ::

A _____ is the temporary suspension or permanent termination of employment of an employee or, more commonly, a group of employees for business reasons, such as personnel management or downsizing an organization. Originally, _____ referred exclusively to a temporary interruption in work, or employment but this has evolved to a permanent elimination of a position in both British and US English, requiring the addition of "temporary" to specify the original meaning of the word. A _____ is not to be confused with wrongful termination. Laid off workers or displaced workers are workers who have lost or left their jobs because their employer has closed or moved, there was insufficient work for them to do, or their position or shift was abolished . Downsizing in a company is defined to involve the reduction of employees in a workforce. Downsizing in companies became a popular practice in the 1980s and early 1990s as it was seen as a way to deliver better shareholder value as it helps to reduce the costs of employers . Indeed, recent research on downsizing in the U.S., UK, and Japan suggests that downsizing is being regarded by management as one of the preferred routes to help declining organizations, cutting unnecessary costs, and improve organizational performance. Usually a _____ occurs as a cost cutting measure.

Exam Probability: **High**

40. *Answer choices:*
(see index for correct answer)

- a. Offshore custom software development
- b. Programmers Guild
- c. Antex
- d. Nearshoring

Guidance: level 1

:: ::

The _____ to Fight AIDS, Tuberculosis and Malaria is an international financing organization that aims to "attract, leverage and invest additional resources to end the epidemics of HIV/AIDS, tuberculosis and malaria to support attainment of the Sustainable Development Goals established by the United Nations." A public-private partnership, the organization maintains its secretariat in Geneva, Switzerland. The organization began operations in January 2002. Microsoft founder Bill Gates was one of the first private foundations among many bilateral donors to provide seed money for the partnership.

Exam Probability: **Medium**

41. *Answer choices:*
(see index for correct answer)

- a. Character
- b. similarity-attraction theory
- c. Global Fund
- d. surface-level diversity

Guidance: level 1

:: ::

MCI, Inc. was an American telecommunication corporation, currently a subsidiary of Verizon Communications, with its main office in Ashburn, Virginia. The corporation was formed originally as a result of the merger of _____ and MCI Communications corporations, and used the name MCI _____ , succeeded by _____ , before changing its name to the present version on April 12, 2003, as part of the corporation's ending of its bankruptcy status. The company traded on NASDAQ as WCOM and MCIP . The corporation was purchased by Verizon Communications with the deal finalizing on January 6, 2006, and is now identified as that company's Verizon Enterprise Solutions division with the local residential divisions being integrated slowly into local Verizon subsidiaries.

Exam Probability: **Medium**

42. *Answer choices:*
(see index for correct answer)

- a. hierarchical
- b. cultural

- c. surface-level diversity
- d. co-culture

Guidance: level 1

:: ::

In ecology, a _____ is the type of natural environment in which a particular species of organism lives. It is characterized by both physical and biological features. A species' _____ is those places where it can find food, shelter, protection and mates for reproduction.

Exam Probability: **Low**

43. *Answer choices:*
(see index for correct answer)

- a. co-culture
- b. surface-level diversity
- c. Habitat
- d. deep-level diversity

Guidance: level 1

:: Fraud ::

In law, _____ is intentional deception to secure unfair or unlawful gain, or to deprive a victim of a legal right. _____ can violate civil law , a criminal law , or it may cause no loss of money, property or legal right but still be an element of another civil or criminal wrong. The purpose of _____ may be monetary gain or other benefits, for example by obtaining a passport, travel document, or driver's license, or mortgage _____ , where the perpetrator may attempt to qualify for a mortgage by way of false statements.

Exam Probability: **Low**

44. *Answer choices:*
(see index for correct answer)

- a. Hitler Diaries
- b. misleading advertising
- c. Age fabrication
- d. Shell corporation

:: Law ::

_____ is a body of law which defines the role, powers, and structure of different entities within a state, namely, the executive, the parliament or legislature, and the judiciary; as well as the basic rights of citizens and, in federal countries such as the United States and Canada, the relationship between the central government and state, provincial, or territorial governments.

Exam Probability: **Low**

45. *Answer choices:*
(see index for correct answer)

- a. Constitutional law
- b. Legal case

:: Business ethics ::

A _____ is a person who exposes any kind of information or activity that is deemed illegal, unethical, or not correct within an organization that is either private or public. The information of alleged wrongdoing can be classified in many ways: violation of company policy/rules, law, regulation, or threat to public interest/national security, as well as fraud, and corruption. Those who become _____ s can choose to bring information or allegations to surface either internally or externally. Internally, a _____ can bring his/her accusations to the attention of other people within the accused organization such as an immediate supervisor. Externally, a _____ can bring allegations to light by contacting a third party outside of an accused organization such as the media, government, law enforcement, or those who are concerned. _____ s, however, take the risk of facing stiff reprisal and retaliation from those who are accused or alleged of wrongdoing.

Exam Probability: **High**

46. *Answer choices:*
(see index for correct answer)

- a. Product stewardship
- b. Whistleblower
- c. Surface Transportation Assistance Act
- d. CUC International

Guidance: level 1

:: Nepotism ::

_____ is the granting of favour to relatives in various fields, including business, politics, entertainment, sports, religion and other activities. The term originated with the assignment of nephews to important positions by Catholic popes and bishops. Trading parliamentary employment for favors is a modern-day example of _____ . Criticism of _____ , however, can be found in ancient Indian texts such as the Kural literature.

Exam Probability: **Low**

47. *Answer choices:*
(see index for correct answer)

- a. Cronyism
- b. Wasta
- c. Nepotism
- d. Crachach

Guidance: level 1

:: ::

Competition law is a law that promotes or seeks to maintain market competition by regulating anti-competitive conduct by companies. Competition law is implemented through public and private enforcement. Competition law is known as " _____ law" in the United States for historical reasons, and as "anti-monopoly law" in China and Russia. In previous years it has been known as trade practices law in the United Kingdom and Australia. In the European Union, it is referred to as both _____ and competition law.

Exam Probability: **Medium**

48. *Answer choices:*
(see index for correct answer)

- a. corporate values

- b. empathy
- c. Antitrust
- d. cultural

Guidance: level 1

:: ::

The _____ , the Calvinist work ethic or the Puritan work ethic is a work ethic concept in theology, sociology, economics and history that emphasizes that hard work, discipline and frugality are a result of a person's subscription to the values espoused by the Protestant faith, particularly Calvinism. The phrase was initially coined in 1904–1905 by Max Weber in his book The Protestant Ethic and the Spirit of Capitalism.

Exam Probability: **Low**

49. *Answer choices:*
(see index for correct answer)

- a. Protestant work ethic
- b. interpersonal communication
- c. imperative
- d. levels of analysis

Guidance: level 1

:: Social philosophy ::

The _____ describes the unintended social benefits of an individual's self-interested actions. Adam Smith first introduced the concept in The Theory of Moral Sentiments, written in 1759, invoking it in reference to income distribution. In this work, however, the idea of the market is not discussed, and the word "capitalism" is never used.

Exam Probability: **High**

50. *Answer choices:*
(see index for correct answer)

- a. Veil of Ignorance
- b. Freedom to contract
- c. Societal attitudes towards abortion
- d. vacancy chain

:: Corporate scandals ::

The _____ was a privately held international group of financial services companies controlled by Allen Stanford, until it was seized by United States authorities in early 2009. Headquartered in the Galleria Tower II in Uptown Houston, Texas, it had 50 offices in several countries, mainly in the Americas, included the Stanford International Bank, and said it managed US$8.5 billion of assets for more than 30,000 clients in 136 countries on six continents. On February 17, 2009, U.S. Federal agents placed the company into receivership due to charges of fraud. Ten days later, the U.S. Securities and Exchange Commission amended its complaint to accuse Stanford of turning the company into a "massive Ponzi scheme".

Exam Probability: **High**

51. *Answer choices:*
(see index for correct answer)

- a. Stanford Financial Group
- b. Petters Group Worldwide
- c. Central Energy Italian Gas Holding
- d. Terra Securities scandal

:: ::

A _____ is an astronomical body orbiting a star or stellar remnant that is massive enough to be rounded by its own gravity, is not massive enough to cause thermonuclear fusion, and has cleared its neighbouring region of _____ esimals.

Exam Probability: **Medium**

52. *Answer choices:*
(see index for correct answer)

- a. imperative
- b. Sarbanes-Oxley act of 2002
- c. Planet
- d. functional perspective

:: Auditing ::

_____ refers to the independence of the internal auditor or of the external auditor from parties that may have a financial interest in the business being audited. Independence requires integrity and an objective approach to the audit process. The concept requires the auditor to carry out his or her work freely and in an objective manner.

Exam Probability: **Medium**

53. *Answer choices:*
(see index for correct answer)

- a. Auditor independence
- b. Verified Audit Circulation
- c. Lease audit
- d. ISACA

:: Criminal law ::

_____ is the body of law that relates to crime. It proscribes conduct perceived as threatening, harmful, or otherwise endangering to the property, health, safety, and moral welfare of people inclusive of one's self. Most _____ is established by statute, which is to say that the laws are enacted by a legislature. _____ includes the punishment and rehabilitation of people who violate such laws. _____ varies according to jurisdiction, and differs from civil law, where emphasis is more on dispute resolution and victim compensation, rather than on punishment or rehabilitation. Criminal procedure is a formalized official activity that authenticates the fact of commission of a crime and authorizes punitive or rehabilitative treatment of the offender.

Exam Probability: **Medium**

54. *Answer choices:*
(see index for correct answer)

- a. Criminal law
- b. Mala prohibita
- c. mitigating factor
- d. Self-incrimination

:: Dutch inventions ::

The Fairtrade certification initiative was created to form a new method for economic trade. This method takes an ethical standpoint, and considers the producers first.

Exam Probability: **Medium**

55. *Answer choices:*
<small>(see index for correct answer)</small>

- a. Fair Trade Certified
- b. Fairtrade

:: ::

The _____ is an 1848 political pamphlet by the German philosophers Karl Marx and Friedrich Engels. Commissioned by the Communist League and originally published in London just as the Revolutions of 1848 began to erupt, the Manifesto was later recognised as one of the world's most influential political documents. It presents an analytical approach to the class struggle and the conflicts of capitalism and the capitalist mode of production, rather than a prediction of communism's potential future forms.

Exam Probability: **High**

56. *Answer choices:*
<small>(see index for correct answer)</small>

- a. Communist Manifesto
- b. deep-level diversity
- c. interpersonal communication
- d. corporate values

:: Monopoly (economics) ::

The _____ of 1890 was a United States antitrust law that regulates competition among enterprises, which was passed by Congress under the presidency of Benjamin Harrison.

Exam Probability: **Medium**

57. *Answer choices:*

- a. Regulatory economics
- b. Demonopolization
- c. Herfindahl index
- d. Wartime Law on Industrial Property

Guidance: level 1

:: Electronic feedback ::

_____ occurs when outputs of a system are routed back as inputs as part of a chain of cause-and-effect that forms a circuit or loop. The system can then be said to feed back into itself. The notion of cause-and-effect has to be handled carefully when applied to _____ systems.

Exam Probability: **Medium**

58. *Answer choices:*

- a. Positive feedback
- b. feedback loop

Guidance: level 1

:: Water law ::

The _____ is the primary federal law in the United States governing water pollution. Its objective is to restore and maintain the chemical, physical, and biological integrity of the nation's waters; recognizing the responsibilities of the states in addressing pollution and providing assistance to states to do so, including funding for publicly owned treatment works for the improvement of wastewater treatment; and maintaining the integrity of wetlands. It is one of the United States' first and most influential modern environmental laws. As with many other major U.S. federal environmental statutes, it is administered by the U.S. Environmental Protection Agency, in coordination with state governments. Its implementing regulations are codified at 40 C.F.R. Subchapters D, N, and O.

Exam Probability: **Medium**

59. *Answer choices:*
(see index for correct answer)

- a. Water right
- b. Return flow
- c. Correlative rights doctrine
- d. Clean Water Act

Guidance: level 1

Accounting

Accounting or accountancy is the measurement, processing, and communication of financial information about economic entities such as businesses and corporations. The modern field was established by the Italian mathematician Luca Pacioli in 1494. Accounting, which has been called the "language of business", measures the results of an organization's economic activities and conveys this information to a variety of users, including investors, creditors, management, and regulators.

:: United States federal income tax ::

Under United States tax law, the _____ is a dollar amount that non-itemizers may subtract from their income before income tax is applied. Taxpayers may choose either itemized deductions or the _____ , but usually choose whichever results in the lesser amount of tax payable. The _____ is available to US citizens and aliens who are resident for tax purposes and who are individuals, married persons, and heads of household. The _____ is based on filing status and typically increases each year. It is not available to nonresident aliens residing in the United States . Additional amounts are available for persons who are blind and/or are at least 65 years of age.

Exam Probability: **High**

1. *Answer choices:*

(see index for correct answer)

- a. Nonrecognition provisions
- b. Rabbi trust
- c. Filing status
- d. Standard deduction

Guidance: level 1

The U.S. _____ is an independent agency of the United States federal government. The SEC holds primary responsibility for enforcing the federal securities laws, proposing securities rules, and regulating the securities industry, the nation's stock and options exchanges, and other activities and organizations, including the electronic securities markets in the United States.

Exam Probability: **Medium**

2. *Answer choices:*
(see index for correct answer)

- a. Securities and Exchange Commission
- b. empathy
- c. open system
- d. process perspective

Guidance: level 1

:: Income taxes ::

An _____ is a tax imposed on individuals or entities that varies with respective income or profits . _____ generally is computed as the product of a tax rate times taxable income. Taxation rates may vary by type or characteristics of the taxpayer.

Exam Probability: **High**

3. *Answer choices:*
(see index for correct answer)

- a. Hall income tax
- b. Income tax
- c. Rouanet Law
- d. Individual income tax in Singapore

Guidance: level 1

:: Generally Accepted Accounting Principles ::

In accounting, an economic item's _____ is the original nominal monetary value of that item. _____ accounting involves reporting assets and liabilities at their _____ s, which are not updated for changes in the items' values. Consequently, the amounts reported for these balance sheet items often differ from their current economic or market values.

Exam Probability: **Low**

4. *Answer choices:*

- a. Shares outstanding
- b. Earnings before interest, taxes and depreciation
- c. Chinese accounting standards
- d. Historical cost

Guidance: level 1

:: Types of accounting ::

Various _____ systems are used by various public sector entities. In the United States, for instance, there are two levels of government which follow different accounting standards set forth by independent, private sector boards. At the federal level, the Federal Accounting Standards Advisory Board sets forth the accounting standards to follow. Similarly, there is the _____ Standards Board for state and local level government.

Exam Probability: **Medium**

5. *Answer choices:*

- a. Personal environmental impact accounting
- b. Product control
- c. Governmental accounting

Guidance: level 1

:: Management accounting ::

_____ are costs that are not directly accountable to a cost object .
_____ may be either fixed or variable. _____ include administration,
personnel and security costs. These are those costs which are not directly
related to production. Some _____ may be overhead. But some overhead
costs can be directly attributed to a project and are direct costs.

Exam Probability: **Low**

6. *Answer choices:*

(see index for correct answer)

- a. Fixed assets management
- b. Invested capital
- c. Certified Management Accountants of Canada
- d. Direct material price variance

Guidance: level 1

:: Bank regulation ::

_____ is a measure implemented in many countries to protect bank
depositors, in full or in part, from losses caused by a bank`s inability to pay
its debts when due. _____ systems are one component of a financial system
safety net that promotes financial stability.

Exam Probability: **Low**

7. *Answer choices:*

(see index for correct answer)

- a. Asset quality
- b. Institute for Law and Finance
- c. Capitis deminutio
- d. Deposit insurance

Guidance: level 1

:: Inventory ::

_____ is the maximum amount of goods, or inventory, that a company can
possibly sell during this fiscal year. It has the formula.

8. *Answer choices:*

(see index for correct answer)

- a. Cost of goods available for sale
- b. Specific identification
- c. Stock keeping unit
- d. LIFO

Guidance: level 1

:: Production and manufacturing ::

_____ consists of organization-wide efforts to "install and make permanent climate where employees continuously improve their ability to provide on demand products and services that customers will find of particular value." "Total" emphasizes that departments in addition to production are obligated to improve their operations; "management" emphasizes that executives are obligated to actively manage quality through funding, training, staffing, and goal setting. While there is no widely agreed-upon approach, TQM efforts typically draw heavily on the previously developed tools and techniques of quality control. TQM enjoyed widespread attention during the late 1980s and early 1990s before being overshadowed by ISO 9000, Lean manufacturing, and Six Sigma.

9. *Answer choices:*

(see index for correct answer)

- a. Feeder line
- b. Transfer line
- c. Mockup
- d. Total quality management

Guidance: level 1

:: ::

_____ is the income that is gained by governments through taxation. Taxation is the primary source of income for a state. Revenue may be extracted from sources such as individuals, public enterprises, trade, royalties on natural resources and/or foreign aid. An inefficient collection of taxes is greater in countries characterized by poverty, a large agricultural sector and large amounts of foreign aid.

Exam Probability: **High**

10. *Answer choices:*
(see index for correct answer)

- a. surface-level diversity
- b. personal values
- c. imperative
- d. Sarbanes-Oxley act of 2002

Guidance: level 1

:: Financial ratios ::

In finance, the _____ , also known as the acid-test ratio is a type of liquidity ratio which measures the ability of a company to use its near cash or quick assets to extinguish or retire its current liabilities immediately. Quick assets include those current assets that presumably can be quickly converted to cash at close to their book values. It is the ratio between quickly available or liquid assets and current liabilities.

Exam Probability: **High**

11. *Answer choices:*
(see index for correct answer)

- a. Quick ratio
- b. Import ratio
- c. Asset turnover
- d. Incremental capital-output ratio

Guidance: level 1

:: Debt ::

A _____ is a monetary amount owed to a creditor that is unlikely to be paid and, or which the creditor is not willing to take action to collect for various reasons, often due to the debtor not having the money to pay, for example due to a company going into liquidation or insolvency. There are various technical definitions of what constitutes a _____ , depending on accounting conventions, regulatory treatment and the institution provisioning. In the USA, bank loans with more than ninety days' arrears become "problem loans". Accounting sources advise that the full amount of a _____ be written off to the profit and loss account or a provision for _____ s as soon as it is foreseen.

Exam Probability: **Medium**

12. *Answer choices:*
(see index for correct answer)

- a. Bad debt
- b. Vulture fund
- c. Museum of Foreign Debt
- d. gearing

Guidance: level 1

:: ::

A work order is usually a task or a job for a customer, that can be scheduled or assigned to someone. Such an order may be from a customer request or created internally within the organization. Work orders may also be created as follow ups to Inspections or Audits. A work order may be for products or services.

Exam Probability: **High**

13. *Answer choices:*
(see index for correct answer)

- a. Job order
- b. cultural
- c. deep-level diversity
- d. empathy

Guidance: level 1

:: Business economics ::

_____ is one of the constituents of a leasing calculus or operation. It describes the future value of a good in terms of absolute value in monetary terms and it is sometimes abbreviated into a percentage of the initial price when the item was new.

Exam Probability: **High**

14. *Answer choices:*
(see index for correct answer)

- a. Trade sale
- b. Business ecosystem
- c. Conglomerate merger
- d. Residual value

Guidance: level 1

:: ::

_____ is capital that is contributed to a corporation by investors by purchase of stock from the corporation, the primary market, not by purchase of stock in the open market from other stockholders . It includes share capital as well as additional _____ .

Exam Probability: **Medium**

15. *Answer choices:*
(see index for correct answer)

- a. Paid-in capital
- b. similarity-attraction theory
- c. co-culture
- d. surface-level diversity

Guidance: level 1

:: Management ::

The _____ is a strategy performance management tool – a semi-standard structured report, that can be used by managers to keep track of the execution of activities by the staff within their control and to monitor the consequences arising from these actions.

16. *Answer choices:*

(see index for correct answer)

- a. Balanced scorecard
- b. Enterprise planning system
- c. Best practice
- d. Value proposition

Guidance: level 1

:: ::

_____ are electronic transfer of money from one bank account to another, either within a single financial institution or across multiple institutions, via computer-based systems, without the direct intervention of bank staff.

Exam Probability: **Low**

17. *Answer choices:*

(see index for correct answer)

- a. corporate values
- b. cultural
- c. Electronic funds transfer
- d. co-culture

Guidance: level 1

:: Management accounting ::

The _____ is a professional membership organization headquartered in Montvale, New Jersey, United States, operating in four global regions: The Americas, Asia/Pacific, Europe, and Middle East/India.

Exam Probability: **Medium**

18. *Answer choices:*

(see index for correct answer)

- a. Direct material usage variance
- b. Institute of Management Accountants
- c. Financial statement analysis
- d. Invested capital

:: Income ::

_____ is a ratio between the net profit and cost of investment resulting from an investment of some resources. A high ROI means the investment's gains favorably to its cost. As a performance measure, ROI is used to evaluate the efficiency of an investment or to compare the efficiencies of several different investments. In purely economic terms, it is one way of relating profits to capital invested. _____ is a performance measure used by businesses to identify the efficiency of an investment or number of different investments.

Exam Probability: **Medium**

19. *Answer choices:*
(see index for correct answer)

- a. Trinity study
- b. Income earner
- c. Family income
- d. Imputed income

:: Expense ::

_____ relates to the cost of borrowing money. It is the price that a lender charges a borrower for the use of the lender's money. On the income statement, _____ can represent the cost of borrowing money from banks, bond investors, and other sources. _____ is different from operating expense and CAPEX, for it relates to the capital structure of a company, and it is usually tax-deductible.

Exam Probability: **High**

20. *Answer choices:*
(see index for correct answer)

- a. Interest expense
- b. Operating expense
- c. Corporate travel
- d. expenditure

:: Investment ::

In economics, _____ is spending which increases the availability of fixed capital goods or means of production and goods inventories. It is the total spending on newly produced physical capital and on inventories —that is, gross investment—minus replacement investment, which simply replaces depreciated capital goods. It is productive capital formation plus net additions to the stock of housing and the stock of inventories.

Exam Probability: **Medium**

21. *Answer choices:*
(see index for correct answer)

- a. IFund
- b. Portable alpha
- c. Short-term investment fund
- d. Net investment

Guidance: level 1

:: Taxation ::

A _____ is a person or organization subject to pay a tax. _____ s have an Identification Number, a reference number issued by a government to its citizens.

Exam Probability: **Low**

22. *Answer choices:*
(see index for correct answer)

- a. Indirect tax
- b. Income tax and gambling losses
- c. Optimal taxation
- d. Taxpayer

Guidance: level 1

:: Financial accounting ::

_____ is a financial metric which represents operating liquidity available to a business, organisation or other entity, including governmental entities. Along with fixed assets such as plant and equipment, _____ is considered a part of operating capital. Gross _____ is equal to current assets. _____ is calculated as current assets minus current liabilities. If current assets are less than current liabilities, an entity has a _____ deficiency, also called a _____ deficit.

Exam Probability: **Medium**

23. *Answer choices:*
(see index for correct answer)

- a. Accounting identity
- b. Working capital
- c. Financial Condition Report
- d. Carry

Guidance: level 1

:: Commerce ::

Continuation of an entity as a _____ is presumed as the basis for financial reporting unless and until the entity's liquidation becomes imminent. Preparation of financial statements under this presumption is commonly referred to as the _____ basis of accounting. If and when an entity's liquidation becomes imminent, financial statements are prepared under the liquidation basis of accounting .

Exam Probability: **Medium**

24. *Answer choices:*
(see index for correct answer)

- a. Group buying
- b. Going concern
- c. Fast track
- d. Purchase discount

Guidance: level 1

:: Ethically disputed business practices ::

_____ , in accounting, is the act of intentionally influencing the process of financial reporting to obtain some private gain. _____ involves the alteration of financial reports to mislead stakeholders about the organization's underlying performance, or to "influence contractual outcomes that depend on reported accounting numbers."

Exam Probability: **Medium**

25. *Answer choices:*
(see index for correct answer)

- a. Earnings management
- b. Insider trading
- c. Designer drug
- d. Wrongful dismissal

Guidance: level 1

:: Accounting terminology ::

_____ or capital expense is the money a company spends to buy, maintain, or improve its fixed assets, such as buildings, vehicles, equipment, or land. It is considered a _____ when the asset is newly purchased or when money is used towards extending the useful life of an existing asset, such as repairing the roof.

Exam Probability: **Medium**

26. *Answer choices:*
(see index for correct answer)

- a. Chart of accounts
- b. Share premium
- c. outstanding balance
- d. Record to report

Guidance: level 1

:: Labour law ::

In law, _____ is to give an immediately secured right of present or future deployment. One has a vested right to an asset that cannot be taken away by any third party, even though one may not yet possess the asset. When the right, interest, or title to the present or future possession of a legal estate can be transferred to any other party, it is termed a vested interest.

Exam Probability: **Low**

27. *Answer choices:*
(see index for correct answer)

- a. Transfers of Undertakings Directive
- b. Maximum medical improvement
- c. Core Labor Standards
- d. Vesting

Guidance: level 1

:: Accounting systems ::

In accounting, a business or an organization and its owners are treated as two separately identifiable parties. This is called the _____ . The business stands apart from other organizations as a separate economic unit. It is necessary to record the business's transactions separately, to distinguish them from the owners' personal transactions. This helps to give a correct determination of the true financial condition of the business. This concept can be extended to accounting separately for the various divisions of a business in order to ascertain the financial results for each division. Under the business _____ , a business holds separate entity and distinct from its owners. "The entity view holds the business `enterprise to be an institution in its own right separate and distinct from the parties who furnish the funds"

Exam Probability: **High**

28. *Answer choices:*
(see index for correct answer)

- a. Substance over form
- b. Waste book
- c. Single-entry bookkeeping system
- d. Accounting practice

Guidance: level 1

:: Financial statements ::

In financial accounting, a _____ or statement of financial position or statement of financial condition is a summary of the financial balances of an individual or organization, whether it be a sole proprietorship, a business partnership, a corporation, private limited company or other organization such as Government or not-for-profit entity. Assets, liabilities and ownership equity are listed as of a specific date, such as the end of its financial year. A _____ is often described as a "snapshot of a company's financial condition". Of the four basic financial statements, the _____ is the only statement which applies to a single point in time of a business' calendar year.

Exam Probability: **Medium**

29. *Answer choices:*
(see index for correct answer)

- a. Statement of retained earnings
- b. Consolidated financial statement
- c. Clean surplus accounting
- d. Balance sheet

Guidance: level 1

:: Management accounting ::

An _____ allows a company to provide a monetary value for items that make up their inventory. Inventories are usually the largest current asset of a business, and proper measurement of them is necessary to assure accurate financial statements. If inventory is not properly measured, expenses and revenues cannot be properly matched and a company could make poor business decisions.

Exam Probability: **High**

30. *Answer choices:*
(see index for correct answer)

- a. Factory overhead
- b. Investment center
- c. Accounting management
- d. Backflush accounting

:: Valuation (finance) ::

The _____ is one of three major groups of methodologies, called valuation approaches, used by appraisers. It is particularly common in commercial real estate appraisal and in business appraisal. The fundamental math is similar to the methods used for financial valuation, securities analysis, or bond pricing. However, there are some significant and important modifications when used in real estate or business valuation.

Exam Probability: **Medium**

31. *Answer choices:*
(see index for correct answer)

- a. Value date
- b. Income approach
- c. Pre-money valuation
- d. The Appraisal Foundation

:: Organizational behavior ::

_____ is the state or fact of exclusive rights and control over property, which may be an object, land/real estate or intellectual property. _____ involves multiple rights, collectively referred to as title, which may be separated and held by different parties.

Exam Probability: **High**

32. *Answer choices:*
(see index for correct answer)

- a. Ownership
- b. Self-policing
- c. Counterproductive norms
- d. Burnout

:: Business models ::

A _____ , _____ company or daughter company is a company that is owned or controlled by another company, which is called the parent company, parent, or holding company. The _____ can be a company, corporation, or limited liability company. In some cases it is a government or state-owned enterprise. In some cases, particularly in the music and book publishing industries, subsidiaries are referred to as imprints.

Exam Probability: **Medium**

33. *Answer choices:*
(see index for correct answer)

- a. Subsidiary
- b. Lawyers on Demand
- c. IASME
- d. Gratis

Guidance: level 1

:: Taxation in the United States ::

The Modified Accelerated Cost Recovery System is the current tax depreciation system in the United States. Under this system, the capitalized cost of tangible property is recovered over a specified life by annual deductions for depreciation. The lives are specified broadly in the Internal Revenue Code. The Internal Revenue Service publishes detailed tables of lives by classes of assets. The deduction for depreciation is computed under one of two methods at the election of the taxpayer, with limitations. See IRS Publication 946 for a 120-page guide to _____ .

Exam Probability: **Medium**

34. *Answer choices:*
(see index for correct answer)

- a. Cigarette tax stamp
- b. Qualified Production Activities Income
- c. Taxpayer Identification Number
- d. Carryover basis

Guidance: level 1

:: ::

From an accounting perspective, _____ is crucial because _____ and _____ taxes considerably affect the net income of most companies and because they are subject to laws and regulations .

35. *Answer choices:*
(see index for correct answer)

- a. cultural
- b. functional perspective
- c. deep-level diversity
- d. Payroll

Guidance: level 1

:: Financial ratios ::

The _____ is a financial ratio indicating the relative proportion of equity used to finance a company's assets. The two components are often taken from the firm's balance sheet or statement of financial position , but the ratio may also be calculated using market values for both, if the company's equities are publicly traded.

36. *Answer choices:*
(see index for correct answer)

- a. Equity ratio
- b. Theoretical ex-rights price
- c. Return on tangible equity
- d. Debt service ratio

Guidance: level 1

:: Inventory ::

Costs are associated with particular goods using one of the several formulas, including specific identification, first-in first-out , or average cost. Costs include all costs of purchase, costs of conversion and other costs that are incurred in bringing the inventories to their present location and condition. Costs of goods made by the businesses include material, labor, and allocated overhead. The costs of those goods which are not yet sold are deferred as costs of inventory until the inventory is sold or written down in value.

Exam Probability: **High**

37. *Answer choices:*

- a. Inventory bounce
- b. Buffer stock
- c. Cost of goods sold
- d. Reorder point

Guidance: level 1

:: Business ::

The seller, or the provider of the goods or services, completes a sale in response to an acquisition, appropriation, requisition or a direct interaction with the buyer at the point of sale. There is a passing of title of the item, and the settlement of a price, in which agreement is reached on a price for which transfer of ownership of the item will occur. The seller, not the purchaser typically executes the sale and it may be completed prior to the obligation of payment. In the case of indirect interaction, a person who sells goods or service on behalf of the owner is known as a _____ man or _____ woman or _____ person, but this often refers to someone selling goods in a store/shop, in which case other terms are also common, including _____ clerk, shop assistant, and retail clerk.

Exam Probability: **High**

38. *Answer choices:*

- a. Free trade
- b. Serviced office broker
- c. Sales
- d. Closure

:: Management accounting ::

_____ is a professional business study of Accounts and management in which we learn importance of accounts in our management system.

Exam Probability: **High**

39. *Answer choices:*
(see index for correct answer)

- a. Accounting management
- b. Cash and cash equivalents
- c. Contribution margin
- d. Cost accounting

:: Accounting source documents ::

A _____ is a commercial document and first official offer issued by a buyer to a seller indicating types, quantities, and agreed prices for products or services. It is used to control the purchasing of products and services from external suppliers. _____ s can be an essential part of enterprise resource planning system orders.

Exam Probability: **High**

40. *Answer choices:*
(see index for correct answer)

- a. Air waybill
- b. Invoice
- c. Purchase order
- d. Remittance advice

:: Accounting ::

_____ are key sources of information and evidence used to prepare, verify and/or audit the financial statements. They also include documentation to prove asset ownership for creation of liabilities and proof of monetary and non monetary transactions.

Exam Probability: **Medium**

41. *Answer choices:*
(see index for correct answer)

- a. Accounting records
- b. History of accounting
- c. Special journals
- d. European training programs

Guidance: level 1

:: Business law ::

A _____ is a business entity created by two or more parties, generally characterized by shared ownership, shared returns and risks, and shared governance. Companies typically pursue _____ s for one of four reasons: to access a new market, particularly emerging markets; to gain scale efficiencies by combining assets and operations; to share risk for major investments or projects; or to access skills and capabilities.

Exam Probability: **High**

42. *Answer choices:*
(see index for correct answer)

- a. Bulk sale
- b. Joint venture
- c. Statutory liability
- d. Fraud deterrence

Guidance: level 1

:: Management ::

Business _____ is a discipline in operations management in which people use various methods to discover, model, analyze, measure, improve, optimize, and automate business processes. BPM focuses on improving corporate performance by managing business processes. Any combination of methods used to manage a company's business processes is BPM. Processes can be structured and repeatable or unstructured and variable. Though not required, enabling technologies are often used with BPM.

Exam Probability: **Medium**

43. *Answer choices:*
(see index for correct answer)

- a. Managerial prerogative
- b. Process Management
- c. Communications management
- d. Gemba

Guidance: level 1

:: Financial ratios ::

_____ is the difference between revenue and cost of goods sold divided by revenue. _____ is expressed as a percentage. Generally, it is calculated as the selling price of an item, less the cost of goods sold . _____ is often used interchangeably with Gross Profit, but the terms are different. When speaking about a monetary amount, it is technically correct to use the term Gross Profit; when referring to a percentage or ratio, it is correct to use _____ . In other words, _____ is a percentage value, while Gross Profit is a monetary value.

Exam Probability: **Low**

44. *Answer choices:*
(see index for correct answer)

- a. Dividend yield
- b. Average propensity to consume
- c. Jaws ratio
- d. Gross margin

Guidance: level 1

:: Password authentication ::

A _____ , or sometimes redundantly a PIN number, is a numeric or alpha-numeric password used in the process of authenticating a user accessing a system.

Exam Probability: **High**

45. *Answer choices:*
(see index for correct answer)

- a. Zero-knowledge password proof
- b. Password synchronization
- c. Personal identification number
- d. LM hash

Guidance: level 1

:: Corporate crime ::

_____ LLP, based in Chicago, was an American holding company. Formerly one of the "Big Five" accounting firms , the firm had provided auditing, tax, and consulting services to large corporations. By 2001, it had become one of the world's largest multinational companies.

Exam Probability: **High**

46. *Answer choices:*
(see index for correct answer)

- a. Arthur Andersen
- b. Arthur Andersen LLP v. United States
- c. Walter Forbes
- d. backdating

Guidance: level 1

:: ::

An _____ is an asset that lacks physical substance. It is defined in opposition to physical assets such as machinery and buildings. An _____ is usually very hard to evaluate. Patents, copyrights, franchises, goodwill, trademarks, and trade names. The general interpretation also includes software and other intangible computer based assets are all examples of _____ s. _____ s generally—though not necessarily—suffer from typical market failures of non-rivalry and non-excludability.

Exam Probability: **High**

47. *Answer choices:*
(see index for correct answer)

- a. corporate values
- b. process perspective
- c. Character
- d. Intangible asset

Guidance: level 1

:: Accounting source documents ::

An _____ , bill or tab is a commercial document issued by a seller to a buyer, relating to a sale transaction and indicating the products, quantities, and agreed prices for products or services the seller had provided the buyer.

Exam Probability: **High**

48. *Answer choices:*
(see index for correct answer)

- a. Remittance advice
- b. Credit memo
- c. Parcel audit
- d. Invoice

Guidance: level 1

:: Management accounting ::

An _____ is a classification used for business units within an enterprise. The essential element of an _____ is that it is treated as a unit which is measured against its use of capital, as opposed to a cost or profit center, which are measured against raw costs or profits.

Exam Probability: **High**

49. *Answer choices:*
(see index for correct answer)

- a. Indirect costs
- b. Investment center
- c. Managerial risk accounting
- d. Environmental full-cost accounting

Guidance: level 1

:: Budgets ::

An _____ is the annual budget of an activity stated in terms of Budget Classification Code, functional/subfunctional categories and cost accounts. It contains estimates of the total value of resources required for the performance of the operation including reimbursable work or services for others. It also includes estimates of workload in terms of total work units identified by cost accounts.

Exam Probability: **Low**

50. *Answer choices:*
(see index for correct answer)

- a. Budget set
- b. Operating budget
- c. Zero-based budgeting
- d. Personal budget

Guidance: level 1

:: Options (finance) ::

A _____ bond is a type of bond that allows the issuer of the bond to retain the privilege of redeeming the bond at some point before the bond reaches its date of maturity. In other words, on the call date, the issuer has the right, but not the obligation, to buy back the bonds from the bond holders at a defined call price. Technically speaking, the bonds are not really bought and held by the issuer but are instead cancelled immediately.

Exam Probability: **Medium**

51. *Answer choices:*

(see index for correct answer)

- a. Interest rate guarantee
- b. Credit default option
- c. Callable
- d. Barrier option

Guidance: level 1

:: Generally Accepted Accounting Principles ::

Financial statements prepared and presented by a company typically follow an external standard that specifically guides their preparation. These standards vary across the globe and are typically overseen by some combination of the private accounting profession in that specific nation and the various government regulators. Variations across countries may be considerable, making cross-country evaluation of financial data challenging.

Exam Probability: **Low**

52. *Answer choices:*

(see index for correct answer)

- a. Profit
- b. Engagement letter
- c. Shares outstanding
- d. Generally Accepted Accounting Principles

Guidance: level 1

:: Money ::

In economics, _____ is money in the physical form of currency, such as banknotes and coins. In bookkeeping and finance, _____ is current assets comprising currency or currency equivalents that can be accessed immediately or near-immediately . _____ is seen either as a reserve for payments, in case of a structural or incidental negative _____ flow or as a way to avoid a downturn on financial markets.

Exam Probability: **Medium**

53. *Answer choices:*
(see index for correct answer)

- a. Love of money
- b. Allowance
- c. Constant dollar
- d. Coin of account

Guidance: level 1

:: Business law ::

An _____ is a natural person, business, or corporation that provides goods or services to another entity under terms specified in a contract or within a verbal agreement. Unlike an employee, an _____ does not work regularly for an employer but works as and when required, during which time they may be subject to law of agency. _____ s are usually paid on a freelance basis. Contractors often work through a limited company or franchise, which they themselves own, or may work through an umbrella company.

Exam Probability: **High**

54. *Answer choices:*
(see index for correct answer)

- a. Independent contractor
- b. General assignment
- c. Stick licensing
- d. Arbitration clause

Guidance: level 1

:: Management accounting ::

In _____ or managerial accounting, managers use the provisions of accounting information in order to better inform themselves before they decide matters within their organizations, which aids their management and performance of control functions.

55. *Answer choices:*
(see index for correct answer)

- a. Management accounting
- b. Semi-variable cost
- c. Institute of Certified Management Accountants
- d. Dual overhead rate

Guidance: level 1

:: Generally Accepted Accounting Principles ::

Paid-in capital is capital that is contributed to a corporation by investors by purchase of stock from the corporation, the primary market, not by purchase of stock in the open market from other stockholders . It includes share capital as well as additional paid-in capital.

56. *Answer choices:*
(see index for correct answer)

- a. Indian Accounting Standards
- b. Contributed capital
- c. Consolidation
- d. Operating income before depreciation and amortization

Guidance: level 1

:: Management accounting ::

A _____ is a cost that differs between alternatives being considered. In order for a cost to be a _____ it must be.

57. *Answer choices:*
(see index for correct answer)

- a. Investment center
- b. Dual overhead rate
- c. Relevant cost
- d. Net present value

Guidance: level 1

:: Asset ::

_____ s, also known as tangible assets or property, plant and equipment , is a term used in accounting for assets and property that cannot easily be converted into cash. This can be compared with current assets such as cash or bank accounts, described as liquid assets. In most cases, only tangible assets are referred to as fixed. IAS 16 defines _____ s as assets whose future economic benefit is probable to flow into the entity, whose cost can be measured reliably. _____ s belong to one of 2 types:"Freehold Assets" – assets which are purchased with legal right of ownership and used,and "Leasehold Assets" – assets used by owner without legal right for a particular period of time.

Exam Probability: **High**

58. *Answer choices:*
(see index for correct answer)

- a. Fixed asset
- b. Current asset

Guidance: level 1

:: ::

_____ is the collection of mechanisms, processes and relations by which corporations are controlled and operated. Governance structures and principles identify the distribution of rights and responsibilities among different participants in the corporation and include the rules and procedures for making decisions in corporate affairs. _____ is necessary because of the possibility of conflicts of interests between stakeholders, primarily between shareholders and upper management or among shareholders.

59. *Answer choices:*

- a. information systems assessment
- b. Corporate governance
- c. levels of analysis
- d. functional perspective

Guidance: level 1

INDEX: Correct Answers

Foundations of Business

1. d: Ownership

2. a: Interest rate

3. : Cash

4. a: Marketing strategy

5. b: Arbitration

6. d: Description

7. c: Project

8. : Retail

9. c: Cooperation

10. d: Interview

11. d: Manufacturing

12. c: Revenue

13. d: Office

14. a: Return on investment

15. : Venture capital

16. a: Bankruptcy

17. c: Market segmentation

18. c: Free trade

19. b: Customs

20. a: Planning

21. a: Bribery

22. d: Payment

23. a: Credit

24. b: Resource

25. d: Financial crisis

26. c: Raw material

27. : Focus group

28. : Solution

29. d: Incentive

30. d: Economic Development

31. d: Number

32. c: Franchising

33. : Selling

34. d: Internal Revenue Service

35. d: Capitalism

36. : Market research

37. a: Scheduling

38. : Frequency

39. b: Sustainability

40. : Competitive advantage

41. b: Duty

42. : ITeM

43. c: Interest

44. d: Strategy

45. d: Evaluation

46. b: Globalization

47. b: E-commerce

48. a: Small business

49. a: Recession

50. c: Energies

51. c: Sony

52. a: Credit card

53. c: Demand

54. b: Direct investment

55. : Strategic alliance

56. a: Common stock

57. : Market value

58. c: Feedback

59. : Schedule

Management

1. d: Merger

2. a: Product life cycle

3. d: European Union

4. c: Glass ceiling

5. c: Inventory control

6. a: Career

7. b: Ratio

8. a: Feedback

9. a: Delegation

10. b: Industrial Revolution

11. c: Goal setting

12. : Organization chart

13. b: Efficiency

14. b: Entrepreneurship

15. : Problem

16. d: Supervisor

17. b: Theory X

18. c: Virtual team

19. d: Description

20. b: Employment

21. : Performance appraisal

22. d: Cost leadership

23. a: Cross-functional team

24. b: Negotiation

25. c: Overtime

26. b: Asset

27. a: Dimension

28. : E-commerce

29. : General manager

30. a: Dilemma

31. : Schedule

32. d: Utility

33. : Offshoring

34. b: Human resource management

35. c: Autonomy

36. : Halo effect

37. : Sales

38. c: Simulation

39. c: Strategic planning

40. b: Strategic management

41. : Policy

42. b: Training and development

43. b: Specification

44. b: Resource

45. b: Organizational commitment

46. a: Variable cost

47. c: Business process

48. c: Committee

49. d: Statistical process control

50. c: Recession

51. : Job analysis

52. c: Bargaining

53. c: Meeting

54. b: Chief executive officer

55. c: Employee stock

56. b: Vendor

57. c: Scheduling

58. b: Size

59. d: Discipline

Business law

1. b: Comparative negligence

2. c: Shares

3. a: Social responsibility

4. a: Merchant

5. d: Assumption of risk

6. a: Jury Trial

7. c: Partnership

8. b: Security

9. b: Authority

10. : Sherman Act

11. a: Writ

12. : Statute of limitations

13. d: Collective bargaining

14. b: Shareholder

15. c: Misdemeanor

16. c: Mens rea

17. : Uniform Electronic Transactions Act

18. d: Federal Trade Commission

19. b: Free trade

20. a: Misrepresentation

21. : Arbitration clause

22. c: World Trade Organization

23. c: Petition

24. b: Perfect tender

25. c: Board of directors

26. b: Offeror

27. c: Labor relations

28. : Preference

29. : Ford

30. a: Utilitarianism

31. b: Insurable interest

32. c: Punitive damages

33. a: Expense

34. b: Warehouse receipt

35. : Brand

36. b: Limited liability

37. b: Appeal

38. c: Stock

39. : Treaty

40. a: Personnel

41. : Contract law

42. a: Creditor

43. c: Corporation

44. b: Statutory Law

45. d: Computer fraud

46. b: Operating agreement

47. : Economic espionage

48. a: Disclaimer

49. c: Criminal law

50. a: Risk

51. b: Directed verdict

52. a: Berne Convention

53. : Regulation

54. b: Assignee

55. b: Insider trading

56. : Delegation

57. : Credit

58. c: Summary judgment

59. a: Environmental Protection

Finance

1. d: Forecasting

2. a: Gross margin

3. a: Pension

4. d: Payback period

5. d: Accrual

6. c: General journal

7. d: Value Line

8. d: Rate of return

9. : Finance

10. d: Brand

11. a: Cost allocation

12. c: Free cash flow

13. d: Stock exchange

14. c: Debt

15. a: Cash management

16. a: Long-term liabilities

17. a: Bank account

18. : Callable bond

19. : Historical cost

20. b: Annuity

21. : Cash flow

22. d: Audit

23. d: Securities and Exchange Commission

24. c: Shareholder

25. d: Accounting

26. b: Mortgage

27. c: Double taxation

28. d: Matching principle

29. b: Stock

30. a: Marketing

31. : Government bond

32. a: Net worth

33. : Exchange rate

34. c: Risk assessment

35. d: Sinking fund

36. a: Cost object

37. d: Compound interest

38. d: Market price

39. a: Accrued liabilities

40. : Operating lease

41. d: Capital budgeting

42. b: Compounding

43. a: Operating expense

44. a: Social security

45. d: Balance sheet

46. b: Capital gain

47. d: Fraud

48. b: Risk premium

49. : Policy

50. b: Dividend

51. a: Working capital

52. : Gross profit

53. : Opportunity cost

54. : Security

55. b: Enron

56. b: Rate risk

57. a: Stock price

58. a: WorldCom

59. a: Market value

Human resource management

1. : Conformity

2. a: Virtual team

3. d: Mining

4. a: Restricted stock

5. a: Sexual orientation

6. a: Reinforcement

7. b: Employee Free Choice Act

8. a: Employee stock ownership plan

9. c: Executive compensation

10. d: Online assessment

11. a: Internship

12. a: Piece rate

13. a: Social loafing

14. c: Performance measurement

15. b: Foreign worker

16. c: Organizational structure

17. c: Job sharing

18. a: Workforce planning

19. c: Learning organization

20. d: Wage curve

21. a: Impression management

22. : Content validity

23. : Recruitment

24. c: Career management

25. : Kaizen

26. b: Employee Polygraph Protection Act

27. b: Mission statement

28. a: Service Employees International Union

29. : E-HRM

30. d: Cafeteria plan

31. d: Committee

32. : Business model

33. : Goal setting

34. b: Resignation

35. b: Brainstorming

36. c: Bureau of Labor Statistics

37. : Ricci v. DeStefano

38. : Arbitration

39. a: Glass ceiling

40. c: Local union

41. a: Aggression

42. d: Human resource management

43. a: Retraining

44. a: Job satisfaction

45. d: Pay grade

46. a: Best practice

47. c: Disability insurance

48. b: Resource management

49. a: Locus of control

50. : Trainee

51. b: Interactional justice

52. a: Needs assessment

53. a: Bargaining unit

54. b: Graveyard shift

55. a: Occupational Safety and Health Act

56. : Persuasion

57. d: Outplacement

58. a: Drug test

59. d: Unemployment benefits

Information systems

1. d: Enterprise information system

2. c: Viral marketing

3. c: Supply chain

4. b: Consumerization

5. b: Information ethics

6. b: Documentation

7. b: Mouse

8. d: Content management system

9. b: Computer-integrated manufacturing

10. d: Phishing

11. c: One Laptop per Child

12. c: Credit card

13. d: Disaster recovery

14. a: YouTube

15. : Freemium

16. c: Porter five forces analysis

17. b: Mobile payment

18. a: Competitive advantage

19. d: Service level agreement

20. d: Fault tolerance

21. b: Business process reengineering

22. a: Operational system

23. : Consumer-to-business

24. a: Bit rate

25. c: Resource management

26. c: Search engine optimization

27. : Google Docs

28. c: Threat

29. a: Output device

30. : Wiki

31. : Groupware

32. a: Social commerce

33. c: Wide Area Network

34. : Netflix

35. a: Downtime

36. d: Picasa

37. : Payment card

38. : Government-to-government

39. a: Accessibility

40. b: Questionnaire

41. a: Service-oriented architecture

42. a: Virtual world

43. a: Automation

44. a: Kinect

45. c: Interoperability

46. a: AdWords

47. : Crowdsourcing

48. c: Throughput

49. a: Data file

50. c: Data element

51. : Flash memory

52. : Service level

53. a: Availability

54. : Innovation

55. c: Top-level domain

56. b: Property

57. b: Diagram

58. b: Online transaction processing

59. : Drill down

Marketing

1. : Investment

2. b: Communication

3. d: Property

4. : Subsidiary

5. b: Resource

6. c: Presentation

7. b: Product manager

8. : Penetration pricing

9. a: Disintermediation

10. : Retail

11. c: Electronic data interchange

12. d: Public

13. d: Comparative advertising

14. : Business-to-business

15. c: Price

16. a: Copyright

17. b: Mass media

18. a: Negotiation

19. d: Persuasion

20. a: Standing

21. c: Brand

22. d: Brand equity

23. : Interest

24. b: Frequency

25. d: Manager

26. a: Information system

27. c: Organizational culture

28. a: Trade association

29. c: Microsoft

30. d: Exchange rate

31. : Productivity

32. a: Customer

33. : Star

34. a: Industry

35. a: Sales

36. : Publicity

37. a: Buyer

38. : New product development

39. : Pricing

40. d: Services marketing

41. b: Creative brief

42. a: Market development

43. : Social networking

44. c: Advertisement

45. a: Problem Solving

46. c: Sales promotion

47. b: Advertising

48. c: Primary data

49. b: Strategy

50. b: Performance

51. d: Creativity

52. a: Empowerment

53. d: Authority

54. d: Innovation

55. a: Variable cost

56. c: Infomercial

57. b: Shopping

58. : Consideration

59. a: E-commerce

Manufacturing

1. b: Risk management

2. d: Control chart

3. a: Supply chain management

4. : Opportunity cost

5. b: Request for proposal

6. d: Purchasing manager

7. : Value engineering

8. : Interaction

9. a: Quality Engineering

10. b: Supply chain network

11. c: Project manager

12. d: Bullwhip effect

13. a: Turbine

14. b: Kanban

15. : Steel

16. b: Glass

17. b: Chemical reaction

18. d: Raw material

19. : Inspection

20. c: Supply chain

21. d: Customer

22. c: Perfect competition

23. d: Steering committee

24. a: Initiative

25. b: Asset

26. d: Durability

27. : Lead

28. : Quality function deployment

29. d: Reboiler

30. c: Rolling Wave planning

31. c: Flowchart

32. b: Quality costs

33. d: Production schedule

34. d: Catalyst

35. c: Sensitivity analysis

36. c: Root cause

37. c: E-procurement

38. a: Project management

39. b: Third-party logistics

40. : Sputnik

41. b: Obsolescence

42. b: Vendor relationship management

43. d: New product development

44. c: Service quality

45. a: Metal

46. c: Cash register

47. : Estimation

48. c: Prize

49. : Control limits

50. c: Change control

51. a: Process flow diagram

52. a: Furnace

53. : Thomas Register

54. : Check sheet

55. c: Dimension

56. b: Electronic data interchange

57. : Retail

58. d: Mary Kay

59. : Joint Commission

Commerce

1. b: Staff position

2. b: Drawback

3. d: Economic development

4. c: Manufacturing

5. d: Customer satisfaction

6. : Mining

7. a: Logo

8. b: Performance

9. b: Organizational structure

10. d: British Airways

11. : Wage

12. b: Innovation

13. d: Authentication

14. d: Insurance

15. : Chief executive officer

16. c: Online advertising

17. d: Good

18. d: Market structure

19. c: Merger

20. a: Real estate

21. d: Vickrey auction

22. d: Charter

23. d: E-commerce

24. c: Bottom line

25. b: Supranational

26. a: Trade

27. c: Pension

28. a: Value-added network

29. : Graduation

30. a: Shares

31. d: Level of service

32. b: Encryption

33. : Sexual harassment

34. c: International trade

35. c: Automation

36. : Industry

37. d: Antitrust

38. : Tariff

39. a: Cash flow

40. d: Amazon Payments

41. b: Interest

42. a: American Express

43. c: Risk management

44. a: Outsourcing

45. : Electronic data interchange

46. c: Market research

47. d: Trial

48. : Budget

49. b: WebSphere Commerce

50. b: Security

51. d: Utility

52. a: Labor union

53. c: Market segmentation

54. d: Logistics Management

55. c: Disney

56. b: Production line

57. d: Transaction cost

58. b: Leadership

59. a: Resource

Business ethics

1. a: Environmental audit

2. d: Recovery Act

3. : Individualistic culture

4. c: Dress code

5. c: Lead

6. : Marketing

7. a: Corporate citizenship

8. c: Electronic waste

9. a: Federal Trade Commission

10. c: Edgewood College

11. : Workplace bullying

12. : Catholicism

13. : Internal control

14. b: Lawsuit

15. b: Forest Stewardship Council

16. d: Transformational leadership

17. b: Principal Financial

18. d: Sustainable

19. : Ethical leadership

20. a: Supply Chain

21. : Medicare fraud

22. b: Kyoto Protocol

23. a: Petroleum

24. d: Locus of control

25. c: Wall Street

26. b: Great Depression

27. a: Risk assessment

28. b: Marijuana

29. : Micromanagement

30. c: Hedonism

31. c: Occupational Safety and Health Administration

32. d: Volcker Rule

33. a: Referent power

34. a: Pyramid scheme

35. : Parental leave

36. c: Social responsibility

37. d: Endangered Species Act

38. : Better Business Bureau

39. c: Junk bond

40. : Layoff

41. c: Global Fund

42. : WorldCom

43. c: Habitat

44. : Fraud

45. a: Constitutional law

46. b: Whistleblower

47. c: Nepotism

48. c: Antitrust

49. a: Protestant work ethic

50. : Invisible hand

51. a: Stanford Financial Group

52. c: Planet

53. a: Auditor independence

54. a: Criminal law

55. a: Fair Trade Certified

56. a: Communist Manifesto

57. : Sherman Antitrust Act

58. c: Feedback

59. d: Clean Water Act

Accounting

1. d: Standard deduction

2. a: Securities and Exchange Commission

3. b: Income tax

4. d: Historical cost

5. c: Governmental accounting

6. : Indirect costs

7. d: Deposit insurance

8. a: Cost of goods available for sale

9. d: Total quality management

10. : Tax revenue

11. a: Quick ratio

12. a: Bad debt

13. a: Job order

14. d: Residual value

15. a: Paid-in capital

16. a: Balanced scorecard

17. c: Electronic funds transfer

18. b: Institute of Management Accountants

19. : Return on investment

20. a: Interest expense

21. d: Net investment

22. d: Taxpayer

23. b: Working capital

24. b: Going concern

25. a: Earnings management

26. : Capital expenditure

27. d: Vesting

28. : Entity concept

29. d: Balance sheet

30. : Inventory valuation

31. b: Income approach

32. a: Ownership

33. a: Subsidiary

34. : MACRS

35. d: Payroll

36. a: Equity ratio

37. c: Cost of goods sold

38. c: Sales

39. a: Accounting management

40. c: Purchase order

41. a: Accounting records

42. b: Joint venture

43. b: Process Management

44. d: Gross margin

45. c: Personal identification number

46. a: Arthur Andersen

47. d: Intangible asset

48. d: Invoice

49. b: Investment center

50. b: Operating budget

51. c: Callable

52. d: Generally Accepted Accounting Principles

53. : Cash

54. a: Independent contractor

55. a: Management accounting

56. b: Contributed capital

57. c: Relevant cost

58. a: Fixed asset

59. b: Corporate governance

CPSIA information can be obtained
at www.ICGtesting.com
Printed in the USA
LVHW031343301019
635717LV00009B/1091/P